HOUGHTON MIFFLIN RESEARCH SERIES

THE

Age of Elizabeth

HOUGHTON MIFFLIN RESEARCH SERIES

Number 1

THE

Age of Elizabeth

SELECTED SOURCE MATERIALS IN

ELIZABETHAN SOCIAL AND LITERARY HISTORY

Edited by

John I. McCollum, Jr.

UNIVERSITY OF MIAMI

HOUGHTON MIFFLIN COMPANY · BOSTON

The Riverside Press Cambridge

PUBLISHER'S NOTE

The use of selected research materials no longer needs justification — if indeed it ever did. That they ease the strain on overtaxed libraries and aid the instructor in teaching the heart of the research method by giving him control of material which all his class is using, there is no dispute. But there are other advantages worth noting.

A genuine grasp of research method is of life-long value. The habit of sifting evidence, weighing bias, winnowing fact from opinion, assessing the judgments of others, and reaching an opinion of one's own with due regard for the possibility that new-found evidence may change it tomorrow — this is far more than a means to better grades and better papers; it is a way of mature and responsible thinking which can affect one's competence in every aspect of living. It is the aim of this book, and of the others in the Houghton Mifflin Research Series, to help the student take a stride in this direction.

The aim has been to pack into these pages enough central documentary material to give useful practice in choosing a limited topic within a broader area, scanning a large body of material, and hence in learning to reject that which is not immediately relevant and to select that which is. The major emphasis is thus placed, as it should be, on the selection, evaluation, organization, and synthesis of materials. The mechanics of notetaking, outlining, and footnote and bibliographical form are treated in every handbook and rhetoric and are not discussed here. For accurate documentation, however, the page numbers of original sources are given in heavy type immediately *after* the material from the page.

Within the limits of these broad aims the book can be used in many ways: (a) for short practice papers stressing the mechanics of research technique; (b) for full-length research papers using only materials here provided; and (c) as a springboard for papers which involve use of the library and additional reading, either historical or literary. Literature as such has been generally excluded, partly for reasons of length and of general student interest, and partly because only the gifted or the specially trained student can at this stage competently handle the very different problems of research and of criticism at the same time. For such students there is ample opportunity to step from the present materials into the relevant literature of special interest to him.

The editor of this book has appended two lists of suggested topics for shorter and longer papers, limited to materials in this book or using additional materials from other sources. It is hoped that these lists will serve as a guide to the instructor and the student and lead to the kinds of reading and thinking essential to competent research in any field.

PREFACE

This volume attempts to represent by means of selected readings from contemporary sources something of the literary and social temper of the Elizabethan age. Like the Italian Renaissance, the English Renaissance has captured and held the world's imagination. In a sense, the reign of Elizabeth was the fulfillment of a century or more of promise. England under Elizabeth established her position as a leader in the realm of politics; she actively contested for the New World; and in literature no modern nation has surpassed her achievement. This exciting period — England's Golden Age — produced some of the most fascinating figures in history, and the lustre of the queen, her courtiers, and her poets has not dimmed.

Many of these figures and much of the social and literary activity of the age may be glimpsed through the documents here reproduced. The era is revealed variously by the polished, charmingly self-effacing letters of Sir Philip Sidney, by William Harrison's homely descriptions of middle class life, by Hentzner's candid comments on the physical appearance of Queen Elizabeth, even to her black teeth and false red hair. Debate and controversy over the value and art of poetry, over dress, and over foreign travel and the adoption of foreign manners are discovered in the comments of Gosson, Sidney, Stubbes, and Ascham, among others. One may observe not only the achievement and perfection of Elizabethan English but a little of the struggle to develop an efficient and beautiful language and the experimentation with literary forms. There are casual glimpses of the theatre and the conduct of play-goers. And with the courtiers, the scholars, and the poets, there are the fops, the dandies, the rogues and thieves. There are the bodies dangling from the gibbets as reminders to the populace, and the heads of traitors on pikes surmounting London Bridge. On the political scene, one may glance at two of the most important events of the period, the victory over the Spanish Armada and the death of the Queen herself, with its attendant struggle for power: all represented by people who saw the events, criticized the actions, argued the causes, and debated the issues.

These pages, then, contain some of the primary materials out of which histories are written. Thus the student may begin where the scholar should begin — with the words of men who lived in the age and observed the events under consideration. As might be expected, the writers represented here do not always agree in their views on a given subject. These miscellaneous materials, therefore, must be sorted, analyzed, interpreted, and synthesized meaningfully. Such a task is in itself an impulse to discovery — one which challenges the critical judgment and the imagination, the indispensable powers of the scholar.

That the student might make the discoveries for himself, the documents are, for the most part, arranged alphabetically by author rather than by date or by subject matter. The spelling, syntax, and punctuation of the texts used are retained. The student will in many instances, therefore, find the *Oxford English Dictionary* an invaluable aid in discovering sixteenth-century meanings.

I am indebted to the staff of the University of Miami Library for many courtesies. I have, in addition, made use of the facilities of the University of Florida Library and, through inter-library loan privileges, of the University of North Carolina Library.

JOHN I. McCOLLUM, JR.

Coral Gables, Florida

CONTENTS

THE

Age of Elizabeth

Roger Ascham (1515–68), humanist, educator, private tutor to Princess (and later Queen) Elizabeth, was one of the group of distinguished humanists who contributed much to the growth of English scholarship in the sixteenth century. Although he wrote in Latin and insisted that Latin or Greek was more "fit for my trade in study," his most important works were written "in the English tongue for English men."

Toxophilus (1545) is a treatise in dialogue on archery, urging the importance of physical education as a part of a man's general training. The Schoolmaster, first published posthumously by his wife in 1570, is the first modern treatise on education. Writing of the training proper for boys and young men of position, Ascham discusses such subjects as discipline, teaching techniques, Italian travel, and idle attendance at court. Samuel Johnson felt that it was filled with "the best advice that was ever given for the study of languages."

Ascham writes in a graphic and polished manner through which one discerns quite easily his gracious love of learning and things English and godly.

Roger Ascham. *The Schoolmaster* in *The Whole Works of Roger Ascham,* Vol. III. Edited by J. A. Giles, London, 1864.

Preface to the Reader

When the great plague was at London, the year 1563, the queen's majesty, queen Elizabeth, lay at her castle of Windsor, where, upon the tenth day of December, it fortuned, that in Sir William Cecil's chamber, her highness's principal secretary, there dined together these personages: Mr. Secretary himself, Sir William Peter, Sir J. Mason, D. Wotton, Sir Richard Sackville, treasurer of the exchequer, Sir Walter Mildmay, chancellor of the exchequer, Mr. Haddon, master of requests, Mr. John Astley, master of the jewel-house, Mr. Bernard Hampton, Mr. Nicasius, and I. Of which number, the most part were of her majesty's most honourable Privy Council, and the rest serving her in very good place. I was glad then, and do rejoice yet to remember, that my chance was so happy to be there that day, in the company of so many wise and good men together, as hardly then could have been picked out again out of all England beside.

Mr. Secretary hath his accustomed manner; though   **page 78 /**   his head be never so full of most weighty affairs of the realm, yet at dinner-time he doth seem to lay them always aside; and findeth ever fit occasion to talk pleasantly of other matters, but most gladly of some matter of learning, wherein he will courteously hear the mind of the meanest at his table.

Not long after our sitting down, "I have strange news brought me," saith Mr. Secretary, "this morning, that divers scholars of Eton be run away from the school for fear of beating." Whereupon, Mr. Secretary took occasion to wish, that some more discretion were in many schoolmasters, in using correction, than commonly there is; who many times punish rather the weakness of nature, than the fault of the scholar; whereby many scholars, that might else prove well, be driven to hate learning before they know what learning meaneth; and so are made willing to forsake their book, and be glad to be put to any other kind of living.

Mr. Petre, as one somewhat severe of nature, said plainly, That the rod only was the sword, that must keep the school in obedience, and the scholar in good order. Mr. Wotton, a man mild of nature, with soft voice and few words, inclined to Mr. Secretary's judgment, and said, "In mine opinion, the school-house should be in deed, as it is called by name, the house of play and pleasure, and not of fear and bondage; and, as I do remember, so saith Socrates in one place of   page 79 /   Plato. And therefore, if a rod carry the fear of a sword, it is no marvel if those that be fearful of nature, choose rather to forsake the play, than to stand always within the fear of a sword in a fond man's handling."

Mr. Mason, after his manner, was very merry with both parties, pleasantly playing both with the shrewd touches of many courste boys, and with the small discretion of many lewd schoolmasters. Mr. Haddon was fully of Mr. Petre's opinion, and said, That the best schoolmaster of our time was the greatest beater, and named the person. "Though," quoth I, "it was his good fortune to send from his school unto the   page 80 /   University one of the best scholars indeed of all our time, yet wise men do think, that that came

The author of this book.

so to pass, rather by the great towardness of the scholar, than by the great beating of the master: and whether this be true or no, you yourself are best witness." I said somewhat farther in the matter, how, and why young children were sooner allured by love than driven by beating, to attain good learning; wherein I was the bolder to say my mind, because Mr. Secretary courteously provoked me thereunto; or else in such a company, and namely in his presence, my wont is, to be more willing to use mine ears, than to occupy my tongue.

Sir Walter Mildmay, Mr. Astley, and the rest, said very little; only Sir Richard Sackville said nothing at all. After dinner, I went up to read with the queen's Majesty. We read then together in the Greek tongue, as I well remember, that noble oration of Demosthenes against Aeschines, for his false dealing in his embassage to king Philip of Macedonia. Sir Richard Sackville came up soon after, and finding me in her Majesty's privy-chamber, he took me by the hand, and carrying me to a window, said: "Mr. Ascham, I would

Sir R. Sackville's communication with the author of this book.

not for a good deal of money have been this day absent from dinner. Where, though I said nothing, yet I gave as good ear, and do consider as well the talk that passed, as any one did there. Mr. Secretary said very wisely, and most   page 81 /   truly, that many young wits be driven to hate learning, before they know what learning is. I can be good witness to this myself; for a fond schoolmaster, before I was fully fourteen years old, drave me so with fear of beating from all love of learning, as now, when I know what difference it is, to have learning, and to have little or none at all, I feel it my greatest grief, and find it my greatest hurt that ever came to me, that it was my so ill chance to light upon so lewd a schoolmaster. But seeing it is but in vain to lament things past, and also wisdom to look to things to come, surely, God willing, if God lend me life, I will make this my mishap some occasion of good hap to little Robert Sackville, my son's son. For whose bringing up, I would gladly, if it so please you, use especially your good advice. I hear say you have a son much of his age; we will thus deal together: point you out a schoolmaster, who by your order shall teach my son and yours, and for all the rest I will provide, yea though they three do cost me a couple of hundred pounds by year; and beside, you shall find me as fast a friend to you and yours, as perchance any you have." Which promise the worthy gentleman surely kept with me until his dying day.

We had then farther talk together of bringing up of children, of the nature of quick and hard wits, of the right choice of a good wit, of fear and love in teaching children. We passed from children and came to young men, namely, *The chief points of this book.* gentlemen: we talked of their too much liberty to live as they lust; of their letting loose too soon to overmuch experience   page 82 /   of ill, contrary to the good order of many good old commonwealths of the Persians and Greeks; of wit gathered, and good fortune gotten by some, only by experience without learning. And, lastly, he required of me very earnestly to show what I thought of the common going of Englishmen into Italy. "But," saith he, "because this place, and this time will not suffer so long talk, as these good matters require, therefore I pray you, at my request, and at your leisure, put in some order of writing the chief points of this our talk, concerning the right order of teaching, and honesty of living, for the good bringing up of children and young men; and surely, beside contenting me, you shall both please and profit very many others." . . .   page 83 /

The First Book, Teaching The Bringing Up Of Youth.

After the child hath learned perfectly the eight parts of speech, let him then learn the right joining together of substantives with adjectives, the noun with the verb, the relative with the antecedent. And in learning farther his syntaxis, by mine advice, he shall not use the common order in common schools, for making of Latins: whereby the child commonly learneth, first, an evil choice of words, (and "right choice of words," saith Caesar, "is the foundation of eloquence;") then, a wrong placing of words; and lastly, an ill-framing of the sentence, with a perverse judgment, both of words and sentences. These faults, taking once root in youth, be never or hardly pluckt away in age. Moreover, there is no one thing, that   page 88 /   hath more either dulled the wits, or taken away the will of children from learning, than the care they have to satisfy their masters in making of Latins.

For the scholar is commonly beat for the making, when the master were more worthy to be beat for the mending, or rather marring of the same: *Making of Latins marreth children.* the master many times being as ignorant as the child, what to say properly and fitly to the matter.

·   ·   ·   ·   ·   ·   ·   ·   ·   ·   ·   ·   ·   ·   ·   ·   ·

There is a way, touched in the first book of *Cicero de Oratore*, which, wisely brought into schools, truly taught, and constantly used, would not only take wholly away this butcherly fear in making of Latins, but would also with ease and pleasure, and in short time, as I know by good experience, work a true choice and placing of words, a right ordering of sentences, an easy understanding of the tongue, a readiness to speak, a facility to write, a true judgement   page 89 /   both of his own and other men's doings, what tongue soever he doth use.

The way is this. After the three concordances learned, as I touched before, let the master read unto him the Epistles of Cicero, gathered together, and chosen out by Sturmius, for the capacity of children.

The order of teaching.

First, let him teach the child cheerfully and plainly the cause and matter of the letter; then, let him construe it into English so oft, as the child may easily carry away the understanding of it; lastly, parse it over perfitly. This done thus, let the child, by and by, both construe and parse it over again; so that it may appear, that the child doubteth in nothing that his master taught him before. After this, the child must take a paper book, and sitting in some place, where no man shall prompt him, by himself, let him translate into English his former lesson. Then showing it to his master, let the master take

Two paper books.

from him his Latin book, and pausing an hour at the least, then let the child translate his own English into Latin again in another paper book. When the child bringeth it turned into Latin, the master must compare it with Tully's book, and lay them both together; and where the child doth well,

Children learn by praise.

either in choosing or true placing of Tully's words, let the master praise him, and say, "Here ye do well." For I assure you, there is no such whetstone to sharpen a good wit, and encourage a will to learning, as is praise.

But if the child miss, either in forgetting a word, or in changing a good with a worse, or misordering the sentence, I would not have the master either frown or chide with him, if the child have done his   page 90 /   diligence, and used no truantship therein. For I know by good experience, that

Gentleness in teaching.

a child shall take more profit of two faults gently warned of, than of four things rightly hit: for then the master shall have good occasion to say unto him; "N., Tully would have used such a word, not this: Tully would have placed this word here, not there; would have used this case, this number, this person, this degree, this gender: he would have used this mood, this tense, this simple, rather than this compound; this adverb here, not there: he would have ended the sentence with this verb, not with that noun or participle," &c.

.   .   .   .

... This is a lively and perfit way of teaching of   page 91 /   rules; where the common way used in common schools, to read the grammar alone by itself, is tedious for the master, hard for the scholar, cold and uncomfortable for them both.

Let your scholar be never afraid to ask you any doubt, but use discreetly the best allurements ye can to encourage him to the same; lest his overmuch fearing of you drive him to seek some misorderly shift; as to seek to be helped by some other book, or to be prompted by some other scholar; and so go about to beguile you much and himself more.   page 92 /

.   .   .   .

With the common use of teaching and beating in common schools of England, I will not greatly contend; which, if I did, it were but a small grammatical controversy, neither belonging to heresy   page 96 /   nor treason, nor greatly touching God nor the prince; although in very deed, in the end, the good or ill bringing up of children, doth as much serve to the good or ill service of God, our prince, and our whole country, as any one thing doth beside. *Common schools.*

I do gladly agree with all good schoolmasters in these points; to have children brought to good perfitness in learning, to all honesty in manners, to have all faults rightly amended, to have every vice severely corrected: but for the order and way, that leadeth rightly to these points, we somewhat differ. For commonly many schoolmasters, some as I have seen, moe as I have heard tell, be of so crooked a nature, as, when they meet with a hard-witted scholar, they rather break him than bow him, rather mar him than mend him. For when the schoolmaster is angry with some other matter, then will he soonest fall to beat his scholar; and though he himself should be punished for his folly, yet must he beat some scholar for his pleasure, though there be no cause for him to do so, nor yet fault in the scholar to deserve so. These, ye will say, be fond schoolmasters, and few they be that be found to be such. They be fond indeed, but surely over many such be found everywhere. But this will I say, that even the wisest of your great beaters, do as oft punish nature as they do correct faults. Yea, many times the better nature is sorer punished. For, if one by quickness of wit take his lesson readily, another by hardness of wit taketh it not so speedily; the first is always commended, the other is commonly punished: when a wise schoolmaster should rather discreetly consider the right disposition of both their natures, and not so much weigh what either of them is able to   page 97 /   do now, as what either of them is likely to do hereafter. For this I know, not only by reading of books in my study, but also by experience of life abroad in the world, that those which be commonly the wisest, the best learned, and best men also, when they be old, were never commonly the quickest of wit when they were young. . . .   page 98 / *Sharp schoolmasters.* *Nature punished.* *Quick wits for learning.*

. . . .

Learning teacheth more in one year than experience in twenty; and learning teacheth safely, when experience maketh mo[re] miserable, than wise. He hazardeth sore that waxeth wise by experience. An unhappy master he is that is made cunning by many shipwrecks; a miserable merchant, that is neither rich nor wise but after some bankrouts. It is costly wisdom that is bought by experience. We know by experience itself, that it is a marvellous pain to find out but a short way by long wandering. And surely, he that would prove wise by experience, he may be witty indeed, but even like a swift runner, that runneth fast out of his way, and upon the night, he knoweth not whither. And verily they be fewest in number that be happy or wise by unlearned experience. . . .   page 136 / *Learning — experience.*

. . . .

Erasmus, the honour of learning of all our time, said wisely, "That experience is the common schoolhouse of fools and ill men. Men of wit and honesty be otherwise instructed. For there be, that keep them out of fire, and yet was never burned; that be ware of water, and yet was never nigh *Experience the schoolhouse of fools and ill men.*

drowning; that hate harlots, and was never at the stews; that abhor false-hood, and never brake promise themselves."   page 137 /

.   .   .   .

Learning therefore, ye wise fathers, and good bringing up, and not blind and dangerous experience, is the next and readiest way that must lead your children, first to wisdom, and then to worthiness, if ever ye purpose they shall come there.

.   .   .   .

And I do not mean by all this my talk, that young gentlemen should always be poring on a book, and by using good studies should leese honest pleasure, and haunt no good pastime: I mean nothing less. For it is well known that I both like and love, and have always, and do yet still use all exercises and pastimes that be fit for my nature and ability: and beside natural disposition, in judgment also I was never either stoic in doctrine or anabaptist in religion, to mislike a merry, pleasant, and playful nature, if no outrage be committed against law, measure and good order.   page 138 /

Diligent learning ought to be joined with pleasant pastimes, namely, in a gentleman.

Therefore I would wish, that beside some good time fitly appointed, and constantly kept, to increase by reading the knowledge of the tongues and learning; young gentlemen should use, and delight in all courtly exercises, and gentlemanlike pastimes. . . .

The pastimes that be fit for comely gentlemen.

Therefore to ride comely, to run fair at the tilt or ring; to play at all weapons, to shoot fair in bow, or surely in gun; to vault lustily, to run, to leap, to wrestle, to swim; to dance comely, to sing, and play on instruments cunningly; to hawk, to hunt; to play at tennis, and all pastimes generally, which be joined with labour, used in open place, and on the day-light, containing either some fit exercise for war, or some plea-   page 139 /   sant pastime for peace, be not only comely and decent, but also very necessary for a courtly gentleman to use. . . .   page 140 /

.   .   .   .

To join learning with comely exercises, Conte Baldesar Castiglione, in his book *Cortegiane*, doth trimly teach; which book advisedly read and diligently followed but one year at home in England, would do a young gentleman more good, I wiss, than three years' travel abroad spent in Italy. And I marvel this book is no more read in the court than it is, seeing it is so well translated into English by a worthy gentleman, Sir Thomas Hobby, who was many ways well furnished with learning, and very expert in knowledge of divers tongues. page 141 /

The Cortegiane, an excellent book for a gentleman.

And beside good precepts in books, in all kind of tongues, this court also never lacked many fair examples for young gentlemen to follow: and surely one example is more valuable, both to good and ill, than twenty precepts written in books; and so Plato, not in one or two, but divers places, doth plainly teach. . . .

Examples better than precepts.

Present examples of this present time I list not to touch; yet there is one example for all the gentlemen of this court to follow, that may well satisfy them, or nothing will serve them, nor no example move them to goodness and learning.

It is your shame (I speak to you all, you young gentlemen of England) that one maid should go beyond you all in excellency of learning and knowledge of divers tongues. Point forth six of the best given gen- page 142 / tlemen of this court, and all they together show not so much good will, spend not so much time, bestow not so many hours daily, orderly, and constantly, for the increase of learning and knowledge, as doth the Queen's Majesty herself. Yea, I believe, that beside her perfect readiness in Latin, Italian, French, and Spanish, she readeth here now at Windsor more Greek every day, than some prebendary of this church doth read Latin in a whole week. And that which is most praiseworthy of all, within the walls of her privy chamber, she hath obtained that excellency of learning to understand, speak, and write both wittily with head, and fair with hand, as scarce one or two rare wits in both the universities have in many years reached unto. Amongst all the benefits that God hath blessed me withal, next the knowledge of Christ's true religion, I count this the greatest, that it pleased God to call me to be one poor minister in setting forward these excellent gifts of learning in this most excellent prince; whose only example if the rest of our nobility would follow, then might England be for learning and page 143 / wisdom in nobility, a spectacle to all the world beside. . . . page 144 /

. . . .

And in meaner matters, if three or four great ones in court will needs outrage in apparel, in huge hose, in monstrous hats, in garish colours; let the prince proclaim, make laws, order, punish, command every gate in London daily to be watched; let all good men beside do every where what they can; surely the misorder of apparel in mean men abroad shall never be amended, except the greatest in court will order and mend themselves first. I know some great and good ones in court were authors, that honest citizens of London should watch at every gate to take misordered persons in apparel: I know that honest Londoners did so; and I saw (which I saw then, and report now with some grief) that some courtly men were offended with these good men of London: and (that which grieved me most of all) I saw the very same time, for all these good orders commanded from the court and executed in London; I saw, I say, come out of London even unto the presence of the prince, a great rabble of mean and light persons in apparel, for matter against law, for making against order, for fashion, namely hose, so without all order, as he thought himself most brave, that durst do most in breaking order, and was most monstrous in misorder. And for all the great commandments that came out of the court, yet this bold misorder was winked at, and borne withal in the court. I thought it was not well, that some great ones of the court durst declare themselves offended with good men of London for doing their duty, and the good ones of the court would not show themselves offended with ill men of London for breaking good page 145 / order. . . .

Example in apparel.

Masters, ushers and scholars' offence.

Beside apparel, in all other things too, not so much good laws and strait commandments, as the example and manner of living of great men, doth carry all mean men every where to like, and love, and do, as they do. For if but two or three noblemen in the court would but begin to shoot, all young gentlemen, the whole court, all London, the whole realm, would straightway exercise shooting. . . . page 146 /

Example in shooting.

. . . .

Hitherto I have showed what harm over-much fear bringeth to children;

and what hurt ill company and over-much liberty breedeth in youth; meaning thereby, that from seven year old to seventeen, love is the best allurement to learning; from seventeen to seven-and-twenty, that wise men should carefully see the steps of youth surely stayed by good order, in that most slippery time, and especially in the court, a place most dangerous for youth to live in, without great grace, good regard, and diligent looking to.

Travelling into Italy.

Sir Richard Sackville, that worthy gentleman of worthy memory, as I said in the beginning, in the queen's privy chamber at **page 147 /** Windsor, after he had talked with me for the right choice of a good wit in a child for learning, and of the true difference betwixt quick and hard wits, of alluring young children by gentleness to love learning, and of the special care that was to be had to keep young men from licentious living; he was most earnest with me, to have me say my mind also, what I thought concerning the fancy that many young gentlemen of England have to travel abroad, and namely to lead a long life in Italy. His request, both for his authority and good will toward me, was a sufficient commandment unto me, to satisfy his pleasure with uttering plainly my opinion in that matter. "Sir," quoth I, "I take going thither, and living there, for a young gentleman that doth not go under the keep and guard of such a man, as both by wisdom can, and authority dare rule him, to be marvellous dangerous."

And why I said so then, I will declare at large now, which I said then privately, and write now openly; not because I do contemn either the knowledge of strange and divers tongues, and namely the Italian tongue (which,

The Italian tongue.

next the Greek and Latin tongue, I like and love above all other), or else because I do despise the learning that is gotten, or the experience that is gathered in strange countries; or for any private malice that I bear to Italy; which country, and in it namely Rome, I have always specially honoured; because time was, when Italy and Rome have been to the great good of us that now live, the best breeders and bringers up of the worthiest men, not only for wise speaking, but also for well doing, in all civil affairs, that ever was in the world. But now that time is gone; and though the place remain, yet the old and present manners do **page 148 /** differ as far as black and white, as virtue and vice. Virtue once made that country mistress over all the world; vice now maketh that country slave to them that before were glad to serve it. All men seeth it; they themselves confess it, namely such as be best and wisest amongst them. For sin, by lust and vanity, hath and doth breed up every where, common contempt of God's word, private contention in many families, open factions in every city; and so making themselves bond to vanity and vice at home, they are content to bear the yoke of serving strangers abroad. Italy now, is not that Italy that it was wont to be; and therefore now not so fit a place as some do count it, for young men to fetch either wisdom or honesty from thence. For surely they will make others but bad scholars, that be so ill masters to themselves.... **page 149 /**

.   .   .   .

Therefore, if wise men will needs send their sons into Italy, let them do it wisely, under the keep and guard of him who, by his wisdom and honesty, by his example and authority, may be able to keep them safe and sound in the fear of God, in Christ's true religion, in good order, and honesty of living....
page 151 /

I know divers noble personages, and many worthy gentlemen of England, whom all the Siren songs of Italy could never untwine from the mast of God's Word, nor no enchantment of vanity overturn them from the fear of God and love of honesty.

But I know as many, or mo, and some sometime my dear friends (for whose sake I hate going into that country the more), who parting out of England fervent in the love of Christ's doctrine, and well furnished with the fear of God, returned out of Italy worse transformed than ever was any in Circes' court. I know divers, that went out of England, men of innocent life, men of excellent learning, who returned out of Italy, not only with worse manners, but also with less learning; neither so willing to live orderly, nor yet so able to speak learnedly, as they were at home, before they went abroad.... **page 152 /**

But I am afraid, that over-many of our travellers into Italy do not eschew the way to Circes' court, but go, and ride, and run, and fly thither: they make great haste to come to her; they make great suit to serve her; yea, I could point out some with my finger, that never had gone out of England, but only to serve Circes in Italy. Vanity and vice, and any license to ill living in England, was counted stale and rude unto them. And so, being mules and horses before they went, returned very swine and asses home again: yet every where very foxes with subtle and busy heads; and where they may, very wolves, with cruel malicious hearts. A marvellous monster, which for filthiness of living, for dulness to learning himself, for wiliness in dealing with others, for malice in hurting without cause, should carry at once in one body, the belly of a swine, the head of an ass, the brain of a fox, the womb of a wolf. If you think we judge amiss, and write too sore against you, hear what the Italian saith of the Englishmen; what the master reporteth of the scholar, who uttereth plainly what is taught by him, and what is learned by you, saying, *Inglese Italianato è un diabolo incarnato;* that is to say, "You remain men in shape and fashion, but become devils in life and condition." **page 156 /**

A true picture of a Knight of Circes' court.

The Italian judgment of Englishmen brought up in Italy.

... And now choose you, you Italian Englishmen, whether you will be angry with us for calling you monsters, or with the Italians for calling you devils, or else with your own selves, that take so much pains, and go so far, to make yourselves both. If some yet do not well understand what is an Englishman Italianated, I will plainly tell him: "He that by living and travelling in Italy, bringeth home into England out of Italy, the religion, the learning, the policy, the experience, the manners of Italy."

An English-man Italian-ated.

These be the enchantments of Circes, brought out of Italy, to mar men's manners in England; much by example of ill life, but more by precepts of fond books, of late translated out of Italian into English, sold in every shop in London; commended by honest titles, the sooner to corrupt honest manners; dedicated over-boldly to virtuous and honourable personages, the easier to beguile simple and innocent wits.... **page 157 /**

Italian books translated into English.

Our Italians bring home with them other faults from Italy. .... For commonly they come home common contemners of marriage, and ready persuaders of all others to the same; not because they love virginity, nor yet because they hate pretty young virgins, but being free in Italy to go whithersoever lust will carry them, they do not like that law and honesty should be such a bar to their liberty at home in England. And yet they be the greatest makers of love, the daily dalliers with such pleasant words, with such smiling and secret countenances, with such signs, tokens, wagers, purposed to be lost before they were purposed to be made, with bargains of wearing colours, flowers, and herbs, to breed occasion of often meeting of him and her, and bolder talking of this and that, &c. And although I have seen some innocent of all ill, and staid in all honesty, that have used these things without all harm, without all suspicion of harm; yet these knacks were brought first into England by them that learned them before in Italy in Circes' court; and how courtly courtesies soever they be counted now, yet if the meaning and manners of some that do use them were somewhat amended, it were no great hurt neither to themselves nor to others. . . .   **page 165 /**

The Mirror for Magistrates, *planned by William Baldwin of Oxford and George Ferrers, Master of the King's Pastimes in the reign of Henry VIII, was licensed for publication in 1559. The work is a series of poetic narratives in which illustrious men recount the circumstances of their downfall for the edification, advice, and reproof of those who hold magisterial power. Baldwin suggests in his dedication the general indebtedness to Lydgate's version of Boccaccio's* Fall of Princes. *Although the work enjoyed great success during the Elizabethan period, it is not now regarded as having great literary merit. The two dedications included in this collection are examples of the "advice to princes" essays so popular in the sixteenth century.*

William Baldwin *et al.*, *Mirror for Magistrates* (three volumes). Edited by Joseph Haslewood, London, 1815.

"Dedication: To the Nobility and All Other In Office, God Graunt the Increase of wisedome, with all things necessary for preseruation of theyr estates. *Amen.*" Vol. I.

Amongste the wise (right Honorable) whose sentences (for the moste parte) tende either to teache the attayning of vertue or eschuing of vice, Plotinus. *Plotinus* that wonderfull and excellent Philosopher hath these wordes: The property of Temperaunce is to couet nothing which may be repented: not to excede the bands of measure, & to kepe Desire vnder the yoke of Reason. Whiche saying if it were so well knowen, as it is nedefull; so well embraced, as is wished; or so surely fixed in minde, as it is printed in his workes: then certis many Christians might by the instruction of an Ethnicke Philosopher, shun great and daungerous perils. For to couet without consideration, to passe the measure of his degree, and to let will run at randon, is the only destruction of all estates. Else howe were it possible, so many learned, polliticke, wise, renoumed, valiaunt, and victorious personages, might euer haue come to such vtter decay? For example, wee haue *Alexander* the Great, *Caesar*, *Pompey*, *Cyrus*, *Hannibal*, &c. All which (by desier of glorye) felte the reward of Quintus theire immoderate and insatiable lustes: for if *Alexander* had beene content Curtius. with Macedonie, or not beene pufte vp with pride after his triumphes, hee had neuer beene so miserably poysoned. If *Caesar* and *Pompey* had beene satisfied with theire victories, and   **page 3 /**   had not fell to ciuill discention, the one had not beene slaine in the senate with daggers, nor the other abroade, by their frendes procurement. If *Cyrus* had beene pleased with all Persia, and Media, and not thirsted for bloud, hee had neuer com to so infortunate a Iustinus lib. *1.* fall. So if *Hanniball* had not so much delited in glorye of warfare, his coūtrey

11

Plutarchus.
Liuius.
Polibius.

had neyther fell in ruine, nor hee bene miserably forced to poyson himselfe. But you will say, desire of fame, glorye, renowne, and immortalitie (to which all men well nighe by nature are inclined, especially those which excell or haue any singuler gift of fortune or the body) moued them to such daungerous, great, and hardy enterprises, which must needes be confessed as an infallible veritie: and therefore I suerly deeme those Princes aboue specified (cōsidering their fortunes, fame and exploytes) had neuer come to suche ende, but for want of temperance. And now sithe there are three other Cardinall vertues which are requisite in him that should bee in authoritye: that is to saye, Prudence, Iustice, and Fortitude, which so wonderfully adorne and beautifie all estates (If Temperaunce bee with them adioyned, that they moue the very enemies with admiration to prayse them) some peraduenture (as affection leades) will commende one, some another: as *Aristotle* the Prince of Philosophers names Prudence, the mother of vertues, but *Cicero* defines her the knowledge of things which ought to bee desired and followed, and also of them which ought to bee fled and eschewed; yet you shall finde that for want of Temperaunce, some which were coūted very wise fell into wonderfull reproche and infamy. But Iustice that incomparable vertue, (as the auncient Ciuillians define her) is a perpetuall and constant will **page 4 /** which giueth to euery man his right, yet if shee be not constant, which is the gifte of Fortitude; nor equal in discerning right from wrong, wherein is Prudence; nor vse proportion in iudgement and sentence, which pertayneth to Temperaunce: shee can neuer bee called equitie or iustice, but fraude, deceite, iniustice and iniurie. And, to speake of Fortitude, which *Cicero* defineth, a cōsyderate vndertaking of perills, and enduring of labours; if he whome wee suppose stoute, valiaunt, and of good courage, want Prudence, Iustice, or Temperaunce, he is not coūted wise, righteous and constant, but sottish, rude and desperate. For Temperaunce (sayth *Cicero*) is of reason in lust and other euel assaultes of the minde, a suer and moderate dominion & rule. This noble vertue is deuided into three partes, that is Cōtinency, Clemencie, and Modestye, which well obserued and kept (if grace bee to them adioyned) it is impossible for him that is endued with the aboue named vertues euer to fall into the infortunate snares of calamity, or misfortune. But Ambition which is immoderate desire of honour, rule, dominion, and superioritie, (the very distruction of nobility and common weales, as among the Romanes; Sylla, Marius, Carbo, Cinna, Cateline, Pompey, and Caesar, are witnesses) hath brought great decay to our cōtrey, and countreymen.... I haue here (right honorable) in this booke only reproued foly in those which are heedelesse: Iniurie in extortioners, rashnes in venterers, **page 5 /** [trecherie in traytours, riote in rebelles,] [1] and excesse in such as suppresse not vnruly affections.... And thus wishing you Prudence to discerne what is meete for your callings, Iustice in the administration of your functions, Fortitude in the defence of your Countrey, and Temperaunce in moderation of all your affections, with increase of honours, and euerlasting felicity:
I bid you in Christ Iesu farewell. At Winceham the vii. day of December.
1586.

Arist.
Cicero.
Prudence.

Fortitude.
Cicero.

Cicero.
Temperance.

Your most humble in
the Lord,

[1] Not in first edit. [Hazleton]

Iohn Higins. **page 6 /**

"Dedication: Loue and Liue. To All the Nobilitie, and All Other In Office, God Graunt Wisedome and all thinges nedefull for the preseruation of their estates. *Amen.*" Vol. II.

Plato among many of his notable sentences concernyng the gouernement of a common weale hath this: Well is that realme gouerned, in which the ambitious desire not to beare office. Whereby you may perceiue (right honourable) what offices are, where they be duely executed: not gainfull spoyles for the gredy to hunt for, but painefull toyles for the heady to bee charged with. You may perceiue also, by this sentence, there is nothing more necessary in a common weale then that magistrates be diligent and trusty in their charges.

And sure in whatsoeuer realme such prouision is made, that officers be forced to do their duties, there is it as hard a matter to get an officer, as it is in other places to repulse and shift of those that with flattery, brybes, and other shiftes, sue and preace for offices. For the ambitious (that is to saye prollers for power or gayne) seeke not for offices to helpe other, for whych cause officers are ordained: but with the vndoing of other, to enrich themselues. And therfore bar them once of this bayt, and force them to do their dueties, then will they geue more to be rid from their charges, than they did at the first to come by them. For they seeke onely their priuate profite. And therfore where the ambitious seeke no office, there **page 3 /** no doubt offices are duely ministred. And where offices are duely ministred, it cannot be chosen, but the people are good, whereof must nedes follow a good common weale. For if the magistrates be good, the people cannot be ill. Thus the goodnes or badnes of any realme lieth in the goodnes or badnes of the rulers. And therfore not without great cause do the holy appostles so earnestly charg vs to pray for the magistrates: for in dede the wealth and quiet of euery common weale, the disorder also and miseries of the same, come specially thorough them. I neede not go eyther to the *Romaines* or *Greekes* for the profe hereof, neither yet to the *Jewes*, or other nations: whose common weales haue alway florished whyle their magistrates were good, and decayed and ran to ruyne when vicious men had the gouernement.

Our countrey stories (if we reade and marke them) wil show vs examples enow, would God we had not sene mo than enow. I purpose not to stand herevpon the particulars, because they be in parte setforth in the tragedies folowing. Yet by the waye, this I note (wishing all other to doe the like) namely, that as good gouernours haue neuer lacked their deserued praises, so haue not the bad escaped infamy, besides such plagues as are horrible to heare of. For God (the ordeiner of offices) although he suffer them for punishment of the people to be often occupied of such, as are rather spoilers and *Judasses*, than toilers or justices (whom the scriptures cal hypocrits) yet suffereth he them not to scape vnpunished, because they dishonour him. For it is God's own office, yea his chief office which they beare and abuse. For as justice is the chief vertue so is the ministration thereof, the chiefest office: and therfore hath God established it with the chiefest name, honouring and calling kinges and all officers vnder them by his owne name, **page 4 /** gods: ye be all gods, as many as haue in your charge any ministration of iustice. What a foule shame were it for any nowe to take vpon them the name and office of God, and in their doings to shew themselues deuils? God cannot of iustice,

but plague suche shamelesse presumption and hipocrisie, and that with shamful death, diseases, or infamye. Howe he hath plagued euil rulers from time to time, in other nations, you may see gathred in *Bochas*' boke intituled: *The fall of Princes*, translated into English by *Lydgate*, (a monke of the abbey of *Bury* in *Suff.*) How he hath delt with some of our countrymen, your auncestours, for sundry vices not yet left, this boke named *A Mirrour for Magistrates*, shall in parte plalinye set forth before your eyes which boke I humbly offer vnto your honours, beseching you to accept it fauorably. For here, as in a mirror or loking glasse, you shal se if any vice be found, how the like hath ben punished in other heretofore, wherby admonished, I trust it will bee a good occasione to moue men to the soner amendment.... page 5 /
...I moste humbly besech your honours fauourably to accepte this rude worke, and diligentlye to reade and consider it. And although you shal find in it, that some haue for their virtue bin enuied and brought vnto misery: yet cease not you to be vertuous, but do your offices to the vttermost. Embrace vertue and suppresse the contrary, both in your selues and other, so shall God, whose officers you are, eyther so maintaine you that no malice shall preuaile, or if it do, it shall be for your good, and to your eternall glory both here and in heauen which I beseech God you may both seek and attaine. Amen.

Your's most humble
W[illiam]. B[aldwin].   page 6 /

Richard Barnfield (1574–1627) is known for The Affectionate Shepherd *(1594);* Cynthia, with certain Sonnets and the Legend of Cassandra *(1595); and a third volume (1598) in which four pamphlets were bound together:* The Encomion of Lady Pecunia, The Complaint of Poetry, Conscience and Covetousness, *and* Poems in Divers Humours, *in which* A remembrance of some English poets *appears. He was a friend of Thomas Watson, Michael Drayton, and Francis Meres. Although he was not a great poet, he, nevertheless, caught some of the music of his greater contemporaries, and has the curious distinction of having had two of his poems (the sonnet "If music and sweet poetry agree" and the ode "As it fell upon a day") attributed to Shakespeare. He is noted for his praise of other authors, particularly Sidney, Spenser, and Shakespeare.*

Richard Barnfield. "A Remembrance of some English Poets" (1598) in *Shakespeare's Centurie of Prayse*. Edited by C. M. Ingleby, revised by Lucy Toulmin Smith, London, 1879.

A Remembrance of some English Poets.

Live *Spenser* ever, in thy *Fairy Queene:*
Whose like (for deepe Conceit) was never seene.
Crownd mayst thou bee, unto thy more renowne,
(As King of Poets) with a Lawrell Crowne.

And *Daniell*, praised for thy sweet-chast Verse:
Whose Fame is grav'd on *Rosamonds* blacke Herse.
Still mayst thou live: and still be honored,
For that rare Worke, *The White Rose and the Red.*

And *Drayton*, whose wel-written Tragedies,
And sweete Epistles, soare thy fame to skies.
Thy learned Name, is aequall with the rest;
Whose stately Numbers are so well addrest.

And *Shakespeare* thou, whose hony-flowing Vaine,
(Pleasing the World) thy Praises doth obtaine,
Whose *Venus*, and whose *Lucrece* (sweete, and chaste)
Thy Name in fames immortall Booke have plac't.
Live ever you, at least in Fame live ever:
Well may the Bodye dye, but Fame dies never. **page 26 /**

William Camden (1551–1623), antiquarian and historian, is noted chiefly for the Britannia *(1586) and the* Annals *(1615); however, one of the most interesting of the Elizabethan historical works is his* Remains, *a collection of essays on such subjects as language, names, money, apparel, published in 1605. Camden made extensive tours throughout England investigating and collecting antiquities. He wrote principally in Latin. An English translation of the* Britannia *was made by Philemon Holland in 1610, and the* Annals *appeared in English in 1625, 1628, and 1635 by various hands.*

William Camden. *The History of the most Renowned and Victorious Princess Elizabeth, Late Queen of England, Containing All the most Important and Remarkable Passages of State, both at Home, and Abroad (so far as they were linked with* English *Affairs) during her Long and Prosperous Reign.* Third edition, London, 1675.

Excess of Apparel restrained.

In these days a wondrous Excess in Apparel had spred itself all over *England*, and the Habit of our own Countrey, through a peculiar Vice incident to our Apish Nation, grew into such Contempt, that men by their new-fashioned Garments, and too gaudy Apparel, discovered a certain Deformity and Arrogancy of Mind, whilest they jetted up and down in their Silks glittering with Gold and Silver, either imbroidered or laced. The Queen observing that, to maintain this Excess, a great quantity of Money was carried yearly out of the Land, to buy Silks and other outlandish Wares, to the impoverishing of the Commonwealth; and that many of the Nobility which might be a great Service to the Commonwealth, and others that they might seem of noble Extraction, did, to their own undoing, not onely wast their Estates, but also run so far in Debt, that of necessity they came within the danger of the Law thereby, and attempted to raise Troubles and Commotions when they had wasted their own Patrimonies; although she might have proceeded against them by the Laws of King *Henry* the 8. and Queen *Mary*, and thereby have fined them in great Summs of Money, yet she chose rather to deal with them by way of Command. She commanded therefore by **page 205 /** Proclamation, that every man should within fourteen days conform himself for Apparel to a certain prescribed Fashion, lest they otherwise incurred the Severity of the Laws: and she began the Conformity herself in her own Court. But, through the Untowardness of the Times, both this Proclamation and the Laws also gave way by little and little to this excess of Pride, which grew daily more and more unreasonable: And with it crept in riotous Banquetting, and prodigal Bravery in Building. For now there began more Noblemens

1574

and private mens Houses to be builded here and there through *England*, and those neat, large and sumptuous Edifices, then in any other Age before; and verily to the great Ornament of the Kingdome, but to as great Decay of the glorious Hospitality of the Nation.   **page 206 /**

England beautified with Buildings.

. . . .

In *England*, in the beginning of this Year, the Neck-attire, which we call Ruffs, being unreasonably large, and with huge wide Setts, and Cloaks, reaching down almost to the Ancles, no less uncomely then expensive, were restrained by Proclamation. Swords also were reduced to the length of three Foot, Daggers to twelve inches besides the Handle, and the Pikes in the Bosses of Bucklers to two in- **page 243 /** ches. In like manner, in regard that great Multitudes of people resorted from all parts to *London*, whereby the City and Suburbs were now so much inlarged with Buildings, (while the rest of the Cities and Towns of *England* ran to Decay) that unless it were timely prevented, neither the ordinary Magistrates would suffice to govern the Multitude, nor the Countries round about to feed them, and the Contagion of Pestilence, if any should happen, would spread itself farther and more dangerously by means of the Houses standing so thick together, and being pestered with numbers of Inhabitants; the Queen by Proclamation prohibited any new Dwelling-houses to be built within three miles of the Gates of the City, upon pain of Imprisonment, and loss of the Stuff provided for the Building; and ordered that no more but one Family should dwell in one House.   **page 244 /**

1580 Excess of Apparell restrained.

1580 And new Buildings in the Suburbs of London.

. . . .

The Queen, who had hitherto enjoyed her Health without Impairment, by reason of her Abstinence from Wine and observing a tem- **page 658 /** perate Diet (which she usually said was the noblest part of Physick,) being now in her Climactericall Year, to wit, the Seventieth Year of her Age, began to be sensible of some Weakness and Indisposition both of Health and Old age, which the badness of the Weather increased, whilst upon the last of *January*, which was a very windy and rainy day, she removed from *Westminster* to *Richmond*, there to enjoy and refresh herself in her Old age, and more freely to attend the Serving of God. Upon which day (whether thinking on her Death, or presaging what would ensue,) she happened to say to the Lord Admirall, whom she always dearly affected, *My Throne hath been the Throne of Kings, neither ought any other then he that is my next Heir to succeed me.* And the Courtiers observed, that she never before more frequented Prayers and the Service of God then now. Who also report, that she then commanded that Ring wherewith she had been as it were joyned in Marriage to her Kingdome at her Inauguration, and had never since taken off, to be filed off from her Finger, because it was so grown into the Flesh, that it could not be drawn off. Which was taken as a sad Omen, as if it portended that her Marriage with the Kingdome, contracted by that Ring, would now be dissolved. In the beginning of her Sickness the Almonds in her Throat swelled, and soon abated again; then her Appetite failed her by degrees; and withall she gave herself over wholly to Melancholy, and seemed to be much troubled with a peculiar Grief for some Reason or other: whether it were

The Queen sickneth at Windsor.

1603

Her Inauguration Ring taken off.

She groweth melancholick the probable Reasons thereof.

through the Violence of her Disease; or for want of *Essex*, (as *Essex* his Friends perswaded themselves;) or that, after so great Expenses in the Irish War, she was prevailed with to pardon the Rebell *Tir-Oen;* or that she had heard some Whisperings, and had also been advertised by the French King, that many of the Nobility did by underhand Letters and Messengers seek to curry Favour with the King of *Scots*, that they adored him as the rising Sun, and neglected her as being now ready to set. Which (as the female Sex and Old age are apt to be suspicious) she easily believed, and that not without good Cause: for

The Ungrate-fulness of some of the Courtiers.

some of the Lords of the Court, (to say nothing of the Ladies,) who had the least Reason of all to have done it, ungratefully in a manner forsook her, whilst she altered not from herself, but they from their Opinion of her, and Respect to her; either because they saw her now very aged; or were weary of her long Government, (for things of long Continuance, though never so good, are tedious;) or out of a credulous Desire of Novelty and Change, hoping for better Times, despising the present, and forgetting Favours past, (the Remembrance whereof is a Burthen to Unthankfull persons;) finding Fault with the state of things, haply out of a Mystery and Art of Court, to win Favour with her Successour, falsly believing that the Dispraise of the Predecessour is a gratefull and delightfull Hearing to the Successour. And this they did so openly, that they quarrelled one with another about it! and others propounded to have the Suc- page 659 / cessour sent for, whilst her Recovery was yet doubtfull; so as they seemed to have fled over to him in

The Queen's Complaint.

their Hearts, though their Bodies stayed at Home in *England.* Hereupon she looked upon herself as a miserable forlorn Woman, and her Grief and Indignation extorted from her such Speeches as these: *They have yoaked my Neck; I have none whom I can trust; My Condition is strangely turned upside down.* And, to increase this her Grief and Dissatisfaction, they made her believe that her Authority among the People sensibly decayed: Whereas the people (in whom there is always a murmuring and querulous Dislike of such as are in Authority) complained of nothing so much as that the Power of some near the Queen, if not above her, was grown too great; and that others were too hasty in catching and snatching for themselves (as is usuall in such cases) now they saw her grown old.

The Queen groweth worse.

When the Report now grew daily stronger and stronger that her Sickness increased upon her, and that, as she had done always before in the prime of her Age, so now much more she refused all Help of Physick, incredible it is with what great Speed the Puritans, Papists, Ambitious persons and Flatterers of all kinds, and other sorts of men, all of them prompted by their particular Hopes, poasted night and day by Sea and Land into Scotland, to adore the

The King of Scots courted by all parties.

rising King, and get into his Favour. Whose Title to the Succession the Queen (though out of Prudence she declared it not openly, yet) always really and from her Heart favoured, as Justice and Equity required: the like did all men of all Degrees and Qualities, who with great Satisfaction and Content had fixed their Eyes and Hearts upon him as her undoubted Heir; though false Rumours were spred abroad of a Marriage of the Lady *Arbella,* his Uncle's Daughter; and the French Embassadour did what he could to raise Disturbances, lest the two yet divided Kingdoms of *Britain, England* and *Scotland,* should be united into one. In the beginning of *March* an heavy Dulness, with a Frowardness familiar to Old age, began to seize upon her, insomuch as she would sit silent, refrain from Meat, fixing her Mind wholly upon her Meditations, and would not endure any Talk unless it were with the Archbishop of *Canterbury*, with whom she often prayed with great Fervency and Devotion, untill by little and little her Speech failed her; and after she willingly heard him praying by her. About this time the Lord Admirall telling the rest of the Privy Councill what the Qu. at her departing from *Westminster* had said to him by the Bye concerning her Successour, they all thought good that he with the Lord Keeper and the Secretary should wait upon her, and put her in Mind thereof, and acquaint her that they were come in the name of the rest of the Councill to understand her Pleasure touching her Successour. *The Queen declareth him her Successour.* The Qu. made Answer with a gasping Breath, *I said that my Throne was a Throne of Kings, that I would not have any mean Person succeed me.* The Secretary asking her what she meant by those words; *I will* (said she) *that a King succeed me: and Who Should that be but my nearest Kinsman,* **page 660 /** *the King of Scots?* Then being put in mind by the Archbishop to think upon God; *That I do,* (said she) *neither doth my Mind at all wander from him.* And when she could no longer pray with her Tongue, with Hands and Eyes lift up she directed the Thoughts of her pious Heart to God; and in this very thing she prayed, by sorrowing inwardly that she could not pray, as was plainly to be gathered by some Signs observed by the Standers by.

On the 24. of *March*, being the Eve of the Annunciation of the Blessed Virgin, she (who was born on the Eve of the Nativity of the same Blessed *Her Death.* Virgin) was called out of the Prison of her earthly Body to enjoy an everlasting Country in Heaven, peaceably and quietly leaving this Life after that happy manner of Departure which *Augustus* wished for, having reigned 44 years, 4 months, and in the 70. Year of her Age; to which no King of *England* ever attained before.   **page 661 /**

William Camden. *Remaines, concerning Britaine: But especially England, and the Inhabitants thereof.* London, 1614.

Language.

Hitherto will our sparkefull Youth laugh at their great grandfathers *English*, who had more care to do wel, than to speake minion-like, and left more glorie to vs by their exploiting of great actes, than we shall doe by our forging anew words, and vncuth phrases. . . .   **page 25 /**

The alteration and admiration in our tongue as in al others, hath bene brought in by entrance of Strangers, as *Danes, Normans,* and others which haue swarmed hither; by trafficke, for new words as well as for new wares, haue alwaies come in by the tyranne *Time,* which altereth all vnder heauen by *Vse,* which swayeth most, and hath an absolute command in words, and by *Pregnant* wits: specially since that learning after long banishment, was recalled in the time of king *Henry* the eight, it hath bene beautified and enriched out of other good tongues, partly by enfranchising and endenizing strange words, partly by refining and mollifying olde words, partly by implanting new words with artificiall composition, happily containing **page 27 /** themselues within the bounds prescribed by *Horace*. So that our tongue is (and I doubt not but hath beene) as copious, pithie, and significatiue, as any other tongue in *Europe*. . . .

. . . I thinke that our *English* tongue is (I will not say as sacred as the *Hebrew*, or as learned as the *Greeke*,) but as fluent as the *Latine*, as courteous as the *Spanish*, as courtlike as the *French*, and as amorous as the *Italian* as some Italianated amorous haue confessed. Neither hath any thing detracted more from the dignitie of our tong, than our own affecting of forraine tongues, by admiring, praising, and studying them aboue measure. . . .

As for the *Monosyllables* so rife in our tongue, which **page 28 /** were not so originally, although they are vnfitting for verses and measures, yet are they most fit for expressing briefly the first conceipts of the minde, or *Intentionalia* as they call them in schooles: so that we can set downe more matter in fewer lines, then any other language. Neither do wee or the Welsh so curtall the *Latine*, that wee make all therein *Monosyllables*, as *Ioseph Scaliger* chargeth vs. . . . I cannot yet but confesse that we haue corruptly contracted most names both of men and places, if they were of more then two syllables, and thereby hath ensued no little obscuritie. . . . **page 29 /**

Whereas the *Hebrew Rabbines* say, and that truly, that Nature hath giuen man fiue instruments for the pronouncing of all letters, the lips, the teeth, the tongue, the palate, and throate; I will not denie but some among vs do pro-**page 30 /** nounce more fully, some flatly, some broadly, and few mincingly, offending in defect, excesse, or chāge of letters, which is rather to bee imputed to the persons and their education, than to the language. . . . **page 31 /**

Money.

King *Henry* the eyght, who had infinite wealth left by his prudent and sparing Father, and so enriched himselfe by the spoyles of Abbayes, by first fruits, tenths, exactions, and absenties in Ireland, was yet so impouerished by his pompous profusion, that in his later dayes he first corrupted the rich coyne of this flourishing Kingdome with Copper, to his great dishonour, the dammage of Successors and the people, although for his aduantage for the present. . . . **page 208 /** But Queene *Elizabeth* of thrise happy memory to her euer glorious renowne, considering in the beginning of her raigne by the long sufferance of that base and copper monies, not onelie her crowne, Nobilitie, and subiects of this her Realme to be dayly more & more impouerished, the auncient and singular honour and estimation, which this Realme of England had beyond all other by plenty of monies of Gold and siluer, onely fine and not base, was hereby decayed, but also by reason of these said base monies, great quantity of forged and counterfets were dayly made and brought from beyond Seas, for the which the auncient fine gold and siluer, and the riche Merchandize of this Realme was transported and dayly carried out of the same, to the impouerishing therof and enriching of others. And finally hereby all manner of prices of things in this Realme, necessary for sustentation of the people, grew daily excessiue to the lamentable and manifest hurte and oppression of the state, specially of Pensioners, souldiers, and all hired seruants, and other meane people that liue by any kinde of wages, and not by rents of lands, or trade of Merchandize. Shee, vpon these considerations desirous to refine the coyne not according to the legall but naturall estimation of the metall, first marked the base money some with a grehound, other with a Portcullous, and other with a Lion, Harpe, Rose, or Floure de lys, and after a time calling them to her Minte, repayed so much for them as they conteined in pure siluer; so that by her benefit England enioyeth as fine, or rather finer sterling siluer then euer it was in this Realme by the space of two hundred yeares & more. . . .

page 209 /

Richard Carew (1555–1620) was a poet and antiquary. An Epistle concerning the excellencie of the English tongue *appeared in the second edition of Camden's* Remaines *(1605). Aside from a general comparison of English to other languages, interesting from the standpoint of the history of the English language, the work is important because of Carew's reference, in a comparison of English and foreign writers, to Shakespeare and some of his contemporaries.*

Richard Carew. *The Excellencie of the English tongue by R. C. of Anthony Esquire to W. C.* (1595). Printed by William Camden in *Remaines, concerning Britaine*, London, 1614.

Locutio is defined, *Animi sensus per vocem expressio*. On which ground I build these consequence, that the first and principall point sought in euery language, is that we may expresse the meaning of our mindes aptly each to other. Next that we may do it readily without great adoe. Then fully, so as others may throughly conceiue vs. And last of all handsomly that those to whom we speak may take pleasure in hearing vs, so as whatsoeuer tongue will gaine the race of perfection, must runne on these foure wheeles, *Sig-* page 36 / *nificancie, Easinesse, Copiousnesse*, and *Sweetnesse*, of which the two foremost import a necessitie, the two latter a delight. Now if I can prooue that our English language, for all, or the most, is matchable, if not preferrable before any other in vse at this day, I hope the assent of any impartiall Reader will passe on my side. . . .

Foure points requisite in a language.

To beginne then with the Significancie, it consisteth in the letters, words, and phrases. And because the Greeke and Latine haue euer borne away the prerogatiue from all other tongues, they shall serue as touchstones to make our triall by.

Significancie.

For letters we haue K more then the Greekes, K and Y more then the Latines, and W more then them both, or the French and Italians.

Letters.

. . . .

Now for the significancie of words, as euery *Indiuiduum* is but one, so in our natiue English-Saxon language, wee finde many of them suitably expressed by words of one syllable: those consisting of more are borrowed from other nations, the examples are infinite, and therefore I wil omit them as sufficiently notorious.

Words.

Againe for expressing our passions, our interiections are very apt and forcible. As finding ourselues somewhat agreeued, we crie *Ah*, if more deepely *Oh*, when wee pittie *Alas*, when we bemoane, *Alacke*, neither of them so effeminate as the Italiā *Deh* or the French *Helas*: in detestatiō page 37 / wee say *Phy*, as if therewithall we should spit. In attention *Haa*, in calling *Whowpe*,

Interiections.

22

in hallowing *Wahabowe*, all which (in my eare) seeme to be deriued from the very natures of those seuerall affections.

Grow from hence to the composition of words, and therein our language hath a peculiar grace, a like significancie, and more short then the Greekes, for example in *Moldwarp* wee expresse the nature of that beast. In *handkercher* the thing and his vse. In *vpright* that vertue by a Metaphore. In *Wisedome* and *Doomes-day*, so many sentences as words, and so of the rest, for I giue onely a taste that may direct others to a fuller obseruation of what my sudden memorie cannot represent vnto mee. It may passe also the masters of this significancie, that in a manner all the proper names of our people doe import somewhat which from a peculiar note at first of some one of the progenitors in processe of time inuested it selfe in a possession of the posteritie, euen as wee see like often befall to those whose fathers bare some vncouth Christian names. Yet for the most part wee auoide the blemish giuen by the Romans, in like cases, who distinguished the persons by the imperfections of their bodies, from whence grew their *Nasones, Labeones, Frontones, Dentones*, & such like. . . . Yea so significant are our words that amongst them sundry single ones, serue to expresse diuers things, as by *Bill* is meant a weapon, a scroll, and a birds beake, by *Graue*, sober, a tombe, and to carue, and by *Light, marke, match, file, sore*, and *pray*, the semblable. . . . **page 38 /**

> *Composition of words.*
>
> *Names.*
>
> *Equiuoca.*

Neither may I omit the significancie of our prouerbes concise in words but plentifull in number, briefely pointing at many great matters, and vnder the circuite of a few syllables prescribing sundry auaileable caueats.

> *Prouerbs.*

Lastly, our speech doth not consist onely of words but in a sort euen of deeds, as when wee expresse a matter by Metaphors, wherein the English is verie fruitfull and forcible. . . .

> *Metaphors.*

Now for his easiness in learning . . . , the most part of our words (as I haue touched) are Monasyllables, and so the fewer in tale, and the sooner reduced to memorie, neither are wee loden with those declensions, flexions, and variations, which are incident to many other tongues, but a few articles gouerne all our verbes and Nownes, and so wee read a very short Grammer. . . . **page 39 /**

> *Easines to be learned.*

But I must now enter into the large field of our tongs copiousnesse, and perhaps long wander vp and downe without finding easie way of Issue, and yet leaue many parts thereof vnsurueied.

> *3. Copiousnes.*

My first proofe of our plenty I borrow from the choice which is giuen vs by the vse of diuers languages. The ground of our owne appertaineth to the old Saxon little differing from the present low *Dutch*, because they more then any of their neighbours haue hitherto preserued that speech from any great forreine mixture; here amongst, the Brittons haue left diuers of their words intersowed, as it were thereby making a continuall claime to their auncient possession. Wee may also trace the footsteps of the *Danish* bitter (though not long during) soueraigntie in these parts, and the *Romane* also imparteed vnto vs of his latine riches with no sparing hand. Our neighbours the French, haue bin likewise contented we should take vp by retaile as well their tearmes as their fashions: or rather we retaine yet but some remnant of that which once here bare all the sway, and daily renew the store. So haue our Italian trauailers brought vs acquainted with their sweete

> *Borrowing.*

relished phrases, which (so thier conditions crept not in withall) were the better tolerable, yea euen wee seeke to make our good of our late Spanish enemie, and feare as little the hurt of his tongue as the dint of his sword. Seeing then we borrow (and that not shamefully) from the *Dutch*, the *Britaine*, the *Romane*, the *Dane*, the *French*, the *Italian*, and *Spanyard;* how can our stocke bee other then exceeding plentifull? It may be obiected that such patching maketh *Littletons* hotch-pot of our tongue, and in effect brings the same rather to a Babellish confusion, then any one entire language. **page 40 /**

Answer. It may againe bee answered, that this theft of words is no lesse warranted by the priuiledge of a prescription, auncient and vniuersall, then was that of goods amongst the *Lacedemonians* by an enacted law; for so the Greekes robbed the Hebrewes, the Latins, the Greekes (which filching *Cicero* with a large discourse in his booke *de Oratore* defendeth) and (in a manner) all other Christian Nations the Latine....

Increase on borrowing. For our owne parts, we employ the borrowed ware so farre to our advantage that we raise a profit of new words from the same stocke, which yet in their owne countrey are not merchantable. For example, wee deduce diuers words from the Latine, which in the Latine it selfe cannot bee yeelded, as the verbs, *To Aire, to beard, to crosse, to flame,* and their deriuations, ayring, ayred, bearder, bearding, bearded, &c. as also closer, closely, closenesse, glosingly, hourely, maiesticall, maiestically. In like sort we graffe vpon French words those buds, to which that soile affoordeth no growth, as *chiefly, faulty, slauish, precisenesse.* Diuers words also wee deriue out of the Latine at second hand by the **page 41 /** French, and made good English, though both Latine and French haue their hands closed in that behalfe, as in these verbes, *Pray, Point, Paze, Prest, Rent, &c.* and also in the Aduerbes *Carpingly, Currantly, Actiuely, Colourably,* &c.....

Of Latine the French. Moreouer the copiousnesse of our language appeareth in the diuersitie of our Dialects, for wee haue Court and wee haue Countrey English, wee haue Northerne and Southerne, grosse and ordinarie, which differ each from other, not onely in the terminations, but also in many words, termes, and phrases, and expresse the same things in diuers sorts, yet all right English alike, neither can any tongue (as I am perswaded) deliuer a matter with more varietie then ours, both plainely and by prouerbs and Metaphors: for example, when wee would bee rid of one, wee vse to say, *bee going, trudge, packe, bee faring, hence, away, shift,* and by circumlocution; *Rather your roome then your company, lets see your backe, come againe when I bid you, when you are called, sent for, intreated, willed, desired, inuited, spare vs your place, another in your steed, a shippe of Salt for you, saue your credite, you are next the doore, the doore is open for you, there is no body holdeth you, no body teares your sleeue, &c.* ...

All sorts of verses. And in a word, to close vp these proofs of our copiousnesse, looke into our Imitations of all sorts of verses affoorded by any other language, and you shall finde that **page 42 /** Sir *Philip Sidney*, Maister *Puttenham*, Maister *Stanihurst*, and diuers more haue made vse how farre wee are within compasse of a fore imagined possibilitie in that behalfe.

I come now to the last and sweetest point of the sweetnesse of our

tongue. . . . The Italian is pleasant but without sinewes as a still fleeting water. *Sweetnesse.*
The French, delicate, but euen nice as a woman, scarce daring to open her
lippes for feare of marring her countenance. The Spanish maiesticall, but *Compared*
fulsome, running too much on the O. and terrible like the diuell in a play. *with others.*
The Dutch manlike but withall verie harsh, as one readie at euerie word
to picke a quarrell. Now we in borrowing from them, giue the strength
of consonants to the Italian, the full sound of wordes to the French, the
varietie of terminations to the Spanish, and the mollifying of more vowels
to the Dutch, and so (like Bees) gather the honey of their good properties and leaue the dregges to themselues. . . .

Againe, the long words that we borrow being intermingled with the
short of our owne store, make vp a perfect harmonie, by culling from *Mixture.*
out which mixture (with iudgement) you may frame your speech according to the matter you must worke on, maiesticall, pleasant, delicate, or
manly more or lesse, in what sort you please. Adde hereunto, that whatsoeuer grace any other language carrieth in verse or Prose, in Tropes or
Metaphors, in Ecchoes and Agnominations, they may all bee liuely and
exactly represented in ours: will you haue Platoes veine? reade Sir *Thomas
Smith*, the *Ionicke?* Sir *Thomas Moore. Ciceroes? Ascham, Varro? Chaucer,
Demosthenes?* Sir *Iohn Cheeke* . . . **page 43 /** Will you reade Virgill? take
the Earle of Surrey. *Catullus?* Shakespeare and Barlowes fragment, Ouid?
Daniell, Lucan? Spencer, Martial? Sir Iohn Dauies and others: will you haue
all in all for Prose and verse? take the miracle of our age Sir Philip Sidney.

And thus if mine owne eyes bee not blinded by affection, I haue made
yours to see that the most renowned of other nations haue layed vp, as
in treasure, and entrusted the *Diuisos orbe Britannos,* with the rarest Iewels
of their lips perfections, whether you respect the vnderstanding for signif-
icance, or the memorie for easinesse, or the conceite for plentifulnesse,
or the eare for pleasantnesse. . . . **page 44 /**

Robert Carey (1560?–1639) was a courtier in the courts of both Elizabeth and James I. In March, 1603, he was present at court during the last illness of Elizabeth. On March 19, 1603, he rushed to Edinburgh to assure James that the queen was near death and that he stood ready to serve him. When Elizabeth died on the morning of March 24th, Carey, despite the prohibition of the queen's council, left London to inform James of her death, for which he was temporarily rewarded. Later, however, the king's favor was withdrawn when it seemed apparent that Carey's actions were generally disapproved. He was able to regain his position and to live prosperously at court within a few years. The Memoirs *provide an eyewitness account of two of the most important events of the period: the battle between the English and Spanish fleets in the Channel and the death of Elizabeth with the accompanying political tensions.*

Memoirs of the Life of Robert Carey, Baron of Leppington, and Earl of Monmouth, And now published from an Original Manuscript in the Custody of John Earl of Corke and Orrery. London, 1759.

The next yeare (1588) the King of *Spain*'s great *Armado* came upon our
page 17 / coast, thinking to devour us all. Upon the newes sent to court from *Plimouth* of their certain arrivall, my Lord *Cumberland* and myselfe tooke post horse, and rode streight to *Portsmouth*, where we found a frigot that carried us to sea; and having sought for the fleets a whole day, the night after wee fell amongst them; where it was our fortune to light first on the *Spanish* fleet; and finding ourselves in the wrong, we tackt about, and in short time gott to our own fleet, which was not farre from the other. At our coming aboord our Admirall, wee stay'd there awhile; but finding the ship much pestered, and scant of cabbins, we left the Admirall, and went aboord Captain *Reyman*, where wee stay'd, and were very welcome, and much made of. It was on Thursday that wee came to the fleete. All that page 18 / day wee followed close the *Spanish Armado*, and nothing was attempted on either side: the same course wee held all Friday and Saturday, by which time the *Spanish* fleet cast anchor just before *Calais*. We likewise did the same, a very small distance behind them, and so continued till Munday morning about two of the clocke; in which time our Counsaile of warre had provided six old hulkes, and stuffed them full of all combustible matter fitt for burning, and on Munday at two in the morning they were lett loose, with each of them a man in her to direct them. The tide serving they brought them very near the *Spanish* fleet, so that they could not misse to come amongst the midest of them: then they set fire on them, and came off themselves, having each of them a little boate to bring him off.
page 19 / The ships set on fire, came so directly to the *Spanish* fleet, as they

had no way to avoid them, but to cut all their halsers, and so escape; and their haste was such that they left one of their four great galeasses on ground before *Calais*, which our men took and had the spoil of, where many of the *Spaniards* were slaine with the Governour thereof, but most of them were saved with wading ashore to *Calais*. They being in this disorder, wee made ready to follow them, where began a cruell fight, and wee had such advantage both of wind and tide, as wee had a glorious day of them; continuing fight from foure o'clocke in the morning, till almost five or six at night, where they lost a douzen or fourteene of their best shippes, some sunke, and the rest ranne ashore in diverse parts to keep **page 20 /** themselves from sinking. After God had given us this great victory, they made all the hast they could away, and wee followed them Tuesday and Wednesday, by which time they were gotten as farre as *Hamborough-head*. It was resolved on Wednesday at night, that by four o'clocke on Thursday, wee should have a new fight with them for a farewell; but by two in the morning, there was a flagge of Counsaile hung out in our Vice Admirall, when it was found that in the whole fleet there was not munition sufficient to make halfe a fight; and therefore it was there concluded that we should let them passe, and our fleet to return to the *Downes*. That night wee parted with them, wee had a mighty storme. Our fleet cast anchor, and endured it: but the *Spanish* fleet, wanting their anchors, were **page 21 /** many of them cast ashore on the west of *Ireland*, where they had all their throates cutt by the [18] Kernes; and some of them on *Scotland*, where they were no better used: and the rest (with much adoe) gott into *Spaine* againe.... **page 22 /**

. . . .

... Having little to do, I resolved upon a journey to court, to see my friends and renew my acquaintance there. I tooke my journey about the end of the year.[91] When I came to the court I found the Queene ill disposed, and shee kept her inner lodging; yet shee hearing of my arrivall sent for mee. I found her in one of her withdrawing chambers, sitting low upon her cushions. Shee called mee to her, I kist her hand, and told her it was my chiefest happinesse to see her in safety and in health, which I wished might long continue. Shee tooke mee by the hand, and wrung it hard, and said, "No, *Robin*, I am not well," **page 136 /** and then discoursed with mee of her indisposition, and that her heart had been sad and heavy for ten or twelve dayes, and in her discourse she fetched not so few as forty or fifty great sighes. I was grieved at the first to see her in this plight; for in all my lifetime before I never knew her to fetch a sigh, but when the Queene of *Scottes* was beheaded. Then [92] upon my knowledge she shedd many teares and [93] sighes, manifesting her innocence that she never gave consent to the death of that Queene.

I used the best words I could to persuade her from this melancholy humour; but I found by her it was too deep rooted in her heart, and hardly **page 137 /** to be removed. This was upon a Saturday night, and she gave command

---

[18] Irish foot soldiers.
[91] 1602.
[92] *At that time* — In the year 1587.
[93] They were indeed necessary upon that occasion.

that the great closet should be prepared for her to go to chappell the next morning. The next day, all things being in a readinesse, wee long expected her coming. After eleven o'clock, one of the [94] groomes came out and bade make ready for the private closet, she would not go to the great. There wee stay'd long for her coming, but at the last she had cushions lay'd for her in the privy chamber hard by the closet doore, and there she heard service.

From that day forwards she grew worse and worse. She remained upon her cushions four dayes and nights at the least. All about her could not persuade her either to take any sustenance or go to bed.   page 138 /

I hearing that neither the physitians, nor none about her could persuade her to take any course for her safety, feared her death would soone after ensue. I could not but think in what a wretched estate I should be left, most of my livelyhood depending on her life. And hereupon I bethought myselfe with what grace and favour I was ever received by the King of *Scottes*, whensoever I was sent to him. I did assure myselfe it was neither unjust nor unhonest for me to do for myselfe, if God at that time should call her to his mercy. Hereupon I wrote to the King of *Scottes* (knowing him to be the right heire to the crowne of [95] *England*) and certified him in what state her Majestie   page 139 /   was. I desired him not to stirr from *Edenborough;* if of that sicknesse she should die, I would be the first man that should bring him newes of it.

The Queene grew worse and worse, because she would be so, none about her being able to perswade her to go to bed. My Lord [96] Admirall was sent for (who by reason of my sister's death, that was his wife, had absented himselfe some fortnight from court); what by faire meanes, what by force, he gatt her to bed. There was no hope of her recovery, because she refused all remedies.

On Wednesday the twenty-third of *March*, she grew speechless. That afternoone, by signes, she called for her   page 140 /   Councill, and by putting her hand to her [97] head, when the King of *Scottes* was named to succeed her they all knew hee was the man she desired should reigne after her.

About six at night she made signes for the [98] Archbishop and her Chap-
page 141 /   lains to come to her, at which time I went in with them, and sate upon my knees full of teares to see that heavy sight. Her Majestie lay upon

[94] Of the chambers.

[95] Protestants and papists unanimously allowed his right: not a murmur arose against it.

[96] Charles Howard Earl of Nottingham, married to Catherine eldest daughter of Henry Lord Hunsdon.

[97] The sign here mentioned is a true and indisputable fact, otherwise it would not have been inserted by the plain, sincere, and ingenuous author of these Memoirs, who was present at the time the sign was made. But still it remains a doubt whether the Queen intended it for a sign or not. The Lords present pretended to think it one.

[98] John Whitgift, Archbishop of Canterbury. He was highly esteemed by Queen Elizabeth for his sense, learning, and piety. The Queen, who was particularly wary what concessions she made, and to whom she granted them, allowed Archbishop Whitgift in the year 1579, (then Bishop of Worcester) the power of bestowing the prebends of his church on such persons as he thought fit, which disposal before this time, had not been in the   page 141 /   nomination of the Bishop, but of the Crown; nor did she now give away the right of such disposal to him, and his successors, but only as a particular favour to himself during his continuance in that see. And in the year 1580, the nomination of Justices of the Peace for Worcestershire and Warwickshire was left to his discretion. Such confidence did the Queen repose in the wisdom and integrity of this Bishop. — See the lives of the Archbishops.
— page 142 /

her backe, with one hand in the bed, and the other without. The Bishop kneeled downe by her, and examined her first of her faith, and she so punctually answered all his several questions, by lifting up her eyes and holding up her hand, as it was a comfort to all the beholders. Then the good man told her plainly, what she was, and what she was to page 142 / come to; and though she had been long a great Queene here upon earth, yet shortly she was to yield an accompt of her stewardship to the King of Kings. After this he began to pray, and all that were by did answer him. After he had continued long in prayer, 'till the old man's knees were weary, hee blessed her, and meant to rise and leave her. The Queene made a signe with her hand. My sister [99] *Scroope* knowing her meaning, told the Bishop the Queene desired hee would pray still. Hee did so for a long halfe houre after, and then thought to leave her. The second time she made signe to have him continue in prayer. He did so for halfe an houre more, with earnest cryes to God for her soule's health, page 143 / which he uttered with that fervency of spirit, as the Queene to all our sight much rejoiced thereat, and gave testimony to us all of her christian and comfortable end. By this time it grew late, and every one departed, all but her women that attended her.

This that I heard with my eares, and did see with my eyes, I thought it my duty to set downe, and to affirme it for a truth, upon the faith of a christian, because I know there have beene many false lyes reported of the end and death of that good lady.

I went to my lodging, and left word with one in the Cofferer's chamber to call mee, if that night it was thought shee would die, and gave the porter an angell to let me in at any time when I called. Betweene one and two of the clock on Thursday morning, he that I left in the Cofferer's chamber page 144 / brought mee word the Queene was [1] dead. I rose and made all the hast to the gate to gett in. There I was answered, I could not enter; the Lords of the Councill having been with him, had commanded him that none should go in or out, but by warrant from them. At that very instant, one of the Councill (the Comptroller) asked whether I was at the gate. I said yes. He said to mee, if I pleased hee would let mee in. I desired to know how the Queene did. He answered, pretty well. I bade him good night. He replied, and said, Sir, if you will come in, I will give you my word and credit you shall go out againe at your own pleasure. Upon his word I entered the gate, and page 145 / came up to the Cofferer's chamber, where I found all the ladies weeping bitterly. Hee led mee from thence to the privy chamber, where all the Councill was assembled; there I was caught hold of, and assured I should not go for *Scotland*, till their pleasures were farther knowne. I told them I came of purpose to that end. From thence they all went to the Secretaryes chamber, and as they went, they gave a speciall command to the porters, that none should go out of the gates but such servants as they should send to prepare their coaches and horses for *London*. There I was left in the middest of the court to think my owne thoughts 'till they had done counsaile. I went to my [2] brother's cham-

[99] Philadelphia Lady Scroope, second daughter of Henry Cary Lord Hunsdon.

[1] She died March 24, soon after the Archbishop had left her, about three o'clock in the morning.

[2] George Lord Hunsdon, a Privy Councellor, Captain of the Band of Pensioners, Governor of the Isle of Wight, and Knight of the Garter.

ber, who **page 146 /** was in bed, having been over-watched many nightes before. I gott him up with all speed, and when the Councill's men were going out of the gate, my brother thrust to the gate. The porter knowing him to be a great officer, lett him out. I pressed after him, and was stayed by the porter. My brother said angrily to the porter, "Let him out, I will answer for him." Whereupon I was suffered to passe, which I was not a little glad of.... **page 147 /**

Thomas Decker (1570?–1632) was a poet, dramatist, and pamphleteer. As a dramatist he wrote for Philip Henslowe's company, frequently in collaboration with other well-known dramatists. His best known plays are The Shoemaker's Holiday *and* Old Fortunatus. *As a pamphleteer he wrote extensively.* The Gull's Hornbook *is a satire on manners, in which the fops and gallants of the Elizabethan society are ridiculed under the guise of ironic instructions to a would-be gallant from the country. Chapter VI, "How a Gallant Should Behave Himself in a Playhouse," is not only an amusing satire but an interesting source of information concerning the Elizabethan theater.*

Thomas Decker. *The Gull's Hornbook* in *The Old Book Collector's Miscellany*, Vol. II. Edited by Charles Hindley, London, 1872.

CHAPTER VI

How a gallant should behave himself in a playhouse.

Since then the place is so free in entertainment, allowing a stool as well to the farmer's son as to your templar: that your stinkard has the selfsame liberty to be there in his tobacco-fumes, which your sweet courtier hath; and that your carman and tinker claim as strong a voice in their suffrage, and page 53 / sit to give judgment on the play's life and death, as well as the proudest *Momus* among the tribes of critic: it is fit that he, whom the most tailors' bills do make room for, when he comes, should not be basely, like a viol, cased up in a corner.

Whether therefore the gatherers of the public, or private playhouse stand to receive the afternoon's rent; let our gallant, having paid it, presently advance himself up to the throne of the stage; I mean not into the lords' room, which is now but the stage's suburbs; no; those boxes, by the iniquity of custom, conspiracy of waiting-women and gentlemen-ushers that there sweat together, and the covetousness of sharers, are contemptibly thrust into the rear; and much new satin is there damned, by being smothered to death in darkness. But on the very rushes [1] where the comedy is to dance, yea, and under the state of *Cambyses* himself, must our feathered ostrich, like a piece of ordinance, be planted valiantly, because impudently, beating down the mews [2] and hisses of the opposed rascality.

For do but cast up a reckoning; what large comings-in are pursed up by

---

[1] Rushes. — The stage was always strewed with *rushes*. [*Footnotes are Hindley's.* — Ed.]
[2] Mews — *i.e.*, Caterwauling. — CAT-CALL. — A kind of whistle used in theatres to interrupt the actors.

sitting on the stage? First a conspicuous eminence is gotten; by which means, the best and most essential parts of a gallant's, **page 54 /** good clothes, a proportionable leg, white hand, the Parisian lock, and a tolerable beard, are perfectly revealed.

By sitting on the stage, you have signed patent to engross the whole commodity of censure, may lawfully presume to be a girder,[1] and stand at the helm to steer the passage of scenes; yet no man shall once offer to hinder you from obtaining the title of an insolent, over-weening coxcomb.

By sitting on the stage, you may, without travelling for it, at the very next door ask whose play it is; and, by that quest of inquiry, the law warrants you to avoid much mistaking; if you know not the author, you may rail against him; and peradventure so behave yourself, that you may enforce the author to know you. . . . **page 55 /**

By spreading your body on the stage, and by being a justice in examining of plays, you shall put yourself into such true scenical authority, that some poet shall not dare to present his muse rudely upon your eyes, without having first unmasked her, rifled her, and discovered all her bare and most mystical parts before you at a tavern; when you most knightly shall, for his pains, pay for both their suppers.

By sitting on the stage, you may, with small cost, purchase the dear acquaintance of the boys; have a good stool for sixpence; at any time know what particular part any of the infants [re]present; get your match lighted; examine the play-suits' lace, **page 56 /** and perhaps win wagers upon laying 'tis copper; &c. . . .

. . . Present not yourself on the stage, especially at a new play, until the quacking Prologue hath by rubbing got colour into his cheeks, and is ready to give the trumpets their cue that he is upon point to enter; for then it is time, as though you were one of the properties, or that you dropped out of the hangings, to creep from behind the arras, with your tripos or three-footed stool in one hand, and a teston[2] mounted **page 57 /** between a forefinger and a thumb in the other; for, if you should bestow your person upon the vulgar, when the belly of the house is but half full, your apparel is quite eaten up, the fashion lost, and the proportion of your body is in more danger to be devoured than if it were served up in the Counter amongst the poultry[1]: avoid that as you would the Bastone.[2] It shall crown you with rich commendation, to laugh aloud in the midst of the most serious and saddest scene of the terriblest tragedy; and to let that clapper, your tongue, be tossed so high, that all the house may ring of it: your lords use it; your knights are apes to the lords, and do so too; your inn-a-court man is zany to the knights, and (many very scurvily) comes likewise limping after it: be thou a beagle to them all, and never lin[3] snuffing till you have scented them: for by talking and laughing, like a ploughman in a morris, you heap *Pelion* upon *Ossa*, glory upon glory; as first, all the eyes in the galleries will leave walking after the players, and only follow you; the simplest dolt in the house snatches up your name, and, when he meets you in

---

[1] Girder. — A jester or satirist.   [2] Teston or *Tester*. — Sixpence.

[1] Counter amongst the poultry. — A punning allusion to the Compter prison, which was situate in the Poultry in Cheapside.

[2] Bastone. — A bastinado.

[3] Lin. — To cease; to stop.

the streets, or that you fall into his hands in the middle of a watch, his word shall be taken for you; he will cry "he's such a gallant," **page 58 /** and you pass: secondly, you publish your temperance to the world, in that you seem not to resort thither to taste vain pleasures with a hungry appetite; but only as a gentleman to spend a foolish hour or two, because you can do nothing else: thirdly, you mightily disrelish the audience, and disgrace the author: Marry; you take up, though it be at the worst hand, a strong opinion of your own judgment, and enforce the poet to take pity of your weakness, and, by some dedicated sonnet, to bring you into a better paradise, only to stop your mouth. . . . **page 59 /**

Before the play begins, fall to cards; you may win or lose, as fencers do in a prize, and beat one another by confederacy, yet share the money when you meet at supper: notwithstanding, to gull the ragamuffins that stand aloof gaping at you, throw the cards, having first torn four or five of them, round about the stage, just upon the third sound,[2] as though you had lost; it skills not if the four knaves lie on their backs, and outface the audience; there's none such fools as dare take exceptions at them; because, ere the play go off, better knaves than they will fall into the company.

Now, sir; if the writer be a fellow that hath either epigrammed you, or hath had a flirt at your mistress, or hath brought either your feather, or your red beard, or your little legs, &c.[3] on the stage; you **page 60 /** shall disgrace him worse than by tossing him in a blanket, or giving him the bastinado in a tavern, if, in the middle of his play, be it pastoral or comedy, moral or tragedy, you rise with a screwed and discontented face from your stool to be gone; no matter whether the scenes be good, or no; the better they are, the worse do you distaste them: and, being on your feet, sneak not away like a coward; but salute all your gentle acquaintance, that are spread either on the rushes, or on stools about you; and draw what troop you can from the stage after you, the mimics are beholden to you for allowing them elbow room: their poet cries, perhaps, "a pox go with you;" but care not for that; there is no music without frets.

Marry: if either the company, or indisposition of the weather bind you to sit it out; my counsel is then that you turn plain ape: take up a rush, and tickle the earnest ears of your fellow gallants, to make other fools fall a laughing; mew at passionate speeches; blare at merry; find fault with the music; whew at the children's action; whistle at the songs; and, above all, curse the sharers, that whereas the same day you had bestowed forty shillings on an embroidered felt and feather, Scotch fashion, for **page 61 /** your mistress in the court, or your punk in the city, within two hours after you encounter with the very same block on the stage, when the haberdasher swore to you the impression was extant but that morning.

---

2 THIRD SOUND. — At the *third sounding*, or flourish of trumpets, the curtain which concealed the stage from the audience, was drawn (opening in the middle) and the play began.

3 FEATHER, RED BEARD, LITTLE LEGS, &c. — Here Decker retorts on Ben Jonson, who in his *The Poetaster*, act iii, sc. 1, makes mention of — "He, with the ash-coloured feather there," "Little Legs," "And shall your hair change like these?" The *blanketting* alludes to the punishment inflicted on him as Horace in the *Satiromastrix*, and the *bastinadoing* to a circumstance of which — whether true or not — several hints are to be found in the same play.

To conclude. Hoard up the finest play-scraps you can get; upon which your lean wit may most savourily feed, for want of other stuff, when the Arcadian and Euphuesed [1] gentlewomen have their tongues sharpened to set upon you.... page 62 /

[1] Arcadian and euphuesed gentlewomen. — Such as had studied Sir Philip Sidney's *Arcadia* and John Lilly's *Euphues*, and *The Anatomy of Wit*, and *Euphues and his England*, 1579–81.

*George Gascoigne (1525?–1577) was highly praised by such of his con-
temporaries as William Webbe, Francis Meres, and Gabriel Harvey as a
wit, poet, dramatist, and satirist.* His Certayne Notes of Instruction in
English Verse *was included in the 1575 volume of* The Poesies of George
Gascoigne, Esquire. *Commenting on such matters as decorum, versification, the use of obsolete and foreign words, and the sacrifice of reason to rime, Gascoigne has the distinction thereby of having written the
earliest critical essay in English. His* Supposes, *an adaptation of Ariosto's*
Suppositi *is the earliest extant comedy in English prose; the* Jocasta,
paraphrased from the Phoenissae *of Euripides and included in* The
Poesies, *is the second earliest blank verse tragedy in English. Gascoigne
thus stands as an important pioneer and experimenter in English literary
history.*

George Gascoigne. *Certayne Notes of Instruction in English Verse* (1575).
   Edited by Edward Arber, London, 1869.

The first and most necessarie poynt that euer I founde meete to be considered
in making of a delectable poeme is this, to grounde it upon some fine inuention. For it is not inough to roll in pleasant woordes, nor yet to thunder in
Rym, Ram, Ruff, by letter (quoth my master *Chaucer*) nor yet to abounde in
apt vocables, or epythetes, vnlesse the Inuention haue in it also *aliquid salis*.
By this *aliquid salis*, I meane some good and fine deuise, shewing the quicke
capacitie of a writer: and where I say some *good and fine inuention*, I meane
that I would haue it both fine and good. For many inuentions are so superfine,
that they are *Vix good*. And againe many Inuentions are good, and yet not
finely handled. And for a general forwarning: what Theame soeuer you do
take in hande, if you do... **page 31 /** neuer studie for some depth of
deuise in ye Inuention, and some figures also in the handlyng thereof: it will
appeare to the skilfull Reader but a tale of a tubbe. To deliuer vnto you
generall examples it were almoste vnpossible, sithence the occasions of
Inuentions are (as it were) infinite: neuerthelesse take in worth mine opinion,
and perceyue my furder meanyng in these few poynts. If I should vndertake
to wryte in prayse of a gentlewoman, I would neither praise hir christal
eye, nor hir cherrie lippe, etc. .... But I would either finde some supernaturall
cause wherby my penne might walke in the superlatiue degree, or els I
would vndertake to aunswere for any imperfection that shee hath, and
therevpon rayse the prayse of hir commendation. Likewise if I should
disclose my pretence in loue, I would eyther make a strange discourse of
some intollerable passion, or finde occasion to pleade by the example of
some historie, or discouer my disquiet in shadowes *per Allegoriam*, or

vse the couertest meane that I could to auoyde the vncomely customes of
common writers. Thus much I aduenture to deliuer vnto you . . . vpon the rule
of Inuention, which of all other rules is most to be marked, and hardest to be
prescribed in certayne and infallible rules, neuerthelesse to conclude therein, I
would haue you stand most vpon the excellencie of your Inuention, and sticke
not to studie deepely for some fine deuise. For that beyng founde, pleasant
woordes will follow well inough and fast inough.

2. Your Inuention being once deuised, take heede that neither pleasure of
rime, nor varietie of deuise, do carie you from it: for as to vse obscure and darke
phrases in a pleasant Sonet, is nothing delectable, so to entermingle merie iests
in a serious matter is an *Indecorum.*

3. I will next aduise you that you hold the iust measure wherwith you begin
your verse, I will not denie but this may seeme a preposterous ordre: but
page 32 / bycause I couet rather to satisfie you particularly, than to
vndertake a generall tradition, I wil not somuch stand vpon the manner as the
matter of my precepts. I say then, remember to holde the same measure
wherwith you begin, whether it be in a verse of sixe syllables, eight, ten, twelue,
etc. and though this precept might seeme ridiculous vnto you, since euery yong
scholler can conceiue that he ought to continue in the same measure wherwith
he beginneth, yet do I see and read many mens Poems now adayes, whiche
beginning with the measure of xij. in the first line, and xiiij. in the second
(which is the common kinde of verse) they wil yet (by that time they haue
passed ouer a few verses) fal into xiiij. and fourtene, *et sic de similibus,* the
which is either forgetfulnes or carelesnes.

4. And in your verses remembre to place euery worde in his natural *Emphasis* or sound, that is to say in such wise, and with such length or shortnesse,
eleuation or depression of sillables, as it is commonly pronounced or vsed. . . .
For example of th' emphasis or natural sound of words, this word *Treasure,*
hath the graue accent vpon the first sillable, whereas if it shoulde be written in
this sorte, *Treasúre,* nowe were the second sillable long, and that were cleane
contrarie to the common vse wherwith it is pronounced. For furder ex-
planation hereof, note you that commonly now a dayes in english rimes (for I
dare not cal them English   **page 33 /**   verses) we vse none other order but
a foote of two sillables, wherof the first is depressed or made short, and the
second is eleuate or made long: and that sound or scanning continueth throughout the verse. We have vsed in times past other kindes of Meeters. . . .

Also our father *Chaucer* hath vsed the same libertie in feete and measures that
the Latinists do vse: and who so euer do peruse and well consider his workes,
he shall finde that although his lines are not alwayes of one selfe same number
of Syllables, yet beyng redde by one that hath vnderstanding, the longest verse
and that which hath most Syllables in it, will fall (to the eare) correspondent
vnto that whiche hath fewest sillables in it: and like wise that whiche hath
in it fewest syllables, shalbe founde yet to consist of woordes that haue
suche naturall sounde, as may seeme equall in length to a verse which
hath many moe sillables of lighter accentes. And surely I can lament that wee
are fallen into suche a playne and simple manner of wryting, that there is none
other foote vsed but one: wherby our Poemes may iustly be called Rithmes,
and cannot by any right challenge the name of a Verse. But since it is so, let vs

take the forde as we finde it, and lette me set downe vnto you suche rules and
precepts that euen in this playne foote of two syllables you wreste no woorde
from his natural and vsuall sounde, I do not meane hereby that you may vse
none other wordes but of twoo sillables, for therein you may vse discretion
according to occasion of matter: but my meaning is, that all the wordes in your
verse be so placed as the first sillable may sound short or be depressed, the
second long or eleuate, the third shorte, the fourth long, the fifth shorte,
etc. . . . **page 34 /**

5. Here by the way I thinke it not amisse to forewarne you that you thrust
as few wordes of many sillables into your verse as may be: and herevnto I
might alledge many reasons: first the most auncient English wordes are of one
sillable, so that the more monasyllables that you vse, the truer Englishman you
shall seeme, and the lesse you shall smell of the Inke-horne. Also wordes of
many syllables do cloye a verse and make it vnpleasant, whereas woordes of
one syllable will more easily fall to be shorte or long as occasion requireth, or
wilbe adapted to become circumflexe or of an indifferent sounde.

6. I would exhorte you also to beware of rime without reason: my meaning
is hereby that your rime leade you not from your first Inuention, for many
wryters when they haue layed the platforme of their inuention, are yet drawen
sometimes (by ryme) to forget it or at least to alter it, as when they cannot
readily finde out a worde whiche maye rime to the first (and yet continue their
determinate Inuention) they do then eyther botche it vp with a worde that will
ryme (howe small reason soeuer it carie with it) or els they alter   **page 35 /**
their first worde and so percase decline or trouble their former Inuention: But
do you alwayes hold your first determined Inuention, and do rather searche the
bottome of your braynes for apte words, than chaunge good reason for
rumbling rime.

7. To help you a little with ryme (which is also a plaine yong schollers
lesson) worke thus, when you haue set downe your first verse, take the last
worde thereof and coumpt ouer all the wordes of the selfe same sounde by order of the Alphabete: As for example, the laste woorde of your firste line is
care, to ryme therwith you haue *bare, clare, dare, fare, gare, hare, and share,
mare, snare, rare, stare*, and *ware, &c.* Of all these take that which best may
serue your purpose, carying reason with rime: and if none of them will serue
so, then alter the laste worde of your former verse, but yet do not willingly alter the meanyng of your Inuention.

8. You may vse the same Figures or Tropes in verse which are vsed in prose,
and in my iudgement they serue more aptly, and haue greater grace in verse
than they haue in prose. . . .

9. Also asmuche as may be, eschew straunge words, . . . vnlesse the Theame do
giue it iust occasion: marie in some places a straunge worde doth drawe attentiue reading, but yet I woulde haue you therein to vse discretion.

10. And asmuch as you may, frame your stile to *perspicuity* and to be sensible: for the haughty obscure verse doth not much delight, and the verse that is
to easie is like a tale of a rosted horse: but let your Poeme be such as may both
delight and draw attentiue readyng, and therewithal may deliuer such matter as
be worth the marking. **page 36 /**

11. You shall do very well to vse your verse after th' englishe phrase, and

not after the manner of other languages: The Latinists do commonly set the
adiectiue after the Substantiue: . . . And yet I will not altogether forbidde it
you, for in some places, it may be borne, but not so hardly as some vse it which
wryte thus:

> *Now let vs go to Temple ours,*
> *I will go visit mother myne &c.*

Surely I smile at the simplicitie of such deuisers which might aswell haue
sayde it in playne Englishe phrase, and yet haue better pleased all eares, than
they satisfie their owne fancies by suche *superfinesse*. Therefore euen as I haue
aduised you to place all wordes in their naturall or most common and vsuall pronunciation, so would I wishe you to frame all sentences in their mother phrase
and proper *Idióma*, and yet sometimes (as I haue sayd before) the contrarie may
be borne, but that is rather where rime enforceth, or *per licentiam Poëticam*, than
it is otherwise lawfull or commendable.

12. This poeticall licence is a shrewde fellow, and couereth many faults in a
verse, it maketh wordes longer, shorter, of mo sillables, of fewer, newer, older,
truer, falser, and to conclude it turkeneth all things at pleasure, for example,
ydone for *done*, *adowne* for *downe*, *orecome* for *ouercome*, *tane* for *taken*,
power for *powre*, *heauen* for *heavn*, *thewes* for good partes or good qualities,
and a numbre of other whiche were but tedious and needelesse to rehearse,
since your owne iudgement and readyng will soone make you espie such ad-
uantages.

13. There are also certayne pauses or restes in a verse whiche may be called
Ceasures, whereof I woulde be lothe to stande long, since it is at discretion of
the wryter, and they haue bene first deuised (as should   page 37 /   seeme)
by the Musicians: but yet thus much I will aduenture to wryte, that in mine
opinion in a verse of eight sillables, the pause will stand best in the middest, in
a verse of tenne it will best be placed at the ende of the first foure sillables: in
a verse of twelue, in the midst, in verses of twelue in the firste and fouretene
in the seconde, wee place the pause commonly in the midst of the first, and at
the ende of the first eight sillables in the second. In Rithme royall, it is at the
wryters discretion, and forceth not where the pause be vntill the ende of the
line.

14. And here bycause I haue named Rithme royall, I will tell you also mine
opinion aswell of that as of the names which other rymes haue commonly borne
heretofore. Rythme royall is a verse of tenne sillables, and seuen such verses make
a staffe, whereof the first and thirde lines do aunswer (acrosse) in like terminations and rime, the second, fourth, and fifth, do likewise answere eche other
in terminations, and the two last do combine and shut vp the Sentence: this hath
bene called Rithme royall, and surely it is a royall kinde of verse, seruing best
for graue discourses. There is also another kinde called Ballade, and thereof
are sundrie sortes: for a man may write ballade in a staffe of sixe lines, euery line
conteyning eighte or sixe sillables, whereof the firste and third, second and fourth
do rime acrosse, and the fifth and sixth do rime togither in conclusion. You
may write also your ballad of tenne sillables rimyng as before is declared, but
these two were wont to be most commonly vsed in ballade, which propre name
was (I thinke) deriued of this worde in Italian *Ballare*, which signifieth to daunce.

And in deed those kinds of rimes serue beste for daunces or light matters. Then haue you also a rondlette, the which doth alwayes end with one self same foote or repeticion, and was thereof (in my iudgement) called a rondelet. This may consist of such measure as best liketh the wryter, then haue you Sonnets, some thinke that all Poemes (being short) may be called   page 38 /   Sonets, as in deede it is a diminutiue worde deriued of *Sonare*, but yet I can beste allowe to call those Sonnets whiche are of fouretene lynes, euery line conteyning tenne syllables. The firste twelue do ryme in staues of foure lines by crosse meetre, and the last two ryming togither do conclude the whole. . . . And the commonest sort of verse which we vse now adayes (*viz.* the long verse of twelue and fourtene sillables) I know not certainly howe to name it, vnlesse I should say that it doth consist of Poulters measure, which giueth .xii. for one dozen and xiiij. for another. But let this suffise (if it be not to much) for the sundrie sortes of verses which we vse now adayes.

15. In all these sortes of verses when soeuer you vndertake to write, auoyde prolixitie and tediousnesse, and euer as neare as you can, do finish the sentence and meaning at the end of euery staffe where you   page 39 /   wright staues, and at the end of euery two lines where you write by cooples or poulters measure: . . . eschue prolixitie and knit vp your sentences as compendiously as you may, since breuitie (so that it be not drowned in obscuritie) is most commendable.

16. I had forgotten a notable kinde of ryme, called ryding rime, and that is suche as our Mayster and Father *Chaucer* vsed in his Canterburie tales, and in diuers other delectable and light enterprises. . . . As this riding rime serueth most aptly to wryte a merie tale, so Rythme royall is fittest for a graue discourse. Ballades are beste of matters of loue, and rondlettes moste apt for the beating or handlyng of an adage or common prouerbe: Sonets serue aswell in matters of loue as of discourse. . . , and the long verse of twelue and fouretene sillables, although it be now adayes vsed in all Theames, yet in my iudgement it would serue best for Psalmes and Himpnes. . . .   page 40 /

Stephen Gosson (1554–1624) is ranked by Meres with Sidney, Chaloner,
Spenser, Fraunce, and Barnfield "amongst us the best" for pastorals.
Gosson himself refers to a career as a playwright. (None of his plays,
however, is extant.) In 1579 he wrote The Schoole of Abuse, *primarily an*
extravagant attack on poets and players, which was inadvisably dedicated to
Sir Philip Sidney, who, according to Spenser, scorned the work. The at-
tack stirred numerous responses; among them Thomas Lodge's A Reply
to Gosson *(1579) and Sidney's* An Apologie for Poetry, *written about*
1580–1582 but not published until 1595. The controversy, which evoked
a number of essays in which the nature and aims of poetry and drama were
examined, thus was the stimulus for the production of the first important
body of English literary criticism, for not until Gosson's time was there
a systematic attempt to examine the principles upon which contemporary
literature was based.

Stephen Gosson. *The Schoole of Abuse* (1579). Edited by Edward Arber,
London, 1869.

. . . The whole practise of Poets, eyther with fables to shew theyr abuses, or with
plaine tearmes to vnfold theyr mischiefe, discouer theyr shame, discredit them
selues, and disperse their poyson through all the worlde. . . . **page 19 /**
I must confesse that Poets are the whetstones of wit, notwithstanding that wit
is dearly bought: where hony and gall are mixed, it will be hard to seuer the one
from the other. The deceitfull Phisition giueth sweete Syrropes to make his
poyson goe downe the smoother: The Iuggler casteth a myst to worke the closer:
The *Syrens* song is the Saylers wrack . . . : Many good sentences are spoken by
Danus, to shadowe his knauery: and written by Poets, as ornamentes to beautifye
their woorkes, and sette theyr trumperie too sale without suspect.
. . . Pul off the visard that Poets maske in, you shall disclose their reproch,
bewray their vanitie, loth their wantonnesse, lament their follie, and perceiue
their sharpe sayings to be placed as Pearles in Dunghils, fresh pictures on rotten
walles, chaste Matrons apparel on common Curtesans. . . . No marueyle though
Plato shut them out of his Schoole, and banished them quite from his common
wealth, as effeminate writers, vnprofitable members, and vtter enimies to vertue.
page 20 /

. . . .

Poetrie and pyping, haue allwaies bene so vnited togither, that til the
Plutarch.   time of *Melanippides,* Pipers were Poets hyerlings. But marke I pray you,
how they are nowe both abused.
The right vse of auncient Poetrie was too haue the notable exploytes
Olde Poets.   of woorthy Captaines, the holesome councels of good fathers, and vertu-

ous liues of predecessors set downe in numbers, and song to the Instrument at solemne feastes, that the sound of the one might draw the hearers from kissing the cupp too often; the sense of the other put them in minde of things past, and chaulk out the way to do the like. . . .

To this end are instruments vsed in battaile, not to tickle the eare, but too teach euery souldier when to strike and when to stay, when to flye, and when to followe. *Chiron* by singing to his instrument, quencheth *Achiles*   Homer. furye; *Terpandrus* with his notes, layeth the tempest, and pacifies the tumult at *Lacedaemon:* *Homer* with his Musicke cured the sick Souldiers in the *Grecians* campe, and purged euery   **page 25 /**   mans Tent of the Plague. Thinke you that those miracles coulde bee wrought with playing of Daunces, Dumpes, Pauins, Galiardes, Measures Fancyes, or new streynes? They neuer came wher this grewe, nor knew what it ment. . . .   **page 26 /**

. . . If you enquire howe manie suche Poetes and Pipers wee haue in our Age, I am perswaded that euerie one of them may creepe through a ring, or daunce the wilde Morice in a Needles eye. We haue infinite Poets, and Pipers, and suche peeuishe cattel among vs in Englande, that liue by merrie begging, mainteyned by almes, and priuily encroch vppon euerie mans purse. But if they that are in authoritie, and haue the sworde in their handes to cut off abuses, shoulde call an accompt to see how many *Chirons, Terpandri,* and *Homers* are heere, they might cast the summe without pen, or counters, and sit downe with *Racha,* to weepe for her Children, because they were not. He that compareth our instruments, with those that were vsed in ancient times, shall see them agree like Dogges and Cattes, and meete as iump as Germans lippes. . . .   **page 27 /**

For as Poetrie and Piping are Cosen germans: so piping and playing are of great affinity, and all three chayned in linkes of abuse.   **page 28 /**

. . . .

Lacon when he sawe the *Atheniens* studie so muche to set out Playes, sayde they were madde. If men for good exercise, and women for theyr credite, be shut from Theaters, whom shall we suffer to goe thither? Litle children? *Plutarch* with a caueat keepeth them out, not so much as admitting the litle crackhalter that carrieth his maisters pantouffles, to set foote within those doores: And alledgeth this reason, that those wanton spectacles of lyght huswiues, drawing gods from the heauens, and young men from them selues to shipwracke of honestie, will hurte them more, then if at the Epicures table, they had nigh burst their guts with ouer feeding. For if the body bee ouercharged, it may bee holpe; but the surfite of the soule is hardly cured. Here I doubt not but some Archplayer or other that hath   *Obiection.* read a litle, or stumbled by chance vpon *Plautus* comedies, will cast me a bone or ii. to pick, saying, yat whatsoeuer these ancient writers haue spoken against plaies is to bee applied too the abuses in olde Comedies, where Gods are broughte in, as Prisoners too beautie, rauishers of Virgins, and seruantes by loue, too earthly creatures. But the Comedies that are exercised in oure daies are better sifted. They shewe no such branne: The first smelte of *Plautus,* these tast of *Menander;* the lewde-   **page 30 /**   ness of Gods, is altered and chaunged to the loue of young men; force, to friendshippe; rapes, too mariage; wooing allowed by assurance of wedding;

priuie meetinges of bachelours and maidens on the stage, not as murderers
that deuour the good name ech of other in their mindes, but as those that
desire to bee made one in hearte. Nowe are the abuses of the worlde re-
uealed, euery man in a play may see his owne faultes, and learne by this
glasse, to amende his manners. . . . Therefore they are either so blinde, that

Answere.
they cannot, or so blunt, that they will not see why this exercise shoulde
not be suffered as a profitable recreation. For my parte I am neither so
fonde a Phisition, nor so bad a Cooke, but I can allowe my patient a cup
of wine to meales, although it be hotte; and pleasaunt sauces to driue downe
his meate, if his stomake bee queasie. Notwithstanding, if people will bee
instructed, (God be thanked) wee haue Diuines enough to discharge that,
and moe by a great many, then are well hearkened to: Yet sith these
abuses are growne too head, and sinne so rype, the number is lesse then I
would it were. . . .   **page 31 /**

Consider with thy selfe (gentle Reader) the olde discipline of Englande,
mark what we were before, and what we are now: . . . cast thine eye backe
to thy Predecessors, and tell mee howe wonderfully wee haue beene
chaunged, since wee were schooled with these abuses. . . . English men could
suffer watching and labor, hunger and thirst, and beare of al stormes with

*Maners of
England in
olde time.*
hed and shoulders, they vsed slender weapons, went naked, and were good
soldiours, they fed vppon rootes and barkes of trees, they would stand vp
to the chin many dayes in marishes without victualles: and they had a kind
of sustenaunce in time of neede, of which if they had taken but the
quantitie of a beane, or the weight of a pease, they did neyther gape after
meate, nor long for the cuppe, a great while after. The men in valure not

*Olde exercise
of England.*
yeelding to *Scithia*, the women in courage passing the *Amazons*. The exercise of both was shootyng and darting, running and wrestling, and trying
such maisteries, as eyther consisted in swiftnesse of feete, agilitie of body,
strength of armes, or Martiall discipline. But the exercise that is nowe among

New England.
vs, is banqueting, playing, pipyng, and dauncing, and all suche delightes
as may win vs to pleasure, or rocke vs a sleepe.

Oh what a woonderfull chaunge is this? Our wreastling at armes, is
turned to wallowyng in Ladies laps, our courage, to cowardice, our running
to ryot, our Bowes into Bolles, and our Dartes to Dishes. We haue robbed
Greece of Gluttonie, *Italy* of wantonnesse, *Spaine* of pride, *Fraunce* of
deceite, and *Dutchland* of quaffing. Compare *London* to *Rome*, and *England*
to *Italy*, you shall finde the Theaters of the one, the abuses of the other,
to be rife among vs. . . .   **page 34 /**   In our assemblies at playes in *London*,
you shall see suche heauing, and shoouing, suche ytching and shouldring,
too sitte by women; Suche care for their garments, that they bee not trode
on: Such eyes to their lappes, that no chippes light in them: Such pillowes
to ther backes, that they take no hurte: Such masking in their eares, I
knowe not what: Such giuing them Pippins to passe the time: Suche playing at foote Saunt without Cardes: Such ticking, such toying, such smiling,
such winking, and such manning them home, when the sportes are ended,
that it is a right Comedie, to marke their behauiour, to watche their con-
ceites. . . . They . . . to celebrate the Sabboth, flock to Theaters, and there keepe
a generall Market of Bawdrie: Not that any filthynesse in deede, is com-

mitted within the compasse of that grounde, . . . but that euery wanton and his Paramour, euery man and his Mistresse, euery John and his Joan, euery knaue and his queane, are there **page 35 /** first acquainted and cheapen the Merchandise in that place, which they pay for elsewhere as they can agree. . . . **page 36 /**

God hath now blessed *England* with a Queene, in vertue excellent, in power mightie, in glorye renowned, in gouerment politike, in possession rich, breaking her foes with the bent of her brow, ruling her subiects with shaking her hand, remouing debate by diligent foresight, filling her chests with the fruites of peace, ministring iustice by order of law, reforming abuses with great regarde. . . . But wee vnworthy seruants of so mild a Mistresse, vnnatural children of so good a mother, vnthankful subiects of so louing a prince, wound her royall hart with abusing her lenitie, and stir *Iupiter* to anger to send vs a Stroke that shal deuoure vs. How often hath her Maiestie with the graue aduise of her honorable Councell, sette downe the limits of apparell to euery degree, and how soone againe hath the pride of our harts ouerflowen the chanel? How many times hath accesse to Theaters beene restrayned, and how boldly againe haue we reentred? Ouerlashing in apparel is so common a fault, that the very hyerlings of some of our Players, which stand at reuersion of vi. s. by the weeke, iet vnder Gentlemens noses in sutes of silke, exercising themselues too prating on the stage, and common scoffing when they come abrode, where they look askance ouer the shoulder at euery man, of whom the sunday before they begged an almes. I speake not this, as though euerye one that professeth the qualitie **page 39 /** so abused him selfe, for it is well knowen, that some of them are sober, discreete, properly learned honest housholders and Citizens well thought on amonge their neighbours at home, though the pryde of their shadowes (I meane those hangebyes whome they succour with stipend) cause them to bee somewhat il talked of abroade. And as some of the Players are farre from abuse: so some of their Playes are without rebuke: which are as easily remembered as quickly reckoned. The twoo prose Bookes plaied at the Belsauage, where you shall finde neuer a woorde without wit, neuer a line without pith, neuer a letter placed in vaine. The *Iew* and *Ptolome*, showne at the Bull, the one representing the greedinesse of worldly chusers, and bloody mindes of Usurers: The other very liuely discrybing howe seditious estates, with their owne deuises, false friendes, with their owne swoordes, and rebellious commons in their owne snares are ouerthrowne: neither with Amorous gesture wounding the eye: nor with slouenly talke hurting the eares of the chast hearers. The *Blacke Smiths daughter*, and *Catilins Conspiracies* vsually brought in to the Theater: The first contayning the trechery of *Turkes*, the honourable bountye of a noble minde, and the shining of vertue in distresse: The last, because it is knowen too be a Pig of myne owne Sowe, I will speake the lesse of it; onely giuing you to vnderstand, that the whole marke which I shot at in that woorke, was too showe the rewarde of traytors in *Catilin*, and the necessary gouerment of learned men, in the person of *Cicero*, which forsees euery danger that is likely to happen, and forstalles it continually ere it take effect. . . . **page 40 /**

The Queenes Maiestie.

Players men.

Some Players modest, if I bee not deceiued.

Some Playes tollerable at sometyme.

Playes are not to be made common.

These Playes are good playes and sweete playes, and of al playes the best playes and most to be liked, woorthy to bee soung of the Muses, or set out with the cunning of *Roscius* himself, yet are they not fit for euery mans dyet: neither ought they commonly to bee shewen. Now if any man aske me why my selfe haue penned Comedyes in time paste, and inueigh so egerly against them here, let him knowe that . . . I haue sinned, and am sorry for my fault. . . . I gaue my self to that exercise in hope to thriue but I burnt one candle to seek another, and lost bothe my time and my trauell, when I had doone. . . .   **page 41 /**

Robert Greene (1560?–92), dramatist and pamphleteer, was one of the most prolific of the Elizabethan writers. His thirty-eight works include plays, romances, and pamphlets. His realistic prose works reveal much of the London middle-class and underworld life — the manners of fops, gulls, thieves, pickpockets, blackmailers, confidence men, etc. "A Quip for an Upstart Courtier" (1592), is an attack on "upstart" urban fashions (symbolized by Velvet-breeches, who is catered to by various tradesmen) which are contrasted unfavourably with solid, old-fashioned virtues (symbolized by Cloth-breeches). The dispute provides a sometimes amusing review of the practices (often improper) of the various trades.

Robert Greene. *A Qvip for an vpstart Courtier: Or, a quaint Dispute between Veluet-breeches and Cloth-breeches; Wherein is plainely set downe the Disorders in all Estates and Trades. London, 1592.* Reprinted in *The Harleian Miscellany: Or, a Collection of Scarce, Curious, and Entertaining Pamphlets and Tracts, As well in Manuscript as in Print, Found in the late Earl of Oxford's Library;* Interspersed with Historical, Political, and Critical Notes. London, 1745, V, 371–396.

. . . Marry, quoth Cloth-breeches, *First*, to the Barber: He can not be but a partiall Man on Veluet-breeches Side, sith he gets more by one Time Dressing of him than by ten time Times Dressing of me. I come plaine to be polde, and to haue my Beard cut, and pay him two Pence: Veluet-breeches, he sits downe in the Chaire, wrapt in fine Cloathes, as though the Barber were about to make him a Footcloth for the Vickar of Saint *Fooles;* then begins hee to take his Sissars in his Hand, and his Comb, and so to snap with them, as if he meant to geue a Warning to all the Lice in his nitty Locks for to prepare themselues, for the Day of their Destruction was at Hande. Then comes he out with his fustian Eloquence, and, making a low Conge, saith, Sir, Will you haue your Worships Hair cut after the *Italian* Manner, short and round, and then frounst with the curling Yrons, to make it looke like to a Halfemoone in a Mist? Or, like a *Spanyard*, long at the Eares, and curled like to the two Endes of an olde cast Perriwig? Or will you be *Frenchefied*, with a Loue Locke downe to your Shoulders? Wherein you may weare your Mistris Fauour: The *English* Cut is base, and Gentlemen scorne it; Nouelty is dainty; speake the Word, Sir; my Sissars are ready to execute your Worships Wil. His Head being once drest, which requires, in Combing and Rubbing, some two Howres, he comes to the Bason; then, being curiously washt with no woorse then a Camphire Bal, he descends as low as his Beard, and asketh, Whether he will haue his Peak cut short and sharpe, amiable like an *Inamorato*, or broad pendant like a Spade, to be

terrible like a Warrior and a Soldado? Whether he will haue his Crates cut lowe
like a Juniper Bush, or his Suberches taken away with a Rasor? If it be his
Pleasure to haue his Appendices primde, or his Mouchaches fostred, to turne
about his Eares like the Branches of a Vine; or cut downe to the Lip with the
Italian Lashe, to make him look like a halfe faced Bauby in Bras? These quaint
Tearms, Barber, you greet Maister Veluet-breeches withal, and, at euery
Word, a Snap with your Sissars, and a Cring with your Knee; wheras, when
you come to poore Cloth-breeches, you either cutte his Beard at your owne
Pleasure, or else, in Disdaine, aske him, if he will be trimd with Christs Cut,
round like the Halfe of a *Holland* Cheese? mocking both Christ and vs. . . . For
you, Maister Surgion, the Statutes of *Englande* exempts you from being of
any Quest; and beside, alas, I sildome fall into your Hands, as being quiet, and
making no Brawls to haue Wounds, as swartrutting Veluet-breeches dooth;
neither doe I frequent Whore-houses to catch the Marbles, and so to grow your
Patient. . . . And, for you, Maister Apoticarie, alas, I looke not once in seauen
Yeare into your Shop, without it be to buy a Peniworth of Wormeseed to giue
my Child to drinke; or a little Triacle to driue out the Measels; or, perhaps,
some Dregs and Powders to make my sicke Horsse a Drench withal; but, for
my selfe, if I be ill at Ease, I take Kitchyn Physicke, I make my Wife my Doctor, and my Garden my Apoticaries Shop; wheras quesie Maister Veluet-
breeches cannot haue a Fart awrye, but he must haue his Purgations, Pils, and
Glisters, or euacuate by Electuaries: He must, if the least Spot of Morphew come
on his Face, haue his Oyle of *Tartar,* his *Lac Virginis,* his Camphir dissolued
in Veriuice, to make the Foole as faire, for sooth, as if he were to playe *Maid-
marian* in a *May* Game, or Moris-daunce. Tush, he cannot disgest his Meat
without Conserues, nor end his Meale without Suckats, nor (Shall I speake
plainely?) please the Trug his Mistres, without he goe to the Apoticaries for
Eringion, *Oleum formicarum alatarum, & Aqua mirabilis* of ten Pound a
Pint. If Maister Veluet-breeches, with drinking these Drugs, hap to haue a
stinking Breath, then, forsooth, the Apoticarie must play the Perfumer to
make it sweet: Nay, What is it about him, that he blameth not Nature for
Framing, and formeth it a new by Art? And, in all this, Who, but Mounsier
the Apoticarie?   **page 382 /**

.   .   .   .

. . . I pray you, Goodman Kilcalfe, what Hauocke playe you with Puffing vp
of Meate, and Blowing with your Pricker, as you flea it? Haue you not your
artificiall Knaueries to set out your Meate with Prickes, and then sweare he
hath more for Mony than euer you bought; to sel a Peece of an olde Cow for a
Chop of a yong Oxe, to wash your old Meat, that hath hung weltring in the
Shop, with new Bloud; to trusse awaye an old Eaw instead of a young Weather, and, altho' you know it is hurtful and forbidden by the Statute to flee your
Hides, Skins, Backes, with Cuts and Slashes, to the Impouerishing of the poore
Shooemaker when he buies it, yet, I pray you, how many Slaughters do you
make in a poore Calues Skin? Oh Butcher, a long *Lent* be your Punishment,
for you make no Conscience in deceiuing the Poore. And you, Maist. Brewer,
that growe to be woorth forty-thousand Pounds by selling of soden Water,
what Subtilty haue you in making your Beere to spare the Malt, and put in the
more of the Hoppe to make your Drinke, be Barly neuer so cheape, not a whit

the stronger, and yet neuer sel a whit the more Measure for Money? You can, when you haue taken all the Harte of the Malt away, then clape on Store of Water, tis cheape inough, and mashe out a Tunning of smalle Beare, that it scoures a Mans Maw like *Rennish* Wine: In your Conscience, how many Barrels draw you out of a Quarter of Malt? . . . .   page 390 /   . . . What, the Vintner! Why, he is a Kinde of Negromancer; for, at Midnight, when all Men are in Bed, then he, forsooth, fals to his Charmes and Spels, so that he tumbles one Hogshead into another, and can make a Cup of Claret, that hath lost his Colour, look high with a Dash of red Wine at his Pleasure; if he hath a strong *Gascoigne* Wine, for Feare it should make his Guests to soone drunke, he can allay it with a smal *Rochel* Wine; he can cherish vp White Wine with Sacke; and, per- haps, if you bide him wash the Pot cleane, when he goes to draw you a Quart of Wine, he wil leaue a little Water in the Bottome, and then draw it full of Wine. And what and if he do? Tis no Harm; Wine and Water is good against the Heat of the Liuer. It were infinit to rehearse the Iugling of Vintners, the Disorder of their Houses, especially of the Persons that frequent them. . . . page 391 /

Little is known of Thomas Harman (fl. 1567). He tells us that he found recreation by questioning vagabonds and various characters of the English underworld about their practices and general way of life. His work sheds much light on the manners, customs, and structure of the lower levels of English society. First printed in 1566, the Caveat *supplied the pamphleteers much of their material, which they pilfered freely and without acknowledgment.*

A Caveat or Warning for Common Cursetors, Vulgarly Called Vagabonds, Set Forth by Thomas Harman, Esquire, in The Old Book Collector's Miscellany, *Vol. I. Edited by Charles Hindley and printed in London, 1871.*

CAP. I.

A Ruffler

The Ruffler, because he is first in degree of this odious order: and is so called in a statute made for the punishment of vagabonds: In the twenty-seventh year of King Henry the Eighth late of most famous memory: He shall be first placed as the worthiest of this unruly rabblement. And he is so called when he goeth first abroad, either he hath served in the wars, or else he hath been a serving man and weary of well doing, shaking off all pain, doth choose him this idle life, and wretchedly wanders about the most shires of this realm. And with stout audacity he demandeth where he thinketh he may be bold, and **page 14 /** circumspect enough, as he seeth cause to ask charity, ruefully and lamentably, that it would make a flinty heart to relent, and pity his miserable estate, how he hath been maimed and bruised in the wars, and peradventure some will show you some outward wound, which he got at some drunken fray, either halting of some privy wound festered with a filthy fiery flankard. For be well assured that the hardiest soldiers be either slain or maimed, either if they escape all hazards, and return home again, if they be without relief of their friends, they will surely desperately rob and steal, or either shortly be hanged or miserably die in prison, for they be so much ashamed and disdain to beg or ask charity, that rather they will as desperately fight for to live and maintain themselves as manfully, and valiantly they ventured themselves in the princes' quarrel. Now, these Rufflers the outcasts of serving men when begging or craving fails, then they pick and pilfer from other inferior beggars that they meet by the way, as Rogues, Palliards, Morts, and Doxies: yea if they meet with a woman alone riding to the market, either old man or boy, that he well knoweth will not resist, such they filch and spoil. These Rufflers, after a year or two at the farthest become Upright men, unless they be prevented by twined hemp.[1]   **page 15 /**

.   .   .   .

Cap. II.

A Upright Man.

A UPRIGHT man the second in sect of this unseemly sort must be next placed, of these ranging rabblement of rascals, some be serving men, artificers, and labouring men, traded up in husbandry: These not minding to get their living with the sweat of their face, but casting off all pain, will wander after their wicked manner, through the most shires of this realm.

As Somersetshire, Wiltshire, Berkshire, Oxfordshire, Hertfordshire, Middlesex, Essex, Suffolk, Norfolk, Sussex, Surrey, and Kent, as the chief and best shires of relief. Yea not without punishment by stocks, whippings, and imprisonment, in most of these places above said: yet notwithstanding they have so good liking in their lewd lecherous loitering, that full quickly all their punishments be forgotten. And repentance is never thought upon, until they climb three trees with a ladder.[1] These unruly   **page 19 /**   rascals in their rolling,[1] disperse themselves into several companies, as occasion serveth, sometime more and sometime less. As if they repair to a poor husbandman's house, he will go alone or one with him, and stoutly demand his charity, either showing how he hath served in the wars and there maimed, either that he seeketh service and saith he would be glad to take pain for his living, although he meaneth nothing less: If he be offered any meat or drink, he utterly refuseth scornfully, and will nought but money, and if he espy young pigs or poultry, he well noteth the place, and then the next night or shortly after, he will be sure to have some of them, which they bring to their stauling-kens, which is their tippling houses. . . . For you must understand every tippling ale house will neither receive them or their wares but some certain houses, in every shire, especially for that purpose, where they shall be better welcome to them, than honester men, for by such have they most gain, and shall be conveyed either into some loft out of the way, or other secret corner not common to any other, and thither repair at accustomed times their harlots which they term Morts and Doxies, not with empty hands, for they be as skilful in picking,   **page 20 /**   rifling and filching, as the upright men, and nothing inferior to them in all kind of wickedness. . . . They bowl and booze one to another, and for the time boozing belly-cheer. And after their roistering recreation if there be not room enough in the house, they have clean straw in some barn or back house near adjoining, where they couch commonly together. . . . These upright men . . . meet at fairs or great markets where they meet to pilfer and steal from stalls, shops, or booths. At these fairs the upright men, use commonly to lie, and linger in highways, bye-

---

[1] TWINED HEMP. — That is, hanged by the neck.
[1] THREE TREES WITH A LADDER — *i.e.,* the gallows; the wooden horse, or three-legged mare.
[1] ROLLING. — Travelling.

lanes, some pretty way or distance from the place, by which ways they be
assured that company passeth still to and fro, and there they will demand with
cap in hand and comely courtesy, the devotion and charity of the people.
They have been much lately whipped at fairs. . . .   page 21 /

.   .   .   .

   These upright men will seldom or never want, for what is gotten by any
Mort or Doxy, if it please him he doth command the same: and if he meet
any beggar, whether he be sturdy or impotent, he will demand of him whether
ever he was stalled to the rogue or no. If he say he was, he will know of whom,
and his name that stalled him. And if he be not learnedly able to show him the
whole circumstance thereof, he will spoil him of his money, either of his
best garment if it be worth any money, and have him to the boozing-ken:
which is, to some tippling house next adjoining and layeth there to gage the
best thing that he hath for twenty pence or two shillings: this man obeyeth
for fear of beating. Then doth this upright man call for a gage of booze, which
is a quart pot of drink and pours the same upon his peld pate,[1] adding these
words I P. G. do stall thee W. T. to the Rogue, and that from henceforth it
shall be lawful for thee to Cant, that is to ask or beg for thy   page 24 /
living in all places. Here you see that the upright man is of great authority
for all sorts of beggars are obedient to his behests, and surmounteth all the
others in pilfering and stealing. . . .   page 25 /

.   .   .   .

CAP. IV.
A Rogue.

   A ROGUE is neither so stout or hardy as the upright man: Many of them
will go faintly and look piteously when they see either meet any person,
having a kercher as white as my shoes tied about their head, with a short staff
in their hand, halting although they need not, requiring alms of such as they
meet or to what house they shall come. But you may easily perceive by their
colour that they carry both health and hypocrisy about them, whereby they
get gain, when others want that cannot feign and dissemble. Others there be
that walk sturdily about the country, and feigneth to seek a brother or kinsman of his, dwelling within some part of the shire either that he hath a letter
to deliver to some honest householder dwelling out of another shire, and will
show you the same fair sealed, with the superscription to the party he speaketh
of, because you shall not think him to run idly about the country, either have
they this shift, they will carry a certificate or passport about   page 30 /
them from some Justice of the Peace, with his hand and seal unto the same,
how he hath been whipped and punished for a vagabond according to the
laws of this realm and that he must return to T, where he was born or last
dwelt, by a certain day limited in the same, which shall be a good long day.
And all this feigned, because without fear they would wickedly wander, and
will renew the same where or when it pleaseth them; for they have of their

―――――――――――

[1] PELD PATE. — Uncovered head.

affinity that can write and read. These also will pick and steal as the upright men, and hath their women and meetings at places appointed, and nothing to them inferior in all kinds of knavery. There be of these Rogues Curtails, wearing short cloaks, that will change their apparel as occasion serveth, and their end is either hanging, which they call Trining in their language, or die miserably of the pox. . . . page 31 /

William Harrison (1534–93), topographer and historian, is noted for his "Description of England" included in Raphael Holinshed's Chronicle. *It has been frequently reprinted separately since the sixteenth century because it is thought to be the most valuable section of the larger work. Book II includes an account of the institutions and inhabitants of England (their food, dress, houses, and customs); Book III describes the products of the land, the inns and fairs, and other aspects of English society. Harrison's work, which is interesting for its literary merit, is also one of the most important sources of information regarding Elizabethan England. It includes a wide variety of subjects, and the descriptions are graphic, candid, and often spiced with personal comment.*

William Harrison. *Description of England*, Book II. London, 1587.

Chapter VI

Of the food and diet of the English.

The situation of our region, lieng neere vnto the north, dooth cause the heate of our stomaches to be of somewhat greater force: therefore our bodies doo craue a little more ample nourishment, than the inhabitants of the hotter regions are accustomed withall, whose digestiue force is not altogither so vehement, bicause their internall heat is not so strong as ours, which is kept in by the coldnesse of the aire, that from time to time (speciallie in winter) dooth enuiron our bodies.

It is no maruell therefore that our tables are oftentimes more plentifullie garnished than those of other nations, and this trade hath continued with vs euen since the verie beginning. . . .   **page 165 /**

In number of dishes and change of meat, the nobilitie of England (whose cookes are for the most part musicall headed Frenchmen and strangers) doo most exceed, sith there is no daie in maner that passeth ouer their heads, wherein they haue not onelie beefe, mutton, veale, lambe, kid, porke, conie, capon, pig, or so manie of these as the season yeeldeth: but also some portion of the red or fallow deere, beside great varietie of fish and wild foule, and thereto sundrie other delicates wherein the sweet hand of the seafaring Portingale is not wanting; so that for a man to dine with one of them, and to tast of euerie dish that standeth before him (which few vse to doo, but ech one feedeth vpon that meat him best liketh for the time, the beginning of euerie dish notwithstanding being reserued vnto the greatest personage that sitteth at the table, to whome it is drawen vp still by the waiters as order requireth, and from whome it descendeth againe euen to the lower end, whereby each one may tast thereof) is rather to yeeld vnto a conspiracie with a great deale of meat for the speedie suppression of naturall health, then the vse of a necessarie meane to satisfie himselfe with a competent repast, to susteine his bodie withall. But as this large feeding is not seene in their gests, no more is it in their owne persons, for sith they haue dailie much resort vnto their tables (and manie times vnlooked for) and thereto reteine great numbers of seruants, it is verie requisit & expedient for them to be somewhat plentifull in this behalfe.

The chiefe part likewise of their dailie prouision is brought in before them (commonlie in siluer vessell if they be of the degree of barons, bishops, and vpwards) and placed on their tables, wherof when they haue taken what it pleaseth them, the rest is reserued, and afterward sent downe to their seruing men and waiters, who feed thereon in like sort with conuenient moderation, their reuersion also being bestowed vpon the poore, which lie readie at their gates in great numbers to receiue the same. This is spoken of the principall tables whereat the nobleman, his ladie and guestes are accustomed to sit, beside which they haue a certeine ordinarie allowance dailie appointed for their hals, where the chiefe officers and household seruants (for all are not permitted by custome to wait vpon their master) and with them such inferiour guestes doo feed as are not of calling to associat the noble man himselfe (so that besides those afore mentioned, which are called to the principall table, there are commonlie fortie or three score persons fed in those hals, to the great reliefe of such poore sutors and strangers also as oft be partakers thereof and otherwise like to dine hardlie. As for drinke it is vsuallie filled in pots, gobblets, iugs, bols of siluer in noble mens houses, also in fine Venice glasses of all formes, and for want of these elsewhere in pots of earth of sundrie colours and moulds whereof manie are garnished with siluer, or at the leastwise in pewter, all which notwithstanding are seldome set on the table, but each one as necessitie vrgeth, calleth for a cup of such drinke as him listeth to haue: so that when he hath tasted of it he deliuered the cup againe to some one of the standers by, who making it cleane by pouring out the drinke that remaineth, restoreth it to the cupbord from whence he fetched the same. By this deuise . . . much idle tippling is furthermore cut off, for if the full pots should continuallie stand at the elbow or neere the trencher, diuerse would alwaies be dealing with them, whereas now they drinke seldome and onelie when necessitie vrgeth, and so auoid the note of great drinking, or often troubling of the seruitours with filling of their bols. Neuerthelesse in the noble mens hals, this order is not vsed, neither in any mans house commonlie vnder the degree of a knight or esquire of **page 166 /** great reuenues. It is a world to see in these our daies, wherin gold and siluer most aboundeth, how that our gentilitie as lothing those mettals (bicause of the plentie) do now generallie choose rather the Venice glasses both for our wine and beere, than anie of those mettals or stone wherein before time we haue beene accustomed to drinke, but such is the nature of man generallie that it most coueteth things difficult to be atteined; & such is the estimation of this stuffe, that manie become rich onelie with their new trade vnto Murana (a towne neere to Venice situat on the Adriatike sea) from whence the verie best are dailie to be had, and such as for beautie doo well neere match the christall or the ancient *Murrhina vasa*, whereof now no man hath knowledge. And as this is seene in the gentilitie, so in the wealthie communaltie the like desire of glasse is not neglected, whereby the gaine gotten by their purchase is yet much more increased to the benefit of the merchant. The poorest also will haue glasse if they may, but sith the Venecian is somewhat too deere for them, they content themselues with such as are made at home of ferne and burned stone, but in fine all go one waie, that is, to shards at the last, so that our great expenses in glasses (beside that they breed much strife toward such as haue the charge of them) are worst of all bestowed in mine opinion, bicause their peeces doo turne vnto no profit.

If the philosophers stone were once found, and one part hereof mixed with fortie of molten glasse, it would induce such a mettallicall toughnesse there-vnto, that a fall should nothing hurt it in any maner, yet it might peraduenture bunch or batter it, neuerthelesse that inconuenience were quickelie to be re-dressed by the hammer. But whither am I slipped?

The gentlemen and merchants keepe much about one rate, and each of them contenteth himselfe with foure, fiue, or six dishes, when they haue but small resort, or peraduenture with one, or two, or three at the most, when they haue no strangers to accompanie them at their tables. And yet their seruants haue their ordinarie diet assigned, beside such as is left at their masters boordes, & not appointed to be brought thither the second time, which neuerthelesse is often seene generallie in venison, lambe, or some especiall dish, whereon the merchant man himselfe liketh to feed when it is cold, or peraduenture for sundrie causes incident to the feeder is better so, than if it were warme or hot. To be short, at such times as the merchants doo make their ordinarie or voluntarie feasts, it is a world to see what great prouision is made of all maner of delicat meats, from euerie quarter of the countrie, wherein beside that they are often comparable herein to the nobilitie of the land, they will seldome regard anie thing that the butcher vsuallie killeth, but reiect the same as not worthie to come in place. In such cases also gelisses of all colours mixed with a varietie in the representation of sundrie floures, herbs, trees, formes of beasts, fish, foules and fruits, and therevnto marchpaine wrought with no small curiositie, tarts of diuerse hewes and sundrie denominations, conserues of old fruits, forren and home-bred, suckets, codinacs, marmilats, marchpaine, sugerbread, gingerbread, florentines, wild foule, venison of all sorts, and sundrie outlandish confections, altogither seasoned with suger (which Plinie calleth *Mel ex arundinibus*, a deuise not common nor greatlie vsed in old time at the table, but onelie in medicine, although it grew in Arabia, India, & Sicilia) doo generallie beare the swaie, besides infinit deuises of our owne not possible for me to remember. Of the potato and such venerous roots as are brought out of Spaine, Portingale, and the Indies to furnish vp our bankets, I speake not, wherin our Mures of no lesse force, and to be had about Crosbie Rauenswath, doo now begin to haue place.

But among all these, the kind of meat which is obteined with most diffi-cultie and cost, is commonlie taken for the most delicat, and therevpon each guest will soonest desire to feed. And as all estats doo exceed herin, I meane for the strangenesse and number of costlie dishes, so these forget not to vse the like excesse in wine, in somuch as there is no kind to be had (neither anie where more store of all sorts than in England, although we haue none grow-ing with vs but yearelie to the proportion of 20000 or 30000 tun and vpwards, notwithstanding the dailie restreincts of the same brought ouer vnto vs) wherof at great meetings there is not some store to be had. Neither doo I meane this of small wines onlie, as Claret, White, Red, French, &c: which amount to about fiftie six sorts, according to the number of regions from whence they come: but also of the thirtie kinds of Italian, Grecian, Spanish, Canarian, &c: whereof Veruage, Catepument, Raspis, Muscadell, Romnie, Bastard Lire, Oseie, Caprike, Clareie & Malmeseie are not least of all ac-compted of, bicause of their strength and valure. For as I haue said in meat, so the stronger the wine is, the more it is desired, by means wherof in old time, the best was called *Theologicum*, bicause it was had from the cleargie and religious men, vnto whose houses manie of the laitie would often send for bottels filled with the same, being sure that they would neither drinke nor be serued of the worst, or such as was anie waies mingled or brued by the vintener: naie the merchant would haue thought that his soule should haue gone streight-waie to the diuell, if he should haue serued them with other than the best. Furthermore when these haue had their course which nature yeeldeth, sundrie sorts of artificiall stuffe, as ypocras & wormewood wine must in like maner succeed in their turnes, beside stale ale and strong beere, which neuerthelesse beare the greatest brunt in drinking, and are of so manie sorts and ages as it pleaseth the bruer to make them.

The beere that is vsed at noble mens tables in their fixed and standing houses, is commonlie of a yeare old, or peraduenture of two yeares tunning or more, but this is not generall. It is also brued in March and therefore called March beere, but for the household it is vsuallie not vnder a moneths age, ech one coueting to haue the same stale as he may, so that it be not sowre, and his bread new as is possible so that it be not hot. *Beere.*

The artificer and husbandman make greatest accompt of such meat as they may soonest come by, and haue it quickliest readie, except it be in London when the companies of euery trade doo meet on their quarter daies, at which time they be nothing inferiour to the nobilitie. Their food also consisteth principallie in beefe and such meat as the butcher selleth, that is to saie, mut-ton, veale, lambe, porke, &c: wherof he findeth great store in the markets adioining, beside souse, brawne, bacon, fruit, pies of fruit, foules of sundrie sorts, cheese, butter, egs, &c: as the other wanteth it not at home, by his owne prouision, which is at the best hand, and commonlie least charge. In feasting also this latter sort, I meane the husbandmen doo exceed after their maner: especiallie at bridales, purifications of women, and such od meetings, where it is incredible to tell what meat is consumed & spent, ech one bringing such a dish, or so manie with him as his wife & he doo consult vpon, but alwaies with this consideration, that the leefer freend shall haue the better prouision. This also is commonlie seene at these bankets, that the good man of the house is not charged with any thing sauing bread, drink, sauce, house-roome and fire. But the artificers in cities and goode townes doo deale far otherwise, for albeit that some of them doo suffer their iawes to *Artificer.*

page 167 /

go oft before their clawes, and diuerse of them by making good cheere doo hinder themselues and other men: yet the wiser sort can handle the matter well inough in these iunkettings, and therfore their frugalitie deserueth commendation. To conclude, both the artificer and the husbandman are sufficientlie liberall, & verie freendlie at their tables, and when they meet, they are so merie without malice, and plaine without inward Italian or French craft and subtiltie, that it would doo a man good to be in companie among them. Herein onelie are the inferiour sort somewhat to be blamed, that being thus assembled, their talke is now and then such as sauoureth of scurrilitie and ribaldrie, a thing naturallie incident to carters and clownes, who thinke themselues not to be merie & welcome, if their foolish veines in this behalfe be neuer so little restreined. This is moreover to be added in these meetings, that if they happen to stumble vpon a peece of venison, and a cup of wine or verie strong beere or ale (which latter they commonlie prouide against their appointed daies) they thinke their cheere so great, and themselues to haue fared so well, as the lord Maior of London, with whome when their bellies be full they will not often sticke to make comparison, because that of a subiect there is no publike officer of anie citie in Europe, that may compare in port and countenance with him during the time of his office.

I haue dined so well as my lord maior.

. . . .

Bread.

The bread through out the land is made of such graine as the soile yeeldeth, neuerthelesse the gentilitie commonlie prouide themselues sufficientlie of wheat for their owne tables, whilest their household and poore neighbours in some shires are inforced to content themselues with rie, or barleie, yea and in time of dearth manie with bread made either of beans, peason, or otes, or of altogither and some acornes among, of which scourge the poorest doo soonest tast, sith they are least able to prouide themselues of better. I will not saie that this extremitie is oft so well to be seene in time of plentie as of dearth, but if I should I could easilie bring my triall. For albeit that there be much more ground eared now almost in euerie place, than hath beene of late yeeres, yet such a price of corne continueth in each towne and market without any iust cause (except it be that landlords doo get licences to carie corne out of the land onelie to keepe vp the preces for their owne priuate gaines and ruine of the common-wealth) that the artificer and poore laboring man, is not able to reach vnto it, but is driuen to content himselfe with horsse corne, I meane, beanes, peason, otes, tares, and lintels: and therefore it is a true prouerbe, and neuer so well verified as now, that hunger setteth his first foot into the horsse manger. If the world last a while after this rate, wheate and rie will be no graine for poore men to feed on, and some catterpillers there are that can saie so much alreadie.

A famine at hand is first seene in the horsse manger when the poore doo fall to horsse corne.

Of bread made of wheat we haue sundrie sorts, dailie brought to the table, whereof the first and most excellent is the mainchet, which we commonlie call white bread, . . . and our good workemen deliuer commonlie such proportion, that of the flower of one bushell with another they make fortie cast of manchet, of which euerie lofe weigheth eight ounces into the ouen and six ounces out, as I haue beene informed. The second is the cheat or wheaton bread, so named bicause the colour therof resembleth the graie or yellowish wheat, being cleane and well dressed, and out of this is the coursest of the

Cheat bread.

bran (vsuallie called gurgeons or pollard) taken. The raueled is a kind of cheat bread also, but it reteineth more of the grosse, and lesse of the pure *Rauelled* substance of the wheat: and this being more sleightlie wrought vp, is vsed in *bread.* the halles of the nobilitie, and gentrie onelie, whereas the other either is or should be baked in cities & good townes of an appointed size (according to such price as the corne dooth beare) and by a statute prouided by king John in that behalfe. The raueled cheat therfore is generallie so made that out of one bushell of meale, after two and twentie pounds of bran be sifted and taken from it (wherevnto they ad the gurgeons that rise from the manchet) they make thirtie cast, euerie lofe weighing eighteene ounces into the ouen and sixteene ounces out: and beside this they so handle the matter that to euerie bushell of meale they ad onelie two and twentie or three and twentie pound of water, washing also in some houses there corne before it go to the mill, whereby their manchet bread is more excellent in colour and pleasing to the eie, than other wise it would be. The next sort is named browne bread of the *Browne bread.* colour, of which we haue two sorts, one baked vp as it cōmeth from the mill, so that neither the bran nor the floure are anie whit diminished. . . . The other hath little or no floure left therein at all, . . . and it is not onlie the woorst and weakest of all the other sorts, but also appointed in old time for seruants, slaues, and the inferiour kind of people to feed **page 168 /** vpon. Here-vnto likewise, bicause it is drie and brickle in the working (for it will hardlie be made vp handsomelie into loaues) some adde a portion of rie meale in our time, whereby the rough drinesse or drie roughnes therof is somwhat qualified, & then it is named miscelin, that is, bread made of mingled corne, albeit that diuerse doo sow or mingle wheat & rie of set purpose at the mill, or before it come there, and sell the same at the markets vnder the aforesaid name.

. . . .

Our drinke, whose force and continuance is partlie touched alreadie, is made of barleie, water, and hops, sodden and mingled togither, by the indus- *Drinke.* trie of our bruers, in a certeine exact proportion. But before our barleie doo come vnto their hands, it susteineth great alteration, and is conuerted into malt. . . .

Our malt is made all the yeare long in some great townes, but in gentle-mens and yeomens houses, who commonlie make sufficient for their owne *Making of* expenses onelie, the winter halfe is thought most meet for that commoditie: *malt.* howbeit the malt that is made when the willow dooth bud, is commonlie worst of all, neuerthelesse each one indeuoureth to make it of the best barleie, which is steeped in a cesterne, in greater or lesse quantitie, by the space of three daies and three nights, vntill it be throughlie soked. This be-ing doone, the water is drained from it by little and little, till it be quite gone. Afterward they take it out, and laieng it vpon the cleane floore on a round heape, it resteth so vntill it be readie to shoote at the root end, which maltsters call *Comming.* When it beginneth therefore to shoot in this maner, they saie it is come, and then foorthwith they spread it abroad, first thicke, and afterward thinner and thinner vpon the said floore (as it commeth), and there it lieth (with turning euerie daie foure or fiue times) by the space of one and twentie daies at the least, the workeman not suffering it in anie wise to take anie heat, whereby the bud end should spire, that bringeth foorth the blade, and by which ouersight or hurt of the stuffe it selfe the malt would be spoiled, and turne small commoditie to the bruer. When it hath gone or beene turned so long vpon the floore, they carie it to a kill couered with haire cloth, where they giue it gentle heats (after they haue spread it there verie thin abroad) till it be drie, & in the meane while they turne it often, that it may be vniformelie dried. For the more it be dried (yet must it be doone with soft fire) the sweeter and better the malt is, and the longer it will continue, whereas if it be not dried downe (as they call it) but slackelie handled, it will breed a kind of worme, called a wiuell, which groweth in the floure of the corne, and in processe of time will so eat out itselfe, that nothing shall remaine of the graine but euen the verie rind or huske.

The best malt is tried by the hardnesse & colour, for if it looke fresh with a yellow hew & thereto will write like a peece of chalke, after you haue bitten a kirnell in sunder in the middest, then you may assure your selfe that it is dried downe. In some places it is dried at leisure with wood alone, or strawe alone, in other with wood and strawe togither, but of all the strawe dried, is the most excellent. For the wood dried malt when it is brued, beside that the drinke is higher of colour, it dooth hurt and annoie the head of him that is not vsed thereto, bicause of the smoake. Such also as vse both indifferentlie doo barke, cleaue, and drie their wood in an ouen, thereby to remooue all moisture that shuld procure the fume, and this malt is in the second place, & with the same likewise, that which is made with dried firze, broome, &c: whereas if they also be occupied greene, they are in maner so preiudiciall to the corne, as is the moist wood. And thus much of our malts, in bruing whereof some grinde the same somewhat groselie, and in seething well the liquor that shall be put vnto it, they adde to euerie nine quarters of mault one of headcorne, which consisteth of sundrie graine, as wheate, and otes groond. . . . Sith I haue taken occasion to speake of bruing, I will exemplifie in such a proportion as I am best skilled in, bicause it is the vsuall rate for mine owne familie, and once in a moneth practised by my wife & hir maid seruants, who proceed withall after this maner, as she hath oft informed me.

Bruing of beere. Hauing therefore groond eight bushels of good malt vpon our querne, where the toll is saued, she addeth vnto it halfe a bushell of wheat meale, and so much of otes small groond, and so tempereth or mixeth them with the malt, that you cannot easilie discerne the one from the other, otherwise these later would clunter, fall into lumps, and thereby become vnprofitable. The first liquor which is full eightie gallons, according to the proportion of our furnace, she maketh boiling hot, and then powreth it softlie into the malt, where it resteth (but without stirring) vntill hir second liquor be almost readie to boile. This doone she letteth hir mash run till the malt be left without liquor, or at the least wise the greatest part of the moisture, which she perceiueth by the staie and soft issue thereof, and by this time hir second liquor in the furnace is ready to seeth, which is put also to the malt as the first woort also againe into the furnace wherevnto she addeth two pounds of the best English hops, and so letteth them seeth togither by the space of two houres in summer, or an houre and an halfe in winter, whereby it getteth an excellent colour, and continuance without impeachment, or anie superfluous

tartnesse. But before she putteth hir first woort into the furnace, or mingleth *Charwoort.*
it with the hops, she taketh out a vessell full, of eight or nine gallons, which
she shutteth vp close, and suffereth no aire to come into it till it become
yellow, and this she reserueth by it selfe vnto further vse, as shall appeare
herafter, calling it Brackwoort, or Charwoort, as she saith it addeth also
to the colour of the drinke, whereby it yeeldeth not vnto amber or fine
gold in hew vnto the eie. By this time also hir second woort is let runne, and
the first being taken out of the furnace and placed to coole, she returneth the
middle woort vnto the furnace, where it is striken ouer, or from whence it
is taken againe, when it beginneth to boile and mashed the second time,
whilest the third liquor is heat (for there are three liquors) and   page 169 /
this last put into the furnace, when the second is mashed againe. When she
hath mashed also the last liquor (and set the second to coole by the first)
she letteth it runne, and then seetheth it againe with a pound and an halfe
of new hops, or peraduenture two pounds as she seeth cause by the goodnesse
or basenesse of the hops, & when it hath sodden in summer two hours & in
winter an houre & an halfe, she striketh it also and reserueth it vnto mixture
with the rest when time dooth serue therefore. Finallie when she setteth hir
drinke togither, she addeth to hir brackwoort or charwoort halfe an ounce of
arras, and halfe & quarterne of an ounce of baiberries finelie powdered, and
then putting the same into hir woort with an handfull of wheat flowre, she
proceedeth in such vsuall order as common bruing requireth. Some in steed
of arras & baies adde so much long pepper onelie, but in hir opinion and my
liking it is not so good as the first, and hereof we make three hoggesheads of
goode beere, such (I meane) as is meet for poore men as I am to liue withall,
whose small maintenance (for what great thing is fortie pounds a yeare *Compu-*
tatis computandis able to performe) may indure no deeper cut, the charges
whereof groweth in this manner. I value my malt at ten shillings, my wood at
foure shillings which I buie, my hops at twentie pence, the spice at two
pence, seruants wages two shillings six pence with meat and drinke, and the
wearing of my vessell at twentie pence, so that for my twentie shillings I haue
ten score gallons of beere or more, notwithstanding the losse in seething,
which some being loth to forgo doo not obserue the time, and therefore speed
thereafter in their successe, and worthilie. The continuance of the drinke is
alwaie determined after the quantitie of the hops, so that being well hopped
it lasteth longer. For it feedeth vpon the hop, and holdeth out so long as the
force of the same continueth, which being extinguished the drinke must be
spent or else it dieth, and becommeth of no value.

In some places of England, there is a kind of drinke made of apples, which *Cider.*
they call it cider or pomage, but that of peares is named pirrie, and both are *Perrie.*
groond and pressed in presses made for the nonce. Certes these two are verie
common in Sussex, Kent, Worcester, and other steeds, where these sorts of
fruits doo abound, howbeit they are not their onelie drinke at all times, but *Metheglin.*
referred vnto the delicate sorts of drinke, as metheglin is in Wales, whereof
the Welshmen make no lesse accompt (and not without cause if it be well
handled) than the Greekes did of their Ambrosia or Nectar. . . . There is a
kind of swish swash made also in Essex, and diuerse other places, with honi-

Mead.

combs and water, which the homelie countrie wiues, putting some pepper and a little other spice among, call mead, verie good in mine opinion for such as loue to be loose bodied at large, or a little eased of the cough. . . . **page 170 /**

Chapter VII

Of their apparell and attire.

An Englishman, indeuoring sometime to write of our attire, made sundrie platformes for his purpose, supposing by some of them to find out one stedfast ground whereon to build the summe of his discourse. But in the end (like an oratour long without exercise) when he saw what **page 171 /** a difficult peece of worke he had taken in hand, he gaue ouer his trauell, and onelie drue the picture of a naked man, vnto whome he gave a paire of sheares in the one hand, and a peece of cloth in the other, to the end he should shape his apparell after such fashion as himselfe liked, sith he could find no kind of garment that could please him anie while togither, and this he

Andrew Boord called an Englishman. Certes this writer (otherwise being a lewd popish hypocrite and vngratious priest) shewed himselfe herein not to be altogether void of iudgement, sith the phantasticall follie of our nation, euen from the courtier to the carter is such, that no forme of apparell liketh vs longer than the first garment is in the wearing, if it continue so long and be not laid aside, to receiue some other trinket newlie deuised by the fickle headed tailors, who couet to have seuerall trickes in cutting, thereby to draw fond customers to

Strange cuts. more expense of monie. For my part I can tell better how to inueigh against this enormitie, than describe anie certeintie of our attire: sithence such is our mutabilitie, that to daie there is none to the Spanish guise, to morrow the French toies are most fine and delectable, ere long no such apparell as that which is after the high Alman fashion, by and by the Turkish maner is generallie best liked of, otherwise the Morisco gowns, the Barbarian sleeues, the mandilion worne to Collie weston ward, and the short French breeches make such a comelie vesture, that except it were a dog in a doublet, you shall not see anie so dignified, as are my countrie men of England. And as these fashions are diuerse, so likewise it is a world to see the costlinesse and the curiositie: the excesse and the vanitie: the pompe and the brauerie: the change and the varietie: and finallie the ficklenesse and the follie that is in all degrees: in somuch that nothing is more constant in England than incon-

Much cost vpon the bodie, and little vpon the soule. stancie of attire. Oh how much cost is bestowed now adaies vpon our bodies and how little vpon our soules! how manie sutes of apparell hath the one and how little furniture hath the other? how long time is asked in decking vp of the first, and how little space left wherin to feed the later? how curious, how nice also are a number of men and women, and how hardlie can the tailor please them in making it fit for their bodies? how manie times must it be sent backe againe to him that made it? what chafing, what fretting, what reprochfull language doth the poore workeman beare awaie? and manie times when he dooth nothing to it at all, yet when it is brought home againe it is verie fit and handsome; then must we put it on, then must the long seames of our hose be set by a plumb-line, then we puffe, then we blow, and finallie sweat till we drop, that our clothes may stand well vpon vs. I will saie nothing of our heads, which sometimes are polled, sometimes curled, or suffered to grow at length like womans lockes, manie times cut off aboue or vnder the eares round as by a woodden dish. Neither will I meddle with our varietie of beards, of which some are shauen from the chin like those of Turks, not a few cut short like to the beard of marques Otto, some made round like a rubbing brush, other with a *pique de vant* (O fine fashion!) or now and then suffered to grow long, the barbers being growen to be so cunning in this behalfe as the tailors. And therfore if a man haue a leane and streight face, a marquesse Ottons cut will make it broad and large; if it be platter like, a long slender beard will make it seeme the narrower; if he be wesell becked, then much heare left on the cheekes will make the owner looke big like a bowdled hen, and so grim as a goose, if Cornelis of Chelmeresford saie true: manie old men doo weare no beards at all. Some lustie courtiers also and gentlemen of courage, doo weare either rings of gold, stones, or pearle in their eares, whereby they imagine the workemanship of God not to be a little amended. But herein they rather disgrace than adorne their persons, as by their nicenesse in apparell, for which I saie most nations doo not vniustlie deride vs, as also for that we doo seeme to imitate all nations round about vs, wherein we be like to the *Polypus* or Chameleon; and thereunto bestow most cost vpon our arses, & much more than vpon all the rest of our bodies, as women doo likewise vpon their heads and shoulders. In women also it is most to be lamented, that they doo now farre exceed the lightnesse of our men (who neuerthelesse are transformed from the cap euen to the verie shoo) and such staring attire as in time past was supposed meet for none but light housewiues onelie, is now become an habit for chast and sober matrones. What should I saie of their doublets with pendant codpeeses on the brest full of iags & cuts, and sleeues of sundrie colours? their galligascons to beare out their bums & make their attire to sit plum round (as they terme it) about them? their fardingals, and diuerslie coloured nether stocks of silke, ierdseie, and such like, whereby their bodies are rather deformed than commended? I haue met with some of these trulles in London so disguised, that it hath passed my skill to discerne whether they were men or women.

Beards.

Excess in women.

Thus it is now come to pass, that women are become men, and men transformed into monsters: and those good gifts which almightie God hath giuen vnto us to releeue our necessities withall (as a nation turning altogither the grace of God into wantonnesse, for

Luxuriant animi rebus plerunque secundis)

not otherwise bestowed than in all excesse, as if we wist not otherwise how to consume and wast them. I praie God that in this behalfe our sinne be not like vnto that of Sodoma and Gomorha, whose errors were pride, excesse of diet, and abuse of Gods benefits aboundantlie bestowed vpon them, beside want of charitie toward the poore, and certeine other points which the pro-

Ezech. 16.

phet shutteth vp in silence. Certes the common-wealth cannot be said to
florish where these abuses reigne, but is rather oppressed by vnreasonable
exactions made vpon rich farmers, and of poore tenants, wherewith to main-
teine the same. Neither was it euer merier with England, than when an Englishman was knowne abroad by his owne cloth, and contented himselfe at
home with his fine carsie hosen, and a meane slop: his coat, gowne, and cloake
of browne blue or puke, with some pretie furniture of veluet or furre, and a
doublet of sad tawnie, or blacke veluet, or other comelie silke, without such
cuts and gawrish colours as are worne in these daies, and neuer brought in
but by the consent of the French, who thinke themselues the gaiest men,
when they haue most diuersities of iagges and change of colours about them.
Certes of all estates our merchants doo least alter their attire, and therefore

*Attire of
merchants.*

are most to be commended: for albeit that which they weare be verie fine
and costlie, yet in forme and colour it representeth a great peece of the ancient
grauitie apperteining to citizens and burgesses, albeit the yoonger sort of
their wiues both in attire and costlie housekeeping can not tell when and how
to make an end, as being women in deed in whome all kind of curiositie
is to be found and seene, and in farre greater measure than in women
of higher calling. I might here name a sort of hewes deuised for the nonce,
wherewith to please phantasticall heads, as gooseturd greene, pease porrige
tawnie, popingaie blue, lustie gallant, the diuell in the head (I should saie
the hedge) and such like: but I passe them ouer **page 172 /** thinking it
sufficient to haue said thus much of apparell generallie, when nothing can
particularlie be spoken of anie constancie thereof. **page 173 /**

Chapter XI

Of sundrie kinds of punishments appointed for malefactors.

In cases of felonie, manslaghter, roberie, murther, rape, piracie, & such
capitall crimes as are not reputed for treason or hurt of the estate, our sentence pronounced vpon the offendor is to hang till he be dead. . . . To vse
torment also or question by paine and torture in these common cases with
vs is greatlie abhorred, sith we are found alwaie to be such as despise death,
and yet abhorre to be tormented, choosing rather frankelie to open our minds
than to yeeld our bodies vnto such seruile halings and tearings as are vsed
in other countries. . . .

The greatest and most greeuous punishment vsed in England, for such as
offend against the state, is drawing from the prison to the place of execution
vpon an hardle or sled, where they are hanged till they be halfe dead, and
then taken downe and quartered aliue, after that their members and bowels
are cut from their bodies, and throwne into a fire prouided neere hand and
within their owne sight, euen for the same purpose. Sometimes, if the tres-
passe be not the more hainous, they are suffered to hang till they be quite

dead. And when soeuer anie of the nobilitie are conuicted of high treason by their peeres, that is to saie, equals (for an inquest of yeoman passeth not vpon them, but onelie of the lords of the parlement) this maner of their death is conuerted into the losse of their heads onelie, notwithstanding that the sentence doo run after the former order. In triall of cases concerning treason, fellonie, or anie other greeuous crime not confessed, the partie accused dooth yeeld, if he be a noble man, to be tried by an inquest (as I haue said) and his peeres: if a gentleman, by gentlemen: and an inferiour, by God and by the countrie, to wit, the yeomanrie (for combat or battell is not greatlie in vse) and being condemned of fellonie, manslaughter, &c: he is eftsoons hanged by the necke till he be dead, and then cut downe and buried. But if he be conuicted of wilfull murther, doone either vpon pretended malice, or in anie notable robberie, he is either hanged aliue in chaines neere the place where the fact was committed (or else vpon compassion taken first strangled with a rope) and so continueth till his bones consume to nothing. We haue vse neither of the wheele nor of the barre, as in other countries; but when wilfull manslaughter is perpetrated, beside hanging, the offendor hath his right hand commonlie striken off before or neere vnto the place where the act was doone, after which he is led foorth to the place of execution, and there put to death according to the law. . . . **page 184 /**

. . . If a woman poison hir husband she is burned aliue, if the seruant kill his master he is to be executed for petie treason, he that poisoneth a man is to be boiled to death in water or lead, although the partie die not of the practise: in cases of murther all the accessaries are to suffer paines of death accordinglie. Periurie is punished by the pillorie, burning in the forehead with the letter P, the rewalting of the trees growing vpon the grounds of the offendors and losse of all his mooueables. Manie trespasses also are punished by the cutting of one or both eares from the head of the offender, as the vtterance of seditious words against the magistrates, fratmakers, petie robbers, &c. Roges are burned through the eares, carters of sheepe out of the land by the losse of their hands, such as kill by poison are either boiled or skalded to death in lead or seething water. Heretikes are burned quicke, harlots and their mates by carting, ducking, and dooing of open penance in sheets, in churches and market steeds are often put to rebuke. Howbeit as this is counted with some either as no punishment at all to speak of, or but smallie regarded of the offendors, so I would with adulterie and fornication to haue some sharper law. For what great smart is it to be turned out of an hot sheet into a cold, or after a little washing in the water to be let lose againe vnto their former trades? Howbeit the dragging of some of them ouer the Thames betweene Lambeth and Westminster at the taile of a boat, is a punishment that most terrifieth them which are condemned therto, but this is inflicted vpon them by none other than the knight marshall, and that within the compasse of his jurisdiction & limits onelie. . . .

Witches are hanged or sometimes burned, but theeues are hanged (as I said before) generallie on the gibbet or gallowes, sauing in Halifax where they are beheaded after a strange maner, and whereof I find this report. *Halifax* There is and hath beene of ancient time a law or rather a custome at Halifax, *law.*

that who soeuer dooth commit anie fellonie, and is taken with the same, or confesse the fact vpon examination: if it be valued by foure constables to amount to the sum of thirteene pence halfe penie, he is foorthwith beheaded vpon one of the next market daies (which fall vsuallie vpon the tuesdaies, thursdaies, & saturdaies) or else vpon the same daie that he is so conuicted, if market be then holden. The engine wherewith the execution is doone, is a square blocke of wood of the length of foure foot and an halfe, which dooth ride vp and downe in a slot, rabet or regall betweene two peeces of timber, that are framed and set vpright of fiue yardes in height. In the neather end of the sliding blocke is an ax keied or fastened with an iron into the wood, which being drawne vp to the top of the frame is there fastned by a woodden pin (with a notch made into the same after the maner of a Samsons post) vnto the middest of which pin also there is a long rope fastened that commeth downe among the people, so that when the offendor hath made his confession, and hath laid his necke ouer the neathermost blocke, euerie man there present dooth either take hold of the rope (or putteth foorth his arme so neere to the same as he can get, in token that he is willing to see true iustice executed) and pulling out the pin in this maner, the head blocke wherein the ax is fastened dooth fall downe with such a violence, that if the necke of the transgressor were so big as that of a bull, it should be cut in sunder at a stroke, and roll from the bodie by a huge distance. If it be so that the offender be apprehended for an ox, oxen, sheepe, kine, horsse, or anie such cattell: the selfe beast or other of the same kind shall haue the end of the rope tied some-where vnto them, so that they being driuen doo draw out the pin wherby the offendor is executed. . . .

    Roges and vagabonds are often stocked and whipped, scolds are ducked *Mute.* vpon cucking stooles in the water. Such fellons as stand mute and speake not at their arraignement are pressed to death by huge weights laid vpon a boord, that lieth ouer their brest, and a sharpe stone vnder their backs, and these commonlie hold their peace, thereby to saue their goods vnto their wiues and children, which if they were condemned should be confiscated to *Cleargie.* the prince. Theeues that are saued by their bookes and cleargie, for the first **page 185 /** offense, if they haue stollen nothing else but oxen, sheepe, monie, or such like, which be no open robberies, as by the high waie side, or assailing of anie mans house in the night, without putting him in feare of his life, or breaking vp of his wals or doores, are burned in the left hand, vpon the brawne of the thombe with an hot iron, so that if they be apprehended againe, that marke bewraieth them to haue been arraigned of fellonie before, *Pirates.* whereby they are sure at that time to haue no mercie. . . . Pirats and robbers by sea are condemned in the court of the admeraltie, and hanged on the shore at lowe water marke, where they are left till three tides haue ouerwashed them. Finallie, such as hauing wals and banks neere vnto the sea, and doo suffer the same to decaie (after conuenient admonition) whereby the water entereth and drowneth vp the countrie, are by a certeine ancient custome apprehended, condemned, and staked in the breach, where they remaine for euer as parcell of the foundation of the new wall that is to be made vpon them, as I haue heard reported. **page 186 /**

William Harrison. *Description of England,* Book III. London, 1587.

CHAPTER XVI

Of our innes and thorowfaires.

Those townes that we call thorowfaires haue great and sumptuous innes builded in them, for the receiuing of such trauellers and strangers as pass to and fro. The manner of harbouring wherein, is not like to that of some other countries, in which the host or goodman of the house dooth chalenge a lordlie authoritie ouer his ghests, but cleane otherwise, sith euerie man may vse his inne as his owne house in England, and haue for his monie how great or little varietie of vittels, and what other seruice himselfe shall thinke expedient to call for. Our innes are also verie well furnished with naperie, bedding, and tapisterie, especiallie with naperie: for beside the linnen vsed at the tables, which is commonlie washed dailie, is such and so much as belongeth vnto the estate and calling of the ghest. Ech commer is sure to lie in cleane sheets, wherein no man hath beene lodged since they came from the landresse, or out of the water wherein they were last washed. If the traueller haue an horsse, his bed dooth cost him nothing, but if he go on foot he is sure to paie a penie for the same: but whether he be horsseman or footman if his chamber be once appointed he may carie the kaie with him, as of his owne house so long as he lodgeth there. If he loose oughts whilest he abideth in the inne, the host is bound by a generall custome to restore the damage, so that there is no greater securitie anie where for trauellers than in the gretest ins of England. Their horsses in like sort are walked, dressed, and looked vnto by certeine hostelers or hired seruants, appointed at the charges of the goodman of the house, who in hope of extraordinarie reward will deale verie diligentlie after outward appeerance in this their function and calling. Herein neuerthelesse are manie of them blameworthie, in that they doo not onelie deceiue the beast oftentimes of his allowance by sundrie meanes, except their owners looke well to them; but also make such packs with slipper merchants which hunt after preie (for what place is sure from euill & wicked persons) that manie an honest man is spoiled of his goods as he trauelleth to and fro, in which feat also the counsell of the tapsters or drawers of drinke, and chamberleins is not seldome behind or wanting. Certes I beleeue not that chapman or traueller in England is robbed by the waie without the knowledge of some of them, for when he commeth into the inne, & alighteth from his horsse, the hostler forthwith is verie busie to take downe his budget or capcase in the yard from his sadle bow, which he peiseth slilie in his hand to feele the weight thereof: or if he misse of this pitch, when the ghest hath taken vp his chamber, the chamberleine that looketh to the making of the beds, will be sure to remooue it from the place where the owner hath set it as if it were to set it more conuenientlie some where else, whereby he getteth an inkling whether it be monie or other short wares, & therof giueth warning to such od ghests as hant the house and are of his confederacie, to the vtter vndoing of manie an honest yeoman as he iournieth by the waie. The tapster in like sort for his part dooth marke his behauiour, and what plentie of monie he draweth when he paieth the shot, to the like end: so that it shall be an hard matter to escape all their subtile practises. Some thinke it a gay matter to commit their budgets at their comming to the goodman of the house: but thereby they oft be- page 246 / wraie themselues. For albeit their monie be safe for the time that it is in his hands (for you shall not heare that a man is robbed in his inne) yet after their departure the host can make no warrantise of the same, sith his protection extendeth no further than the gate of his owne house: and there cannot be a surer token vnto such as prie and watch for those booties, than to see anie ghest deliuer his capcase in such maner. In all our innes we haue plentie of ale, beere, and sundrie kinds of wine, and such is the capacitie of some of them that they are able to lodge two hundred or three hundred persons, and their horsses at ease, & therto with a verie short warning make such prouision for their diet, as to him that is vnacquainted withall may seeme to be incredible. Howbeit of all in England there are no worse ins than in London, and yet manie are there far better than the best I haue heard of in anie forren countrie, if all circumstances be dulie considered.... page 247 /

Paul Hentzner, a native of Brandenburg, a jurist and counselor to Duke Charles of Münsterberg and Öls, visited England in August and September, 1598, as a companion and tutor to Christoph Rehdiger, a young Silesian nobleman. His account includes striking descriptions of Queen Elizabeth's court, her dress and manner, the elaborate preparations for her dinner, a quick view of London and its environs. We are intrigued not only by the informal description of England from a foreign visitor's point of view but also by the candid nature of his remarks concerning that which he saw.

Paul Hentzner. *A Journey into England, in the Year M. D. XC. VIII.* Printed at Strawberry Hill, 1757.

This city being very large of itself, has very extensive suburbs, and a fort, called the Tower, of beautiful structure. It is magnificently ornamented, with public buildings and churches, of which there are above 120 parochial.

On the South, is a bridge of stone, 800 feet in length, of wonderful work; it is supported upon 20 piers of square stone, 60 feet high, and 30 broad, joined by arches of about 20 feet diameter. The whole is covered on each side with houses, so disposed, as to have the appearance of a continued street, not at all of a bridge.   **page 4 /**

Upon this is built a tower, on whose top the heads of such as have been executed for high treason, are placed upon iron spikes: We counted above 30.

Paulus Iovius, in his description of the most remarkable towns in England, says, all are obscured by London: . . . the capital of all Britain, famous for the commerce of many nations; it's houses are elegantly built, it's churches fine, it's towns strong, and it's riches and abundance surprizing. The wealth of the world is wafted to it by the Thames, swelled by the tide, and navigable to merchant ships, through a safe and deep channel for 60 miles, from its mouth to the city: It's banks are every where beautified with fine country seats, woods, and farms; below, is the royal palace of Greenwich; above, that of Rich- **page 5 /** mond; and between both, on the West of London, rise the noble buildings of Westminster, most remarkable for the courts of Justice, the Parliament, and St. Peter's church, enriched with the royal tombs. At the distance of 20 miles from London, is the castle of Windsor, a most delightful retreat of the kings of England, as well famous for several of their tombs, and for the ceremonial of the Order of the Garter. The river abounds in Swans, swimming in flocks; the sight of them, and their noise, is vastly agreeable to the fleets that meet them in their course. It is joined to the city by a bridge of stone, wonderfully built; is never encreased by any rains, rising only

with the tide, and is every where spread with nets, for the taking of Salmon
and Shad. *Thus far Paulus Iovius.*   **page 6 /**

.   .   .   .

In WHITEHALL are the following things worthy of observation:

I. The Royal Library, well stored with Greek, Latin, Italian and French
books: Amongst the rest, a little one in French, upon parchment, in the hand
writing of the present reigning queen Elizabeth, thus inscribed:

> *To the most High, Puissant, and redoubted Prince, Henry VIII.*
> *of the Name, King of England, France and Ireland, Defender of*
> *the Faith:*
> *Elizabeth, his most humble Daughter,*
> *Health and Obedience.*

page 30 /

All these books are bound in velvet of different colours, though chiefly red,
with clasps of gold and silver; some have pearls, and precious stones, set in
their bindings.

II. Two little silver cabinets of exquisite work, in which the Queen keeps
her paper, and which she uses for writing boxes.

III. The Queen's bed, ingeniously composed of woods of different colours,
with quilts of silk, velvet, gold, silver, and embroidery.

IV. A little chest ornamented all over with pearls, in which the Queen keeps
her bracelets, ear-rings, and other things of extraordinary value.

V. Christ's passion, in painted glass.

VI. Portraits: Among which are queen Elizabeth at 16 years old. Henry,
Richard,   **page 31 /**   Edward, kings of England; Rosamond; Lucrece, a Grecian bride, in her nuptial habit; the genealogy of the kings of England; a picture of king Edward VI. representing at first sight something quite deformed,
till by looking through a small hole in the cover, which is put over it, you see
it in it's true proportions; Charles V. Emperor; Charles Emanuel Duke of
Savoy, and Catherine of Spain, his wife; Ferdinand Duke of Florence, with
his daughters; one of Philip king of Spain, when he came into England and
married Mary; Henry VII. Henry VIII. and his mother: Besides many more
of illustrious men and women; and a picture of the siege of Malta.

VII. A small Hermitage, half hid in a rock, finely carved in wood.

VIII. Variety of emblems, on paper, cut in the shape of shields, with
mottoes, used by the nobility at tilts and tournaments, hung up here for a
memorial.   **page 32 /**

IX. Different instruments of music, upon one of which two persons may
perform at the same time.

X. A piece of clock-work, an Æthiop riding upon a Rhinoceros, with
four attendants, who all make their obeisance, when it strikes the hour; these
are all put into motion by winding up the machine. . . .   **page 33 /**

.   .   .   .

The government of London is this: The city is divided into 25 Regions, or
Wards; the council is composed of 24 Aldermen, one of which presides over
every Ward. And whereas of old, the chief magistrate, was a Portreve, *i.e.*

Governor of the city: Richard I. appointed two Bailiffs; instead of which,
page 34 /   king John gave a power by grant, of chusing annually a Mayor,
from any of the twelve principal Companies, and to name two Sheriffs, one
of which to be called the King's, the other, the City's. It is scarce credible
how this city encreased, both in public and private buildings, upon establish-
ing this form of government. *Vide Cambden's Britan. Middlesex.*

It is worthy of observation, that every year upon St. Bartholemew's day,
when the Fair is held, it is usual for the Mayor, attended by the 12 principal
Aldermen, to walk in a neighbouring field, dressed in his scarlet gown, and
about his neck a golden chain, to which is hung a* Golden Fleece, and besides,
that† particular ornament, which distinguishes the most noble Order of
the Garter. During the year of his Magistracy, he is obliged to live so magnificently, that Foreigner or Na-   **page 35 /**   tive, without any expence, is
free, if he can find a chair empty, to dine at his table, where there is always the
greatest plenty. When the Mayor goes out of the precincts of the city, a scepter, a sword, and a cap, are born before him, and he is followed by the principal
Aldermen in scarlet gowns, with gold chains; himself and they on horseback: Upon their arrival at a place appointed for that purpose, where a tent
is pitched, the mob begin to wrestle before them, two at a time; the conquerors
receive rewards from the Magistrates. After this is over, a parcel of live
Rabits are turned loose among the crowd, which are pursued by a number of
boys, who endeavour to catch them, with all the noise they can make. While
we were at this shew, one of our company, Thobias Salandar, Doctor of Physic,
had his pocket picked of his purse, with nine crowns du soleil, which without doubt was so cleverly taken from him, by an Englishman who always
kept very close to him, that the Doctor did not in the least perceive it.   **page
36 /**

.   .   .   .

Without the city are some THEATRES, where English Actors represent almost evry day Tragedies and Comedies to very numerous audiences; these
are concluded with excellent music, variety of dances, and the excessive applause of those that are present.   **page 41 /**

.   .   .   .

There is still another place, built in the form of a Theatre, which serves
for the baiting of Bulls and Bears, they are fastened behind, and then worried
by great English bulldogs; but not without great risque to the dogs, from the
horns of the one, and the teeth of the other; and it sometimes happens they are
killed upon the spot; fresh ones are immediately supplied in the places of those
that are wounded, or tired. To this entertainment, there often follows that of
whipping a blinded Bear, which is performed by five or six men, standing
circularly with whips, which they exercise upon him without any mercy, as
he cannot escape from them because of his chain; he defends himself with all
of his force and skill, throwing down all who come within his reach, and are
not active enough to get out of it, and tearing the   **page 42 /**   whips out of
their hands, and breaking them. At these spectacles, and every where else, the

---

* *This probably alluded to the woollen manufacture; Stow mentions his riding through*
the Cloth Fair, on the Eve of St. Bartholemew, p. 651.
  † *The Collar of SS.*

English are constantly smoaking Tobacco, and in this manner; they have pipes on purpose made of clay, into the farther end of which they put the herb, so dry that it may be rubbed into powder, and putting fire to it, they draw the smoak into their mouths, which they puff out again, through their nostrils, like funnels, along with it plenty of phlegm and defluxion from the head. In these theatres fruits, such as apples, pears and nuts, according to the season, are carried about to be sold, as well as ale and wine.   **page 43 /**

. . . .

We arrived next at the royal palace of GREENWICH, reported to have been originally built by Humphrey Duke of Gloucester, and to have received very magnificent additions from Henry VII. It was here Elizabeth, the present queen, was born, and here she generally resides; particularly in summer, for the delightfulness of it's situation. We were admitted by an order Mr. Rogers had procured from the Lord Chamberlain, into the Presence-Chamber, hung with rich tapestry, and the floor after the English fashion, strewed with* hay, through which the Queen commonly passes in her way to chapel: At the door stood a Gentleman dressed in velvet, with a gold chain, whose office was **page 47 /**   to introduce to the Queen any Person of Distinction, that came to wait on her: It was Sunday, when there is usually the greatest attendance of Nobility. In the same hall were the Archbishop of Canterbury, the Bishop of London, a great number of Counsellors of State, Officers of the Crown, and Gentlemen, who waited the Queen's coming out; which she did from her own apartment, when it was time to go to Prayers, attended in the following manner:

First went Gentlemen, Barons, Earls, Knights of the Garter, all richly dressed and bare-headed; next came the Chancellor, bearing the Seals in a red-silk Purse, between Two; one of which carried the Royal Scepter, the other the Sword of State, in a red scabbard, studded with golden Fleurs de Lis, the point upwards: Next came the Queen, in the Sixty-fifth Year of her Age, as we were told, very majestic; her Face oblong, fair, but wrinkled; her Eyes small, yet black and pleasant; her Nose a little hooked; her Lips nar-row, and her Teeth black; (a   **page 48 /**   defect the English seem subject to, from their too great use of sugar) she had in her Ears two pearls, with very rich drops; she wore false Hair, and that red; upon her Head she had a small Crown, reported to be made of some of the gold of the celebrated Lunebourg tablet: Her Bosom was uncovered, as all the English ladies have it, till they marry; and she had on a Necklace of exceeding fine jewels; her Hands were small, her Fingers long, and her Stature neither tall nor low; her air was stately, her manner of speaking mild and obliging. That day she was dressed in white Silk, bordered with pearls of the size of beans, and over it a Mantle of black silk, shot with silver threads; her Train was very long, the end of it born by a Marchioness; instead of a Chain, she had an oblong Collar of gold and jewels. As she went along in all this state and magnificence, she spoke very graciously, first to   **page 49 /**   one, then to another, whether foreign Ministers, or those who attended for different reasons, in English, French and Italian; for besides being well skilled in Greek, Latin, and the Languages I

---

* He probably means rushes. [Source.]
† At this distance of time, it is difficult to say what this was.

have mentioned, she is mistress of Spanish, Scotch, and Dutch: Whoever speaks to her, it is kneeling; now and then she raises some with her Hand. While we were there, W. Slawata, a Bohemian Baron, had letters to present to her; and she, after pulling off her glove, gave him her right Hand to kiss, sparkling with rings and jewels, a mark of particular Favour: Wherever she turned her Face, as she was going along, every body fell down on their* knees. The Ladies of the Court followed next to her, very handsome and well-   page 50 / shaped, and for the most part dressed in white; she was guarded on each side by the Gentlemen Pensioners, fifty in number, with gilt battle-axes; in the Anti-chapel next the Hall where we were, Petitions were presented to her, and she received them most graciously, which occasioned the acclamation of, LONG LIVE QUEEN ELIZABETH! She answered it with, I THANK YOU MY GOOD PEOPLE. In the Chapel was excellent music; as soon as it, and the Service was over, which scarce exceeded half an hour, the Queen returned in the same State and Order, and prepared to go to Dinner. But while she was still at Prayers, we saw her Table set out with the following Solemnity:

A Gentleman entered the room bearing a rod, and along with him another who had a table-cloth, which after they had both kneeled three times, with the utmost veneration, he spread upon the table, and after kneeling again, they both retired. Then came two others, one with the rod again, the other with a salt-seller, a plate, and bread; when   page 51 /   they had kneeled, as the others had done, and placed what was brought upon the table, they too retired with the same ceremonies performed by the first. At last came an unmarried Lady, (we were told she was a Countess) and along with her a married one, bearing a tasting-knife; the former was dressed in white silk, who when she had prostrated herself three times, in the most graceful manner approached the table, and rubbed the plates with bread and salt, with as much awe, as if the Queen had been present: When they had waited there a little while, the Yeoman of the Guard entered, bare-headed, cloathed in scarlet, with a golden rose upon their backs, bringing in at each turn a course of twenty-four dishes, served in plate most of it gilt; these dishes were received by a Gentleman in the same order they were brought, and placed upon the table, while the Lady-Taster gave to each of the guard a mouthful to eat, of the particular dish he had brought, for fear of any poison. During the time that this guard, which consists of the tallest and stoutest men that can   page 52 / be found in all England, being carefully selected for this service, were bringing dinner, twelve trumpets, and two kettle-drums made the hall ring for half an hour together. At the end of all this ceremonial a number of unmarried Ladies appeared, who with particular solemnity lifted the meat off the table, and conveyed it into the Queen's inner and more private chamber, where after she had chosen for herself, the rest goes to the Ladies of the Court.

The Queen dines and sups alone with very few attendance; and it is very seldom that any body, foreigner or native, is admitted at that time, and then only at the intercession of somebody in power. . . .   page 53 /

---

* *Her Father had been treated with the same deference. It is mentioned by Fox in his Acts and Monuments, that when the Lord Chancellor went to apprehend queen Catherine Parr, he spoke to the King on his knees. King James I. suffered his courtiers to omit it.* Bacon's Papers, v. ii. p. 516. [*Source.*]

.   .   .   .

[Oxford]

These Students lead a life almost Monastic; for as the Monks had nothing in the world to do, but when they had said their prayers at stated hours, to employ themselves in instructive studies, no more have these. They are divided into three Tables: The first is called the Fellows Table, to which are admitted Earls, Barons, Gentlemen, Doctors, and Masters of Arts, but very few of the latter; this is more plentifully and expensively served than the others: The Second is for Masters of Arts, Bachelors, some Gentlemen, and eminent Citizens: The Third for people of low condition. While the rest are at dinner or supper in a great Hall, where they are all assembled, one of the Students reads aloud the Bible, which is placed on a desk in the middle of the Hall, and this office every one of them takes upon himself in his turn; as soon as Grace is said after each meal, every one is at liberty, either to retire to his own chambers, or to walk in the College garden, there being none that   page 64 /   has not a delightful one. Their habit is almost the same as that of the Jesuits, their gowns reaching down to their ancles, sometimes lined with furr; they wear square caps; the Doctors, Masters of Arts, and Professors, have another kind of gown that distinguishes them: Every Student of any considerable standing has a key to the College Library, for no College is without one.   page 65 /

Of the *Manners* of the *ENGLISH*.

The English are serious like the Germans, lovers of shew; liking to be followed where-ever they go by whole troops of servants, who wear their masters arms in silver, fastened to their left arms, a ridicule they deservedly lay under: They excell in dancing and music, for they are active and lively, though of a thicker make than the French; they cut their hair close on the middle of the head, letting it grow on either side; they are good sailors, and better pyrates, cunning, treacherous, and thievish; above 300 are said to be hanged annually at London; beheading with them is less infamous than hanging; they give the wall as the place of honour; hawking is the general sport of the gentry; they are more polite in eating than the French, devouring less bread, but more meat, which they roast in perfection; they put a great deal of sugar in their drink; their beds are covered with tapestry, even those of farmers; they are often   page 88 /   molested with the scurvy, said to have first crept into England with the Norman conquest; their houses are commonly of two stories, except in London, where they are of three and four, though but seldom of four; they are built of wood, those of the richer sort with bricks, their roofs are low, and where the owner has money, covered with lead.

They are powerful in the field, successful against their enemies, impatient of any thing like slavery; vastly fond of great noises that fill the ear, such as the firing of cannon, drums, and the ringing of bells, so that it is common for a number of them, that have got a glass in their heads, to go up into some belfry, and ring the bells for hours together, for the sake of exercise. If they see a foreigner, very well made or particularly handsome, they will say, *It is a pity he is not an* ENGLISHMAN.   page 89 /

Ben Jonson (1573–1637) attended Westminster School under William Camden, to whom he owed his future in scholarship. In 1597 he began working for Henslowe's company as a player and playwright. By the end of Elizabeth's reign, he was second only to Shakespeare as a dramatist and second to none as a dramatic satirist. The comedy Every Man in his Humour *was acted in 1598 with Shakespeare taking a part. Its success established Jonson as one of the leading dramatists of the day. In addition to comedy he was a major writer of masques, notable for their quality, variety, and scenic display. His lyrics show rare beauty and grace.* Timber, or Discoveries *is a commonplace book in which he recorded numerous translations, comments about works read, various recollections, among them remarks concerning writers of the Elizabethan age. He listed among his acquaintances all the remarkable men of his time: Camden, Chapman, Bacon, Drayton, Donne, Beaumont, and Fletcher, to name only a few. There was no man of letters so highly regarded as Jonson. After his death, his influence was still apparent in the poetry of such men as Herrick, Suckling, Thomas Carew — "sons of Ben." Although in praise of his own age Dryden was at times critical of Jonson, he expressed confidence that no age would reach some of his excellencies.*

Ben Jonson. *Every Man in his Humour* (1598) in *The Works of Ben Jonson.* London, 1692.

Prologue

Though Need make many Poets, and some such
As Art and Nature have not better'd much;
Yet ours, for want, hath not so lov'd the Stage,
As he dare serve th'ill Customs of the Age,
Or purchase your delight at such a rate,
As, for it, he himself must justly hate:
To make a child now swadled, to proceed
Man, and then shoot up in one beard and weed,
Past threescore years: or, with three rusty swords,
And help of some few foot- and half-foot words,
Fight over YORK, and LANCASTERS long jars,
And in the Tyring-house bring wounds to scars.
He rather prays, you will be pleas'd to see
One such to day, as other plays should be;
Where neither CHORUS wafts you o're the seas,
Nor creaking Throne comes down, the boys to please;

Nor nimble Squib is seen, to make afeard
The Gentlewomen; nor roul'd Bullet heard
To say, it Thunders; nor tempestuous Drum
Rumbles, to tell you when the Storm doth come;
But Deeds, and Language, such as men do use:
And Persons, such as Comoedy would chuse,
When she would shew an Image of the Times,
And sport with Humane Follies, not with Crimes.
Except, we make 'em such by loving still
Our popular Errors, when we know th'are ill.
I mean such Errors as you'll all confess
By laughing at them, they deserve no less:
Which when you heartily do, there's hope left, then,
You, that have so grac'd Monsters, may like Men.   **page 1 /**

Ben Jonson. *TIMBER: or DISCOVERIES, Made upon Men and Matter* in *The Works of Ben Jonson.* London, 1692.

Censura de
Poetis.

Nothing in our Age, I have observ'd, is more preposterous, than the *running Judgments* upon *Poetry* and *Poets;* when we shall hear those things commended, and cry'd up for the best Writings, which a Man would scarce vouchsafe, to wrap any wholsom Drug in; he would never light his *Tabaco* with them. And those Men almost nam'd for *Miracles,* who yet are so vile, that if a Man should go about, to examine, and correct them, he must make all they have done, but one blot. . . .

Cestius.
Cicero.

Yet their Vices have not hurt them: Nay, a great many they have profited; for they have been lov'd for nothing else. And this false Opinion grows strong against the best Men: if once it take Root with the *Ignorant. Cestius* in his time, was preferr'd to *Cicero;* so far, as the Ignorant durst. They learn'd him without Book, and had him often in their Mouths: But a Man cannot imagine that thing so foolish, or rude, but will find, and enjoy an Admirer; at least, a Reader, or *Spectator.* The Puppets are seen

Heath.
Taylor.

now in despight of the Players: *Heath's Epigrams,* and the *Skuller's Poems* have their Applause. There are never wanting, that dare prefer the worst *Preachers,* the worst *Pleaders,* the worst *Poets:* not that the better have left to write, or speak better, but that they that hear them judge worse. . . . Nay,

Spencer.

if it were put to the question of the Water-rimers Works, against *Spencer's;* I doubt not, but they would find more *Suffrages;* because the most favour common Vices, out of a Prerogative the vulgar have, to lose their Judgments; and like that which is naught.

Poetry in this latter Age, hath prov'd but a mean *Mistris,* to such as have wholly addicted themselves to her; or given their Names up to her Family. They who have but saluted her on the by; and now and then tendred their Visits, she hath done much for, and advanced in the way of their own Professions (both the *Law,* and the *Gospel*) beyond all they could have hoped, or done for themselves, without her favour. . . .

Indeed, the multitude commend Writers, as they do Fencers; or Wrastlers;

who if they come in robustiously, and put for it, with a deal of violence, are received for the *Braver-fellows:* when many times their own rudeness is a Cause of their disgrace; and a slight touch of their Adversary, gives all that boisterous Force the foil. But in these things, the unskilful are naturally deceiv'd, and judging wholly by the Bulk, think rude things greater than polish'd; and scatter'd more numerous, than compos'd: Nor think this only to be true in the sordid   page 698 /   Multitude but the neater sort of our *Gallants:* for all are the Multitude; only they differ in Cloaths, not in Judgment or Understanding.

I remember, the Players have often mentioned it as an honour to *Shakespeare,* that in his Writing, (whatsoever he penn'd) he never blotted out a Line. My answer hath been, Would he had blotted a thousand. Which they thought a malevolent Speech. I had not told Posterity this, but for their ignorance, who chose that Circumstance to commend their Friend by, wherein he most faulted. And to justifie mine own Candor, (for I lov'd the Man, and do honour his Memory (on this side Idolatry) as much as any.) He was (indeed) honest, and of an open and free Nature: had an excellent *Phantsie;* brave Notions, and gentle Expressions: wherein he flow'd with that facility, that sometime it was necessary he should be stop'd.... His Wit was in his own Power; would the Rule of it had been so too. Many times he fell into those things, could not escape laughter: As when he said in the Person of *Caesar,* one speaking to him; *Caesar thou dost me wrong.* He reply'd; *Caesar did never wrong, but with just Cause:* and such like; which were ridiculous. But he redeemed his Vices with his Vertues. There was ever more in him to be praised, than to be pardoned....   page 699 /   [*Erroneously numbered 669.* — Ed.]

Cicero is said to be the only Wit, that the People of *Rome* had equall'd to their *Empire. Ingenium par imperio.* We have had many, and in their several Ages, (to take in but the former *Seculum*) Sir *Thomas Moore,* the elder *Wiat, Henry* Earl *Surrey, Chaloner, Smith, Cliot, B. Gardiner,* were for their times admirable; and the more, because they began Eloquence with us. Sir *Nico. Bacon* was singular, and almost alone, in the beginning of Queen *Elizabeth's* time. Sir *Philip Sidney,* and Mr. *Hooker,* (in different Matter) grew great Masters of Wit and Language, and in whom all vigour of Invention, and strength of Judgment met. The Earl of *Essex,* noble and high; and Sir *Walter Rawleigh,* not to be contemn'd, either for Judgment, or Style. Sir *Henry Savile,* grave and truly letter'd; Sir *Edwin Sands,* excellent in both; Lord *Egerton,* the Chancellor, a grave and great Orator; and best, when he was provok'd. But his learned and able (though unfortunate) *Successor,* is he who hath fill'd up all Numbers, and perform'd that in our Tongue, which may be compar'd, or preferr'd, either to insolent *Greece,* or haughty *Rome.* In short, within his view, and about his times, were all the Wits born, that could honour a Language, or help Study....
page 701 /

De
Shakespeare
nostrat.

Scriptorum
Catalogus.
Sir Thomas
Moore.
Sir Thomas
Wiat.
Henry *Earl of*
Surrey.
Sir Thomas
Chaloner.
Sir Thomas
Smith.
Sir Thomas
Cliot.
B. Gardiner.
Sir Nic.
Bacon. *L. K.*
Sir Philip
Sidney.
M. Richard
Hooker.
Robert *Earl
of* Essex
Sir Walter
Rawleigh.
Sir Henry
Savile.
Sir Edwin
Sands.
Sir Thomas
Egerton *L. C.*
Sir Francis
Bacon *L. C.*
De Augmentis
Scientiarum.

John Marston (1575?–1643) began his career as a satirist and drama-tist, but later renounced the stage to take holy orders. In 1598 he pub-lished Pygmalion's Image, *an erotic poem of the type popularized by* Venus and Adonis *and* Hero and Leander, *though he later claimed that his effort was intended to burlesque the fashion. In the same year he published* The Scourge of Villainy *in which he satirized social vices, literary rivals and affectations. After both these books were suppressed in 1599, he devoted himself to drama. Sometime before 1616 he took holy orders and held a country living until 1631. Meres lists him among the chief English satirists of the age.*

John Marston. *The Scourge of Villanie* (1599) in *The Works of John Marston*, Vol. III. Edited by J. O. Halliwell, London, 1856.

Satyre VI.

Curio, know'st me? Why, thou bottle-ale,
Thou barmie froth! O stay me, least I raile
Beyond Nil ultra! to see this butterfly,
This windy bubble, taske my balladry
With senselesse censure. Curio, know'st my sp'rite?
Yet deem'st that in sad seriousnesse I write
Such nasty stuffe as is *Pigmalion?*
Such maggot-tainted, lewd corruption!
   Ha, how he glavers with his fawning snowt,
And sweares he thought I meant but faintly flowt
My fine smug rime. O barbarous dropsie noule!
Think'st thou that genius that attends my soule,
And guides my fist to scourge magnificoes,
Wil daigne my minde be rank't in Paphian showes?
Thinkst thou that I, which was create to whip
Incarnate fiends, will once vouchsafe to trip
A Paunis traverse, or will lispe "Sweet love,"
Or pule "Aye me," some female soule to move?
Think'st thou that I in melting poesie
Will pamper itching sensualitie?   **page 274 /**
(That in the bodies scumme all fatally
Intombes the soules most sacred faculty.)
   Hence, thou misjudging censor: know I wrot
Those idle rimes to note the odious spot
And blemish that deformes the lineaments

Of moderne poesies habiliments.
Oh that the beauties of invention,
For want of judgements disposition,
Should all be spoil'd! O that such treasurie,
Such straine of well-conceited poesie,
Should moulded be in such a shapelesse forme,
That want of art should make such wit a scorne!
   Here's one must invocate some lose-leg'd dame,
Some brothel drab, to help him stanzaes frame,
Or els (alas!) his wits can have no vent,
To broch conceits industrious intent.
Another yet dares tremblingly come out;
But first he must invoke good Colin Clout.
   Yon's one hath yean'd a fearful prodigy,
Some monstrous mishapen Balladry;
His guts are in his braines, huge jobbernoule,
Right gurnets-heads; the rest without all soule.
Another walkes, is lazie, lies downe,
Thinkes, reades, at length some wonted slepe doth crowne
His new-falne lides, dreames, straight, ten pound to one,
Out steps some fayery with quick motion,
And tells him wonders of some flowry vale;
Awakes, straight rubs his eyes, and prints his tale.
   Yon's one whose straines have flowne so high a pitch,
That straight he flags and tumbles in a ditch.
His sprightly hot high-soring poesie
Is like that dreamed of imagery,   **page 275 /**
Whose head was gold, brest silver, brassie thigh,
Lead leggs, clay feete; O faire fram'd poesie!
   Here's one, to get an undeserv'd repute
Of deepe deepe learning, all in fustian sute
Of ill past, farre-fetch't words attireth
His period, that sense forsweareth.
   Another makes old Homer Spencer cite,
Like my *Pigmalion*, where, with rage, delight,
He cryes, O Ovid! This caus'd my idle quill,
The world's dull eares with such lewd stuff to fill,
And gull with bumbast lines the witlesse sense
Of these odde nags, whose pates circumference
Is fill'd with froth. O the same buzzing gnats
That sting my sleeping browes, these Nilus rats,
Halfe dung, that have their life from putrid slime —
These that do praise my loose lascivious rime!
For these same shades, I seriously protest,
I slubbered up that chaos indigest,
To fish for fooles, to stalke in goodly shape;
"What, though in velvet cloake, yet still an ape."
Capro reads, sweares, scrubs, and sweares againe,

Now by my soule an admirable straine;
Strokes up his haire, cries, "Passing passing good;"
Oh, there's a line incends his lustfull blood!
    Then Muto comes, with new glasse-set face,
And with his late-kist hand my booke doth grace,
Straight reades, then smiles, and lisps, "Tis pretty good,"
And praiseth that he never understood.
But roome for Flaccus, he'le my Satyres read;
O how I trembled straight with inward dread!
But when I sawe him read my fustian,
And heard him sweare I was a Pythian,   page 276 /
Yet straight recald, and sweares I did but quote
Out of Xilinum to that margents note,
I could scarce hold and keepe myselfe conceal'd,
But had well-nigh myselfe and all reveal'd.
Then straight comes Friscus, that neat gentleman,
That newe discarded academian,
Who, for he could cry *Ergo* in the schoole,
Straight-way with his huge judgment dares controule
Whatso'ere he views: "That's pretty good;
That epithite hath not that sprightly blood
Which should enforce it speake; that's Persius vaine;
That's Juvenal's; heere's Horace crabbid straine;"
Though he nere read one line in Juvenall,
Or, in his life, his lazie eye let fall
On duskie Persius. O, indignitie
To my respectlesse free-bred poesie!
    Hence, ye big-buzzing little-bodied gnats,
Yee tatling ecchoes, huge-tongu'd pigmy brats:
I meane to sleepe: wake not my slumbring braine
With your malignant, weake, detracting vaine.
    What though the sacred issue of my soule
I here expose to idiots controule;
What though I beare to lewd opinion,
Lay ope to vulgar prophanation,
My very genius, — yet know, my poesie
Doth scorne your utmost, rank'st indignitie;
    My pate was great with child, and here tis eas'd;
    Vexe all the world, so that thy selfe be pleas'd.   page 277 /

Fynes Moryson (1566–1630) received license to travel in 1589. His Itinerary is generally devoted to continental Europe, but he includes a description of the English countryside, the inns, food, and costume, which he frequently contrasts with those of other nations. His work is valuable for its minute detail and its comparisons.

Fynes Moryson. *An Itinerary, Containing His Ten Yeeres Travell Throvgh the Twelve Domjnions of Germany, Bohmerland, Sweitzerland, Netherland, Denmarke, Poland, Jtaly, Turky, France, England, Scotland, and Ireland*, Part III, Chapter 3. London 1617.

Of England. . . .

The ayre of *England* is temperate, but thicke, cloudy and misty, and *Caesar* witnesseth, that the cold is not so piercing in *England* as in *France*. For the Sunne draweth vp the vapours of the Sea which compasseth the Iland, and distills them vpon the earth in frequent showers of raine, so that frosts are somewhat rare; and howsoeuer Snow may often fall in the Wintertime, yet in the Southerne parts (especially) it seldome lies long on the ground. Also the coole blasts of Sea winds, mittigate the heat of Summer. By reason of this temper, Lawrell and Rosemary flourish all Winter, especially in the Southerne parts, and in the Summer time *England* yeelds Abricots plentifully, Muske **page 146 /** melons in good quantity, and Figges in some places, all which ripen well, and happily imitate the taste and goodnesse of the same fruites in *Italy*. And by the same reason all beasts bring forth their young in the open fields, euen in the time of Winter; and *England* hath such abundance of Apples, Peares, Cherries, and Plummes, such variety of them, and so good in all respects, as no countrie yeelds more or better, for which the Italians would gladly exchange their Citrons and Oranges. But vpon the Sea coast, the winds many times blast the fruits in the very flower.

The English are so naturally inclined to pleasure, as there is no Countrie, wherein the Gentlemen and Lords haue so many and large Parkes onely reserued for the pleasure of hunting, or where all sorts of men alot so much ground about their houses for pleasure of Gardens and Orchards. The very Grapes, especially towards the South and West are of a pleasant taste, and I haue said, that in some Counties, as in *Glostershire*, they made Wine of old, which no doubt many parts would yeeld at this day, but that the inhabitants forbeare to plant Vines, aswell because they are serued plentifully, and at a good rate with French wines, as for that the hilles most fit to beare Grapes, yeeld more commoditie by feeding of Sheepe and Cat-

The situation.

The fertility and trafficke.

tell. *Caesar* writes in his Commentaries, that *Britany* yeelds white Leade
within land, and Iron vpon the Sea-coasts. No doubt *England* hath vnexhaust-
ible vaines of both, and also of Tinne, and yeelds great quantitie of
Brasse, and of Allom and Iron, and abounds with quarries of Free-stone,
and Fountaines of most pure Salt; and I formerly said that it yeelds some
quantity of Siluer, and that the Tinne and Leade is mingled with Siluer,
but so, as it doth not largely quit the cost of the labour in seperating or
trying it. Two Cities yeeld medicinall Baths, namely, *Buxstone* and *Bathe*,
and the waters of *Bathe* especially, haue great vertue in many diseases.
England abounds with Sea-coales vpon the Sea-coast, and with Pit coales
within land. But the Woods at this day are rather frequent and pleasant then
vast, being exhausted for fier, and with Iron-milles, so as the quantity of wood
and charcoale for fier, is much diminished, in respect of the old abundance, and in some places, as in the Fennes they burne Turffe, and the
very dung of Cowes. Yet in the meane time *England* exports great quantity of Seawale to forraine parts. In like sort *England* hath infinite quantity,
as of Mettalls, so of Woolls, and Woollen cloathes to be exported. The English Beere is famous in *Netherland* and lower *Germany*, which is made
of Barley and Hops; for *England* yeelds plenty of Hops, howsoeuer they also
vse Flemish Hops. The Cities of lower *Germany* vpon the sea, forbid the
publike selling of English Beere, to satisfie their owne brewers, yet pri-
uately swallow it like Nectar. But in *Netherland*, great and incredible
quantity thereof is spent. *England* abounds with corne, which they may
transport, when a quarter (in some places containing sixe, in others eight
bushels) is sold for twenty shillings, or vnder; and this corne not onely
serues *England*, but also serued the English Army in the ciuil warres of
Ireland, at which time they also exported great quantity thereof in to forraigne parts, and by Gods mercy *England* scarce once in ten yeeres needes
supply of forraigne Corne, which want commonly proceeds of the couetous-
nesse of priuate men, exporting or hiding it. Yet I must confesse, that
daily this plenty of Corne decreaseth, by reason that priuate men finding
greater commoditie in feeding of Sheepe and Cattell, then in the Plough,
requiring the hands of many seruants, can by no Law be restrained from
turning corne fields into inclosed Pastures, especially since great men are
the first to breake these Lawes. *England* abounds with all kinds of foule,
aswell of the Sea, as of the land, and hath more tame Swannes swimming
in the Riuers, then I did see in any other part. It hath multitudes of hurtfull birds, as Crowes, Rauens, and Kytes, and they labor not to destroy the
Crowes, consuming great quantity of Corne, because they feede on Wormes
and other things hurting the Corne. And in great Cities it is forbidden to
kill Kytes or Rauens, because they deuoure the filth of the streetes. *England* hath very great plenty of Sea and Riuer fish, especiallie aboue all other
parts abundance of Oysters, Makrell, and Herrings, and the English are
very industrious in fishing. . . . **page 147 /**

. . . .

. . . The World affoords not such Innes as *England* hath, either for good
and cheape entertainement after the Guests owne pleasure, or for humble
attendance on passengers, yea, euen in very poore Villages, where if *Curculio*

of *Plautus*, should see the thatched houses, he would fall into a fainting of
his spirits, but if he should smell the variety of meates, his starueling looke
would be much cheared: For assoone as a passenger comes to an Inne, the
seruants run to him, and one takes his Horse and Walkes him till he be
cold, then rubs him, and giues him meate, yet I must say that they are not
much to be trusted in this last point, without the eye of the Master or
his Seruant, to ouersee them. Another seruant giues the passenger his priuate chamber, and kindles his fier, the third puls of his bootes, and makes
them cleane. Then the Host or Hostesse visits him, and if he will eate
with the Host, or at a common Table with others, his meale will cost him
sixe pence, or in some places but foure pence, (yet this course is lesse
honourable, and not vsed by Gentlemen): but if he will eate in his chamber,
he commands what meate he will according to his appetite, and as much
as he thinkes fit for him and his company, Yea, the kitchin is open to him,
to command the meat to be dressed as he best likes; and when he sits at
Table, the Host or Hostesse will accompany him, or if they haue many
Guests, will at least visit him, taking it for curtesie to be bid sit downe:
while he eates, if he haue company especially, he shall be offred musicke,
which he may freely take or refuse, and if he be solitary, the Musitians
will giue him the good day with musicke in the morning. It is the custome and no way disgraceful to set vp part of supper for his breakefast:
In the euening or in the morning after breakefast, (for the common sort vse
not to dine, but ride from breakefast to supper time, yet comming early to
the Inne for better resting of their Horses) he shall haue a reckoning in
writing, and if it seeme vnreasonable, the Host will satisfie him, either for
the due price, or by abating part, especially if the seruant deceiue him any
way, which one of experience will soone find. . . . Lastly, a Man cannot more
freely command at home in his owne House, then hee may doe in his Inne,
and at parting if he giue some few pence to the Chamberlin & Ostler,
they wish him a happy iourney.   **page 151 /**

Sir Robert Naunton (1563–1635), courtier and political figure, was under the early patronage of the Earl of Essex, who planned for him a diplomatic career. He was Secretary of State under James I, a member of the commission to examine Sir Walter Raleigh in 1618, and by popular report largely responsible for Raleigh's execution. Naunton's Fragmenta Regalia, *though sketchy, is an interesting account of the men around Elizabeth and has the attributes and weaknesses of personal reminiscence. One of the most attractive sketches is that of Elizabeth.*

Sir Robert Naunton. *Fragmenta Regalia: Or, Observations on the late Queen Elizabeth Her Times, and Favourites.* Reprinted by Edward Arber, London, 1870.

To take her in the Originall, She was daughter to *Henry* the eighth, by *Anne Bullen*, the second of six Wives which He had, and one of the Maids of Honour to the divorced Queen *Katherine* of *Austria* (or as they stile it) *Infanta of Spain*, and from thence taken into the Royall Bed.

That She was not of a most Noble and Royall extract by Her Father, will not fall into question: for on that side there was disimbogued into her veines by a confluence of Bloud, the very abstract of all the greatest houses in Christendome; and remarkable it is concerning that violent desertion of the Royall House of the *Britains*, by the invasion of the *Saxons*, and afterwards by the Conquest of the *Normans*, that by the vicissitude of times, and through a discontinuance (almost a thousand yeares) the Royall Scepter should fall back into the Current of the old British Bloud, in page 13 / the person of her renowned Grandfather *Henry* the Seventh, together with whatsoever the *German, Norman, Burgundian, Castalian,* and *French* Atchievements, with the intermarriages, which eight hundred years had acquired, incorporated, and brought back into the old Royall Line.

By her Mother she was of no Soveraign descent, yet Noble, and very ancient in the Name and Family of *Bullen*, though some erroniously brand it with a Citizens rise or originall, which was yet but of a second Brother, who (as it were) divining the greatnesse and lustre to come to his House, was sent into the City to acquire wealth.... Unto whose atchievements (for he was Lord Mayor of *London*) fell in, as it was averred, both the bloud and inheritance of the eldest Brother, for want of issue Male, by which accumulation, the House within a few descents mounted *in Culmen honoris*, and was suddenly elated into the best Families of *England* and *Ireland* as *Howard, Ormund, Sackvile,* and divers others. Having thus toucht, and now leaving her stirp, I come to her Person; and as she came to the

Crown by the decease of her Brother and Sister. Under *Edward* She was his, and one of the darlings of Fortune: for besides the consideration of Bloud, there was between these two Princes a concurrency and sympathy in their natures and affections, together with the Celestiall (conformity in Religion) which made them one, and friends; for the King ever called her his sweetest and dearest Sister, and was scarce his own man, She being absent, which was not so between him and the Lady *Mary*. Under his Sister She found her condition much altered: For it was resolved, and her destiny had decreed to set her an Apprentice in the School of Affliction, and to draw her through the Ordeall fire of tryall, the better to mould and fashion her to rule and Soveraignty; which finished, and Fortune calling to mind, that the time of her servitude was expired, gave up her Indentures, and therewith page 14 / delivered up into her custody a Scepter, as a reward for her patience, which was about the twenty sixth year of her Age; a time in which (as for externals) she was full blown, so was she for her internals grown ripe, and seasoned with adversity, and in the exercise of her Vertue; for it seems Fortune meant no more, than to shew her a piece of her variety, and changeablenesse of her Nature, and so to conduct her to her destined Felicity. She was of personage tall, of hair and complexion fair, and therewith well favoured, but high nosed, of limbs and feature neat, and which added to the lustre of those exteriour Graces, of Stately and Majestick comportment; participating in this more of her Father than Mother, who was of inferiour allay, plausible, or as the French hath it, more *debonaire* and affable, vertues which might well suit with Majesty; and which descending, as Hereditary to the daughter, did render of a more sweeter temper, and endeared her more to the love and liking of the people; who gave her the name and fame of a most gracious and popular Prince; the atrocity of her Fathers nature, being rebated in hers, by the Mothers sweeter inclinations. For to take, and that no more than the Character out of his own mouth; He never spared man in his anger, nor woman in his lust.

If we search further into her intellectuals and abilities, the whole course of Government deciphers them to the admiration of posterity; for it was full of magnanimity, tempered with Justice, and Piety; and to speak truly, noted but with one act or taint; all her deprivations either of life or liberty, being legall, and necessitated: She was learned (her sex, and the time considered) beyond common belief; for letters about this time, and somewhat before, began to be of esteem and in fashion, the former ages being overcast with the mists and fogs of the Romane ignorance; and it was the maxime that over-ruled the foregoing times, that ignorance was the mother of devotion. Her warres were a long time more in the auxiliary part, in assist- page 15 / ance of forraign Princes and States, than by invasion of any, till common policie advised it for a safer way, to strike first abroad, than at home to expect the warre, in all which she was felicious and victorious. The change and alteration of Religion upon the instant of her accession (the smoak and fire of her Sisters Martyrdomes scarcely quenched) was none of her least remarkable accounts: But the support and establishment thereof, with the meanes of her subsistence, amidst so powerfull enemies abroad, and those many domestique practises, were (me thinks) works of inspiration, and of no humane providence, which on her Sisters departure she most religiously acknowledged, ascribing the glory of her deliverance to God alone: for she received the news both of the Queens death, and her Proclamation, by the generall consent of the House, and the publike suffrage of the people, whereat, falling on her knees (after a good time of respiration) she uttered this Verse of the Psalms, *A Domino factum est istud, et est mirabile in oculis nostris,* which we find to this day on the stamp of her gold, with this on her silver, *Posui Deum adjutorem meum....*

The principall note of her Reign will be, that she ruled much by faction and parties, which her self both made, upheld, and weakened, as her own great judgement advised. . . . **page 16 /**

. . . She was absolute and soveraign Mistress of her Graces; and . . . all those, to whom she distributed her favours, were never more than Tenants at will, and stood on no better ground than her Princely pleasure, and their own good behaviour. And this also I present as a known observation, that she was (though very capable of Counsell) absolute enough in her own resolutions, which was ever apparent even to her last, in that her aversation to grant *Tirone* the least drop of her mercy, though earnestly and frequently advised, yea, wrought only by the whole Councell of State, with very many pressing reasons, and as the state of her Kingdome then stood, (I may speak it with assurance) necessitated Arguments. If we look into her inclination, as it is disposed either to magnificence or frugality, we shall find in them many notable considerations, for all her dispensations were so poysed, as though discretion and justice had both agreed to stand at the beam, and see them weighed out in due proportion, the maturity of her years and judgement meeting in a concurrency, and at such an age as seldome lapseth to excesse. To consider them apart: We have not many presidents of her liberality, or of any large donatives to particular men; my Lord of *Essex* Book of *Parks* only excepted, which was a Princely gift, and some few more of a lesser size to my Lord of *Leicester, Hatton,* and others. Her rewards consisted chiefly in grants of Leases of Offices, Places of Judicature: but for ready money, and in any great summes, she was very sparing; which we partly conceive was a vertue rather than drawn from necessity, than her nature, for she had many layings out, and to her last period. And I am of opinion with S. *Walter Rawliegh,* that those many brave men of our times, and of the *Militia,* tasted little more of her **page 18 /** bounty than in her grace and good word, with their due entertainment, for she ever paid the Souldiers well, which was the honour of her times, and more than her great adversary of *Spain* could perform. So that when we come to the consideration of her frugality, the observation will be little more, than that her bounty and it were so inter-woven together, that the one was suited by an honourable way of spending, the other limited by a necessitated way of sparing. The Irish action we may call a malady, and a consumption of her times, for it accompanied her to her end; and it was of so profuse and vast an expence, that it drew neer a distemperature of State, and of passion in her self: For toward her last she grew hard to please; her Arms being accustomed to prosperity, and the Irish prosecution not answering her expectation and wonted successe for a good while, it was an unthrifty and inauspitious war, which did much disturb and mislead her judgement, and the more, for that it was a president which was taken out of her own pattern: For as the Queen (by way of diversion) had at the coming to the Crown supported the revolted States of *Holland*, so did the King of *Spain* turn the trick on her self towards her going out, by cherishing the Irish rebellion. . . .   **page 19 /**

Leicester.

It will be out of doubt, that my Lord of *Leicester* was one of the first whom she made Master of the Horse: he was the youngest Sonne then living of the Duke of *Northumberland*, beheaded *primo Mariae;* and his Father was that *Dudley*, which our Histories couple with *Empson;* and both so much infamed for the Caterpillars of the Common-wealth, during the reign of *Henry* the seventh, who being of a Noble extract, was executed the first year of *Henry* the eight: but not thereby so extinct, but that he left a plentiful Estate, and such a Son, who, as the vulgar speaks it, could live without the teat; for out of the ashes of his Fathers infamie, he rose to be a Duke, and as high, as subjection could permit, or Soveraignty endure; and though he could not find out any appellation to assume the Crown in his own Person, yet he projected, and very neerly effected it for his Son *Gilbert*, by inter-marriage with the Lady *Iane Grey*, and so by that way to bring it   **page 26 /**   about into his loynes. . . . It may amaze a well setled judgement, to look back into those times, and to consider how this Duke could attain to such a pitch of greatnesse; his Father dying in ignominie, and at the Gallows, his Estate confiscate, and that for peeling and polling, by the clamour, and crucifige of the people; but when we better think upon it, we find that he was given up, but as a Sacrifice to please the people, not for any offense committed against the person of the King; so that upon the matter he was a Martyr of the Prerogative, and the King in honour could doe no lesse, than give back to his Son the priviledges of his bloud, with the acquirings of his Fathers profession, for he was a Lawyer, and of the Kings Counsels at Law, before he came to be *ex interioribus consiliis*, where besides the licking of his own fingers, he got the King a masse of riches, and that not with the hazard, but the losse of his fame and life for the Kings Fathers sake. Certain it is, that his sonne was left rich in purse and brain, which are good foundations, and full to ambition; and it may be supposed, he was on all occasions well heard of the King, as a person of mark and compassion in his eye: but I find not that he did put up for advancement, during *Henry* the eights time, although a vast aspirer, and provident storer. It seems he thought the Kings reign was given to the falling sicknesse: but espying his time fitting, and the Soveraignty in the hands of a pupil Prince, he thought he might as well then put up for it as the best, for having then possession of bloud, and a purse, with a head-piece of a vast extent, he soon got honour, and no sooner there, but he began to side it with the best, even with the Protector, and in conclusion got his, and his Brothers   **page 27 /**   heads; still aspiring, till he expired, in the losse of his own: so that posterity may by reading the Father and Grandfather, make judgement of the Son; for we shall find, that this *Robert* (whose originall we have now traced, the better to present him) was inheritor of the genius and craft of his Father, and *Ambrose* of the estate, of whom hereafter we shall make some short mention.

We take him now as he was admitted into the Court, and the Queens favour, where he was not to seek to play his part well, and dexteriously. But his play was chiefly at the fore-game; not that he was a learner at the latter, but he loved not the after-wit, for they report (and I think not untruly) that he was seldome behind hand with his Gamesters, and that they alwayes went away with the losse.

He was a very goodly person, and singular well featured, and all his youth well favoured, and of a sweet aspect, but high-foreheaded, which I should take it, was of no discommendation: but towards his latter end (which with old men, was but a middle age) he grew high-coloured and red-faced. So that the Queen in this, had much of her Father, for (excepting some of her kindred, and some few that had handsome wits in crooked bodies) she alwayes took personage in the way of her election; for the people hath it to this day in proverb, King *Harry* loved a man. Being thus in her grace, she called to mind the sufferings of his Ancestors, both in her Fathers and sisters reigns, and restored his and his brothers bloud, creating *Ambrose*, the elder, Earl of *Warwick*, and himself Earl of *Leicester*. etc. And he was *ex primitiis*, or of her first choice; for he rested not there, but long enjoyed her favour: and therewith much what he listed, till time and emulation (the companions of great ones) had resolved on his period, and to cover him at his setting in a cloud at *Cornbury*, not by so violent a death, and by the fatall sentence of Judicature, as that of his Fathers and Grandfathers was; but as it is suggested,   **page 28 /**   by that poyson which he had prepared for others, wherein they report him a rare Artist. I am not bound to give credit to all vulgar relations, or to the libels of the times, which are commonly forced, and falsified suitable to the moods and humours of men in passion and discontent: But that which leads me to think him no good man, is amongst others of known truth, that of my Lord of *Essex* death in *Ireland*, and the marriage of his Lady yet living, which I forbear to presse, in regard that he is long since dead, and others living whom it may concern.

To take him in the observations of his Letters and Writings (which should best set him off) for such as fell into my hands, I never yet saw a style or phrase more seeming religious, and fuller of the streames of devotion; and were they not sincere, I doubt much of his well-being; and I may fear he was too well seen in the Aphorismes and principles of *Nicholas* the *Florentine*, and in the reaches of *Caesar Borgia*. Hitherto I have touched him in his Courtship; I conclude him in his Lance. He was sent Governour by the Queen to the United States of *Holland;* where we read not of his wonders; for they say that he had more of *Mercury* than of *Mars;* and that his device might have been, without prejudice to the Great *Caesar*, *Veni, vidi, redii.*   **page 29 /**

Sir Philip Sidney.

He was sonne to Sir *Henery Sidney*, Lord Deputy of *Ireland*, and President of *Wales;* a person of great parts, and in no mean grace with the Queen; his mother was sister to my Lord of *Leicester*, from whence we may conjecture, how the Father stood up in the place of honour and imployment, so that his descent was apparently noble on both sides: For his education, it was such as travell, and the University could afford, or his Tutours infuse; for after an incredible proficiency in all the species of Learning; he left the Academicall life, for that of the Court, whither he came by his Uncles invitation, famed afore-hand by a **page 34 /** noble report of his accomplishments, which together with the state of his person, framed by a naturall propension to Armes, he soon attracted the good opinion of all men, and was so highly prized in the good opinion of the Queen, that she thought the Court deficient without him: And whereas (through the fame of his deserts) he was in the election for the Kingdom of *Pole*, she refused to further his advancement, not out of emulation, but out of fear to lose the jewell of her times: He married the daughter and sole heir of Sir *Francis Walsingham*, then Secretary of State, a Lady destinated to the Bed of honour, who (after his deplorable death at *Zutphen* in the *Netherlands*, where he was Governour of *Flushing* at the time of his Uncles being there) was married to my Lord of *Essex*, and since his death to my Lord of Saint *Albans*, all persons of the sword, and otherwise of great honour and vertue.

They have a very quaint and facetious figment of him, That *Mars* and *Mercury* fell at variance whose servant he should be. And there is an *Epigrammist* that saith, that Art and Nature had spent their excellencies in his fashioning; and fearing they should not end what they begun, they bestowed him on Fortune, and nature stood musing and amazed to behold her own work; but these are the fictions of Poets.

Certain it is, He was a noble and matchless Gentlemen, and it may be justly said without hyperboles of fiction, as it was of *Cato Uticensis*, That he seemed to be born to that onely which he went about. *Versatilis ingenii*, as *Plutarch* hath it. But to speak more of him, were to make him lesse.
page 35 /

Sir Walter Raleigh (1552?–1618), poet, historian, military and naval commander, courtier, statesman, and patron of the arts and sciences, was engaged variously in most of the activities of his age. He has been termed by one biographer "the last of the Elizabethans." Although his poetry has recognized merit, little has survived. His literary reputation, therefore, rests on such prose works as The Truth of the Fight about the Isles of the Azores *(1591) and* The History of the World *(1614). Numerous other essays on political subjects were published after his death, one of which is herein reproduced in part. This work is not uncharacteristic of the advice to princes and collections of* sentientia *recommended for the moral and political discipline of governors and magistrates.*

Sir Walter Raleigh. *The Secrets of Government, and Misteries of State, Plainly laid open, in all the several Forms of Government in the Christian World.* Published by John Milton, Esq. Printed in the year 1697.

Every good and lawful Principality is either Elective or Successive: Of them Election seemeth the more Ancient; but Succession in divers respects the better: *Minore discrimine sumitur Princeps quam quaeritur.* Tac.

The chief and only Endeavor of every good Prince, ought to be the Commodity and Security of the Subjects, as contrariwise the Tyrant seeketh his own private Profit with the Oppression of his People: *Civium non servitus sed tutela tradita est.* Sal.

To the Perfection of every good Prince, two things are necessarily required (*viz.*) Prudence and Vertue; **page 35 /** the one to direct his Doings, the other to govern his Life: *Rex eris si recte feceris.* Hor.

The second care which appertaineth to a good Prince, is to make his Subjects like unto himself; for thereby he is not only honored, but they also the better governed: *Facile imperium in bonos.* Plaut.

Subjects are made good by two means (*viz.*) by constraint of Law, and the Princes Example; for in all Estates, the People do imitate those Conditions whereunto they see the Prince enclined: *Quicquid faciunt principes, praecipere videantur.* Quintil.

All Vertues be required in a Prince, but Justice and Clemency are most necessary; for Justice is a Habit of doing things Justly, as well to himself as others, and giving to every one so much as to him appertaineth: This is that Vertue that preserveth Concord among Men, and whereof they be called good: *Jus & acquit as vincula civitatum.* Cic. **page 36 /**

It is the Quality of this Vertue also, to proceed equally and temperately; it informeth the Prince not to surcharge the Subjects with infinite Laws; for

88

thereof proceedeth the Impoverishment of the Subjects, and the Inriching of Lawyers, a kind of Men which in Ages more Ancient, did seem of no Necessity: *Sine causidicis satis foelices olim fuere futuraeque sunt urbes.* Sal.

The next Vertue required in Princes is Clemency, being an Inclination of the Mind to Lenity and Compassion, yet tempered with Severity and Judgment; this Quality is fit for all great Personages, but chiefly Princes, because their occasion to use it is most; by it also the Love of Men is gained: *Qui vult regnare, languida regnet manu.* Sen.

After Clemency, Fidelity is expected in all good Princes, which is a certain Performance and Observation of Word and Promise; this vertue seemeth to page 37 / accompany Justice, or is as it were the same, and therefore most fit for Princes: *Sanctissimum generis humani bonum.* Liv.

As Fidelity followeth Justice, so doth Modesty accompany Clemency; Modesty is a Temperature of Reason, whereby the Mind of Man is so governed, as neither in Action or Opinion he over-deemeth of himself, or any thing that is his; a quality not common in Fortunate Folk, and most rare in Princes: *Superbia commune nobilitatis malum.* Sal.

This Vertue doth also moderate all External Demonstration of Insolence, Pride and Arrogance, and therefore necessary to be known of Princes, and all others whom Favor or Fortune have advanced: *Impone faelicitati tua fraenos, facilius illam reges.* Curt.

But as Princes are to observe the Bounds of Modesty, so may they not forget the Majesty appertaining to their Supreme Honor, being a certain Reverend Greatness due to Princely Vertue and Royal State; a Grace and Gravity no less beseeming a Prince than Vertue page 38 / it self; for neither over-much Familiarity, nor too great Austerity, ought to be used by Princes: *Facilitas autoritatem, severitas amorem minuit.* Tac.

To these Vertues we may apply Liberality, which doth not only Adorn, but highly Advance the Honor due to Princes; thereby also the good Will of Men is gained; for nothing is more fitting a Prince's Nature than Bounty, the same being accompanied with Judgment, and performed according to the Laws of Liberality: *Perdere multi sciunt, donare nesciunt.* Tac.

It seemeth also that Prudence is not only fit, but also, among other Vertues, necessary in a Prince; for the daily use thereof is in all Humane Actions required, and chiefly in Matters of State and Government: *Prudentia imperantis propria & unica virtus.* Arist.

The Success of all Worldly Proceedings, doth shew that Prudence hath compassed the Prosperous Event of Humane Actions, more than Force of Arms or other Power: *Mens una sapiens plurium vincit manus.* Eurip. page 39 /

Prudence is either natural, or received from others; for whoso can Counsel himself what is fit to be done, needeth not the Advice of others; but they that want such Perfection, and are nevertheless capable, and are willing to know what others inform, ought to be accounted wise enough: *Laudatissimus est qui cuncta videbit, sed laudanus est is qui paret recte monenti.* Hesiod.
page 40 /

Sir Philip Sidney (1554–86), scholar, courtier, statesman, soldier, and writer, was considered one of the flowers of the English Renaissance. He was prominent among the literary figures of the period, a member of the Areopagus — a club composed of such writers as Spenser, Fulke Greville, and Gabriel Harvey and formed chiefly for the purpose of naturalizing the classic meters in English verse. Although Sidney's literary influence was great, none of this own works was published in his lifetime. His Arcadia *is a domesticated pastoral romance. Sidney's sonnets initiated the vogue of sonnet sequences in English, and his* Defence of Poesy *is one of the most important critical statements of the age.*

Noted from his youth for his learning, Sidney received in May, 1572, the queen's permission to undertake a two years' visit to the continent to perfect his knowledge of foreign languages. In 1573, at Frankfort, he met Hubert Languet, the learned Protestant scholar, whom he accompanied to Vienna, where he visited the court of Emperor Maximilian II. In October, when Sidney left Vienna for an extended tour in Italy, the two friends agreed to correspond. The letters reveal the intimacy of the friendship and much of the intellectual concerns of two Renaissance gentlemen. Thus they are valuable not only for the revealing glimpse into the intellectual life of one of the great men of Elizabeth's England but for the general view of the intellectual activity of a young Englishman intent upon securing the best education possible.

The Correspondence of Sir Philip Sidney and Hubert Languet, Now First Collected and Translated From the Latin with Notes and a Memoir of Sidney by Steuart A. Pears. London, 1845.

SIDNEY TO LANGUET

... At present I am learning the sphere, and a little music. My pen I only practise when I write to you; but in truth I begin to find that by writing ill I only learn to write ill, and therefore I wish you would give me some rules for improving my style, and at the same time you may send me those other admonitions which you said you had put off till I should come to you; for I am sure that you will never exhaust **page 8 /** your stock of counsel, and that my blunders will give ample scope to your lectures. ... I wish you would send me Plutarch's works in French, if they are to be bought in Vienna; I would gladly give five times their value for them, and you will be able to send them no doubt by the hand of some trader. Tell

90

me too, in your next, if you have got *L'Historia del mondo di Tarchagnota,** *Lettere de Principi,* † *Lettere de tredici illustri homini,* ‡ *Imprese di Girolamo Ruscelli,*|| *Il stato di Vinegia scritto da* page 9 / *Contarini*§ *e da Donato Gianotti.*¶ All of these are interesting books, and if there are any others you would like to have, I can easily have them sent to you.... Farewell, wholly yours,

Venice, 19th December, 1573.   Ph. Sidney.

LANGUET TO SIDNEY

You ask me to tell you how you ought to form your style of writing. I think you will do well to read both page 19 / volumes of Cicero's letters, not only for the beauty of the Latin, but also for the very important matter they contain. There is nowhere a better statement of the causes which overthrew the Roman Republic. Many persons think it very useful to take one of his letters and translate it into another language; then to shut the book and turn it back into Latin; then again to refer to the book and compare your expressions with Cicero's. But beware of falling into the heresy of those who think that the height of excellence consists in the imitation of Cicero,* and pass their lives in labouring at it.

... If the works of Plutarch were to be bought here, I would spare no money to gratify your desire. I have not ventured to ask Master Vulcobius for the copy which he possesses, because I see that he is his favourite author; but if you desire it, I will get rid of my modesty and ask. When you begin to read Cicero's letters perhaps you will not want Plutarch. You

* Dell' istorie del mondo, le quali con tutte quelle particolarita che bisognano, contengono quanto dal principio del mondo fin a tempi nostri è successo. Published at Venice in four volumes in 1562. The book went through seven editions in a few years. [*All footnotes are from the source.* — Ed.]

† Lettere di Principi, le quali o si scrivono da Principi, o a' Principi, o ragionan di Principi. Lib. 1. Nuovamente Mandato in luce da Girolamo Ruscelli, all Illmo et Rev^mo Cardinal Carlo Borromeo. — Venice, 1562.

‡ Published at Venice, 1560, containing letters of Bembo, Manuzio, Boccaccio, Lorenzo de Medici and others.

|| Le impresse illustri, con esposizioni e discorsi, published 1566. A description with plates of the devices or emblems borne by the most illustrious men of his age, a curious and interesting volume in 4to. Ruscelli was a friend of Tasso, and was one of the first to discover the merit of his earliest poems: he died at Venice, 1566. — Sidney's fine taste in the choice of mottoes and devices both for himself on various occasions and for his heroes in the Arcadia, may have been assisted by these studies.

§ Contarini, a Venetian, was much employed by Clement VII. and other Popes; he was a Cardinal and the Pope's legate to the diet of Ratisbon in 1540, where he presided at the theological discussions. He died in 1542. The title of his history is "de Magistratu ac Republica Venetorum."

¶ Gianotti was Secretary to the Council of State at Florence, Machiavelli being the unsuccessful candidate for the office: he retired to Venice, where he wrote his Republica di Vinegia, and died in 1560. page 10 /

* Languet had probably heard Erasmus speak in the same manner of Cicero. In 1580 Philip writes to his brother Robert, "So you can speak and write Latin not barbarously, I never require great study in Ciceronianism, the chief abuse of Oxford, qui dum verba sectantur, res ipsas negligunt."

are right to pay attention to astronomy; without some knowledge of it, it is impossible to understand cosmography; and he who reads history without a knowledge of this, is very like a man who makes a journey in the dark. The advice I wished to give you is not of a kind which can be safely trusted to writing, and it is not your faults (as **page 20 /** you allege) which give me matter for advice, but your good qualities, which will soon I hope be so conspicuous that men will take notice of what you do and say. . . . **page 21 /**

Vienna, 1st of January, 1574.

SIDNEY TO LANGUET

. . . Your last letter, written on the 1st of January, reached me on the 13th. It brought me no news, for it was filled with instances of your affection, ever pleasant indeed, but long since known and proved, a kind of letter which is above all others delightful and acceptable to me, for while I read, I fancy that I have the very Hubert himself before my eyes and in my hands. I intend to follow your advice about composition, thus; I shall first take one of Cicero's letters and turn it into French; then from French into English, and so once more by a sort of perpetual motion, (but not of Abondius's sort) it shall come round into Latin again. Perhaps, too, I shall improve myself in Italian by the same exercise. For I have some letters translated into the vulgar tongue by the very learned Paolo Manuzio,* and into French by some one else. The volumes of Cicero I will read diligently. There are some things also which I wish to learn of the Greeks, which hitherto I have but skimmed on the surface. But the **page 23 /** chief object of my life, next to the everlasting blessedness of heaven, will always be the enjoyment of true friendship, and there you shall have the chiefest place. . . . As to what you say of the copies of Plutarch, I should be sorry that for so small a matter you should throw off the modesty which nature has implanted in you, nor am I so presumptuous as to disregard the pleasure of my friends, while I seek my own convenience. About Abondius, I am anxiously thinking what I shall send to him in return for the great kindness he has shown to me, but I will see to it shortly. In the mean time I beg you will give him my service.

    . . . — Farewell, yours with all my heart,

                           Philip Sidney.

Padua. 15th of January, 1574.

To the most excellent and illustrious Hubert Languet,

    Always my much esteemed friend, at Vienna. **page 24 /**

---

* The family of Manuzio held the same place at Venice as that of Stephens at Paris; they were the great printers and patrons of learned men. Paul was the son of the famous Aldo Manuzio. He published a fine edition of all Cicero's works with a commentary of his own. He died in Rome on the 6th of April, 1574.

LANGUET TO SIDNEY

I am glad you have decided on going to Padua, where you will easily find better lodging than at Venice, and, I hope, have better acquaintances to amuse yourself with, and to converse with about your studies. You are quite right to learn the elements of astronomy, but I do not advise you to proceed far in the science, because it is very difficult, and not likely to be of much use to you. I do not know whether it is wise to apply your mind to geometry, though it is a noble study and well worthy of a fine understanding; but you must consider your condition in life, how soon you will have to tear yourself from your literary leisure, and therefore the short time which you still have should be devoted entirely to such things as are most essential. I call those things essential to you, which it is discreditable for a man of high birth not to know, and which may, one day, be an ornament and a resource to you. Geometry may, indeed, be of great use to a man of rank, in the fortification or investment of towns, in castrametation and all branches of architecture, but to understand it sufficiently to make it useful would certainly require much time, and I consider it absurd to learn the rudiments of many sciences simply for display and not for use. Besides, you are not over cheerful by nature, and it is a study which will make you still more grave, and as it requires the strongest application of the mind, it is likely to wear out the powers of the intellect, and very much to impair the health; and the greater the ability, the more intense is the interest excited, and therefore the more injurious; and you know you have no health to spare. **page 25 /**

About the Greek language I cannot advise you. It is a beautiful study, but I fear you will have no time to carry it through, and all the time you give to it will be lost to your Latin, which though it is considered a less interesting language than the Greek, is yet much more important for you to know. And therefore as I said before, I do not venture to advise you on the subject. I only recommend you to learn first what is most necessary and most suitable to your condition. You are now acquainted with four languages. If in your hours of amusement you can learn enough German to understand it anyhow, I think you will be employing yourself well. Next to the knowledge of the way of salvation, which is the most essential thing of all, and which we learn from the sacred scriptures, next to this, I believe nothing will be of greater use to you than to study that branch of moral philosophy which treats of justice and injustice. I need not speak to you of reading history, by which more than anything else men's judgments are shaped, because your own inclination carries you to it, and you have made great progress in it. But perhaps you are occupied with other matters, and my tedious letters only weary you. I must however remind you to take good care of your health, and not to injure it with too much study. Nothing excessive lasts long, and a sound mind is not enough unless it dwells in a sound body. Since you are somewhat serious by nature, you should choose companions who can enliven you with becoming entertainment. The noble Count of Hannau and all his suite are greatly attached to you. I advise you to make yourself most intimate with them. There will always be good men who will esteem it a favour if you seek their friendship, and, as long as you remain what you are, you will find men all over the world to love you and show you kindness. . . .

— Farewell.

Vienna, 22nd January, 1574.   **page 26 /**

SIDNEY TO LANGUET

Your last letter was on many accounts most delightful to me, full as it was of your affectionate regard for me. I am glad you approve of my intention of giving up the study of astronomy, but about geometry I hardly know what to determine. I long so greatly to be acquainted with it, and the more so because I have always felt sure that it is of the greatest service in the art of war; nevertheless I shall pay but sparing attention to it, and only peep through the bars, so to speak, into the rudiments of the science. Of Greek literature I wish to learn only so much as shall suffice for the perfect understanding of Aristotle. For though translations are made almost daily, still I suspect they do not declare the meaning of the author plainly or aptly enough; and besides, I am utterly ashamed to be following the stream, as Cicero says, and not go to the fountain head. Of the works of Aristotle, I consider the politics* to be the most worth reading; and I mention this in reference to your advice that I should apply myself to moral philosophy. Of the German language, my dear Hubert, I absolutely **page 28 /** despair. It has a sort of harshness,† you know very well what I mean, so that at my age I have no hope that I shall ever master it, even so as to understand it; nevertheless to please you, I will sometimes, especially at dinner, practise it with my good Delius. I readily allow that I am often more serious ‡ than either my age or my pursuits demand; yet this I have learned by experience, that I am never less a prey to melancholy than when I am earnestly applying the feeble powers of my mind to some high and difficult object. But enough of this.

I am both glad and sorry that you ask me so urgently for my portrait; glad, because a request of this kind breathes the spirit of that sweet and long-tried affection with which you regard me; and sorry that you have any hesitation in asking me so mere a trifle. For even if there were not between us that true and genuine friendship which throws into shade all other feelings, as the sun obscures the lesser lights, still I have received that from you, which gives you a right to demand from me as a debt

---

* In 1579 he writes to his brother, "I think you have read Aristotle's ethics; if you have you know it is the beginning and foundation of all his works."

† "The Dutch so (full) of the other side with consonants, that they cannot yield the sweet sliding fit for verse." — Sidney's Defence of Poesie.

‡ "The curious wits, seeing dull pensiveness
  Bewray itself in my long settled eyes,
  Whence those same fumes of melancholy rise
  With idle pains and missing aim do guess" &c. —
Astrophel and Stella, xxiii.

greater things than this. As soon as ever I return to Venice, I will have
it done either by Paul Veronese,* or by Tintoretto,† who hold by far the
highest **page 29 /** place in the art. . . . Forgive me this letter, full as it is
of blots and scores, for I write in haste. — Farewell, your most loving and
dutiful,

Philip Sidney.

Padua, 4th of February, 1574.

LANGUET TO SIDNEY

I should be glad, as I wrote to you before, if you could acquire such
a knowledge of German as to understand the language when you hear
or read it: learn it perfectly you cannot without **page 30 /** much time and
labour. You English have more intercourse with the Germans than with
any other people, and their authority and power as a nation is already the
greatest in christendom, and no doubt will yet be increased by the folly
of my own country and other neighbouring states. It seems to me quite
absurd that your countrymen should make such a point of speaking Italian
well, since, as far as I know, you derive no advantage from them; on the
other hand they derive the greatest from you; and therefore they ought
rather to learn your language. Perhaps you are afraid you will not persuade them to take your money, unless you speak with perfect fluency.
See, my dearest Sidney, how I trifle with you. . . . **page 31 /**

.   .   .   .

My letters are trifles, which I fear will soon weary you. Farewell, and greet
my friends.

Vienna, 28th January, 1574. **page 34 /**

LANGUET TO SIDNEY

I wrote to you lately what I thought of your studies. I entreat you make
an effort to improve your pronunciation. Nothing is impossible to your
abilities. You will find some little trouble at first, but believe me you will
not need much time to accomplish it, and you will gain the more credit,
because so few of your countrymen take any pains about it. Find out some
man of letters, whose pronunciation pleases you, and converse with him
alone daily for half an hour on various subjects. Take at first the pronunciation of the letter A to correct, and desire your friend to check you when-
ever you say it wrong, and every time you are checked, pay him some

---

* Paolo Cagliari of Verona, born in 1532. — Titian's most celebrated pupil.

† Giacomo Robusti, son of a dyer, hence called Tintoretto, born in 1512; he painted
with great rapidity. In comparing him with Veronese, Pilkington says, "If Tintoretto was
allowed to imitate nature with superior force and vivacity and more truth and colour,
Veronese was acknowledged to have a finer invention, more grace in his figures, more
dignity in his characters and more elegance." — Tintoretto was also a pupil of Titian, who
is said to have been jealous of his abilities and driven him from his studio.

little fine in money, or what you please. I am sure that in five or six days you will find you have spent your time well and will go on to the rest with more alacrity. I would not recommend it to a dull man, but you can do what you wish, and so you need not   page 37 /   answer me with your favourite line* about "nature recurring;" for if you will not do as I ask, I shall lay the blame on the want of will and energy, not on poor innocent nature. Scarcely two months have passed since you began to write to me, and yet in that short time you seem to me to have improved more than many men would in a year. I have watched you closely when you were speaking my own language, but I hardly ever detected you pronouncing a single syllable wrongly; I entreat you, my dear Sidney, for my sake, try this one thing, and then the most ill-natured censors will have no fault to find with you. Pardon the love which makes me trouble you with these admonitions....

Vienna, 5th Feb. 1574.   page 38 /

PHILIP SIDNEY TO HIS BROTHER ROBERT

My dear Brother, for the money you have received, assure yourself (for it is true) there is nothing I spend so pleaseth me, as that which it is for you. If ever I have the ability you will find it, if not, yet shall not any brother living be better beloved than you of me.... For your countenance, I would for no cause have it diminished in Germany; in Italy your greatest expense must be upon worthy men, and not upon householding. Look to your diet (sweet Robin) and hold up your heart in courage and virtue, truly great part of my comfort is in you. I know not myself what I meant by bravery in you, so greatly you may see I condemn you; be careful of yourself, and I shall never have cares. I have written to Mr. Savile,† I wish you kept still together, he is an excellent man; and there may if you list pass good exercises betwixt you and Mr. Nevyle,‡ there is great expectation of you both. For the method of writing history, Boden‖ hath written at large; you may read him and gather out of many words some matter....
page 199 /

.   .   .   .

...Now (dear brother), take delight likewise in the mathematicals; Mr. Savile is excellent in them. I think you understand the sphere; if you do, I care little for any astronomy in you. Arithmetic and geometry, I would wish you well seen in, so as both in the matter of number and measure you might have a feeling and active judgment; I would you did bear the mechanical instruments, wherein the Dutch excel. I write this to you as one, that for myself have given over the delights in the world, but wish to you as much, if not more, than to myself. So you can speak and write Latin, not

* Naturam expellas furcâ, tamen usque recurret. Horace.
† Afterwards the celebrated Sir Henry Savile.
‡ Mr. Alexander Nevyle. For an account of this gentleman, see Warton's History of Poetry, vol. iv. 208, ed. 1824.
‖ Jean Bodin (Johannes Bodinus), born at Angers in 1530, wrote a book entitled "Methodus ad facilem historiarum cognitionem."

barbarously, I never require great study in Ciceronianism, the chief abuse of Oxford, "qui dum verba sectantur, res ipsas negligunt." My toyful books I will send, with God's help, by February, at which time you shall have your money: and for 200 £. a year, assure yourself, if the estates of England remain, you **page 201 /** shall not fail of it: use it to your best profit. ... Now, sweet brother, take a delight to keep and increase your music, you will not believe what a want I find of it in my melancholy times. At horsemanship, when you exercise it, read Crison Claudio, and a book that is called "La gloria del' Cavallo," withal that you may join the thorough contemplation of it with the exercise; and so shall you profit more in a month than others in a year, and mark the bitting, saddling and curing of horses. I would by the way your worship would learn a better hand; you write worse than I, and I write evil enough; once again, have a care of your diet, and consequently of your complexion. ... When you play at weapons, I would have you get thick caps and brasers, and play out your play lustily, for indeed ticks and dalliances are nothing in earnest, for the time of the one and the other greatly differs, and use as well the blows as the thrust: it is good in itself, and besides exerciseth your breath and strength, and will make you a strong man at the tourney and barriers. First in any case practise the single sword, and then with the dagger; let no day pass without an hour or two such exercise: the rest study, or confer diligently, and so shall you come home to my comfort and credit. Lord! how I have babbled: once again farewell, dearest brother. Your most loving and careful brother,

Philip Sidney.

At Leicester House, this 18th of October, 1850.　**page 202 /**

Philip Sidney. *An Apologie for Poetrie* (1595). Edited by Edward Arber, London, 1868.

... I ... in these my not old yeres and idelest times, hauing slipt into the title of a Poet, am prouoked to say somthing vnto you in the defence of that my vnelected vocation. ... I must say, that as I haue iust cause to make a pittiful defence of poore Poetry, which from almost the highest estimation of learning, is fallen to be the laughingstocke of children. So haue I need to bring some more auaileable proofes: sith the former is by no man barred of his deserued credite, the silly latter hath had euen the names of Philosophers vsed to the defacing of it, with great danger of ciuill war among the Muses. And first, truly to al them that professing learning inueigh against Poetry, may iustly be obiected, that they goe very neer to vngratfulnes, to seek to deface that, which in the noblest nations and languages that are knowne, hath been the first light-giuer to ignorance, and first Nurse, whose milk by little and little enabled them to feed afterwards of tougher knowledges. ... Let learned Greece in any of her manifold Sciences, be able to shew me one booke, before *Musaeus, Homer,* and *Hesiodus,* all three nothing els but Poets. Nay, let any historie be brought, that can say any Writers were there before them, if they were not men of the same skil,

as *Orpheus, Linus,* and some other are named: who hauing beene the first
of that Country, that made pens deliuerers of their knowledge to their posterity, may iustly challenge to bee called their Fathers in learning: for not
only in time they had this priority (although in it self antiquity be venerable)
but went before them, as   page 20 /   causes to drawe with their charming
sweetnes, the wild vntamed wits to an admiration of knowledge. So as
Amphion was sayde to moue stones with his Poetrie, to build Thebes. And
Orpheus to be listened to by beastes, indeed, stony and beastly people.
So among the Romans were *Liuius, Andronicus,* and *Ennius.* So in the
Italian language, the first that made it aspire to be a Treasure-house of Sci-
ence, were the Poets *Dante, Boccace,* and *Petrarch.* So in our English were
Gower and *Chawcer.* . . .   page 21 /

Among the Romans a Poet was called *Vates,* which is as much as a Diuiner,
Fore-seer, or Prophet, as by his conioyned wordes *Vaticinium* and *Vaticinari,*
is manifest: so heauenly a title did that excellent people bestow vpon this
hart-rauishing knowledge. And so farre were they carried into the admiration thereof, that they thought in the chaunceable hitting vppon any such
verses, great fore-tokens of their following fortunes were placed. Whereupon grew the worde of *Sortes Virgilianae,* when by suddaine opening
Virgils booke, they lighted vpon any verse of hys making, whereof the
histories of the Emperors liues are full . . . , which although it were a very
vaine, and godles superstition, as also it was to think that spirits were commaunded by such verses, whereupon this word charmes, deriued of *Carmina*
commeth, so yet serueth it to shew the great reuerence those wits were helde
in. And altogether not without ground, since both the Oracles of *Delphos*
and *Sibillas* prophecies, where wholy deliuered in verses. For that same exquisite obseruing of number and measure in words, and that high flying liberty
of conceit proper to the Poet, did seeme to haue some dyuine force in it.

And may not I presume a little further, to shew the reasonablenes of this
worde *Vates?* And say that the holy *Dauids* Psalmes are a diuine Poem?
If I doo, I shall not do it without the testimonie of great learned men, both
auncient and moderne: but euen the name Psalmes will speake for mee, which
being interpreted,   page 23 /   is nothing but songes; Then that it is fully
written in meeter, as all learned Hebricians agree, although the rules be not yet
fully found. Lastly and principally, his handeling his prophecy, which is
meerely poetical. For what els is the awaking his musicall instruments? The
often and free changing of persons? His notable *Prosopopeias,* when he
maketh you as it were, see God comming in his Maiestie. His telling of the
Beastes ioyfulnes, and hills leaping, but a heauenlie poesie: wherein almost
hee sheweth himselfe a passionate louer, of that vnspeakable and euerlasting
beautie to be seene by the eyes of the minde, onely cleered by fayth. But
truely nowe hauing named him, I feare mee I seeme to prophane that holy
name, applying it to Poetrie, which is among vs throwne downe to so ridiculous an estimation: but they that with quiet iudgements will looke a little
deeper into it, shall finde the end and working of it such, as beeing rightly
applyed, deserueth not to bee scourged out of the Church of God.

But now, let vs see how the Greekes named it, and howe they deemed
of it. The Greekes called him a Poet, which name, hath as the most excellent,

gone thorough other Languages. It commeth of this word *Poiein*, which is, to make: wherein I know not, whether by lucke or wisedome, wee English-men haue mette with the Greekes, in calling him a maker: which name, how high and incomparable a title it is, I had rather were knowne by marking the scope of other Sciences, then by my partiall allegation. . . . **page 24 /**

. . . .

Poesie . . . is an arte of imitation, for so *Aristotle* termeth it in his word *Mimesis*, that is to say, a representing, counterfetting, or figuring foorth: to **page 26 /** speake metaphorically, a speaking picture: with this end, to teach and delight; of this haue beene three seuerall kindes. The chiefe both in antiquitie and excellencie, were they that did imitate the incon-ceiuable excellencies of GOD. Such were, *Dauid* in his Psalmes, *Salomon* in his song of Songs, in his Ecclesiastes, and Prouerbs: *Moses* and *Debora* in theyr Hymnes, and the writer of *Iob;* which beside other, the learned *Emanuell Tremilius* and *Franciscus Iunius,* doe entitle the poeticall part of the Scripture. Against these none will speake that hath the holie Ghost in due holy reuerence.

In this kinde, though in a full wrong diuinitie, were *Orpheus, Amphion, Homer* in his hymes, and many other, both Greekes and Romaines: and this Poesie must be vsed, by whosoeuer will follow *S. Iames* his counsell, in singing Psalmes when they are merry: and I knowe is vsed with the fruite of comfort by some, when in sorrowfull pangs of their death-bringing sinnes, they find the consolation of the neuer-leauing goodnesse.

The second kinde, is of them that deale with matters Philosophicall; eyther morrall, as *Tirteus, Phocilides* and *Cato,* or naturall, as *Lucretius* and *Virgils Georgicks:* or Astronomicall, as *Manilius,* and *Pontanus:* or his-torical, as *Lucan:* which who mislike, the faulte is in their iudgements quite out of taste, and not in the sweet foode of sweetly vttered knowledge. But because thys second sorte is wrapped within the folde of the proposed subiect, and takes not the course of his owne inuention, whether they prop-erly be Poets or no, let Gramarians dispute: and goe to the thyrd, indeed right Poets, of whom chiefly this question ariseth; betwixt whom, and these second is such a kinde of difference, as betwixt the meaner sort of Painters, (who counterfet onely such faces as are sette before them) and the more excellent: who hauing no law but wit, bestow that in cullours vpon you which is fittest for the eye to see: **page 27 /** as the constant, though lamenting looke of *Lucrecia,* when she punished in her selfe an others fault.

Wherein he painteth not *Lucrecia* whom he neuer sawe, but painteth the outwarde beauty of such a vertue: for these third be they which most properly do imitate to teach and delight, and to imitate, borrow nothing of what is, hath been, or shall be: but range onely rayned with learned dis-cretion, into the diuine consideration of what may be, and should be. These bee they, that as the first and most noble sorte, may iustly bee termed *Vates,* so these are waited on in the excellen[te]st languages and best vnderstandings, with the fore described name of Poets: for these indeede doo meerely make to imitate: and imitate both to delight and teach: and delight to moue men to take that goodnes in hande, which without delight they would flye as from a stranger. And teach, to make them know that goodnes whereunto they are mooued, which being the noblest scope to which euer any learning was directed, yet want there not idle tongues to barke at them. These be sub-diuided into sundry more speciall denominations. The most notable bee the *Heroick, Lirick, Tragick, Comick, Satirick, Iambick, Elegiack, Pastorall,* and certaine others. Some of these being termed according to the matter they deale with, some by the sorts of verses they liked best to write in, for indeede the greatest part of Poets have apparelled their poeticall inuentions in that num-brous kinde of writing which is called verse: indeed but apparelled, verse being but an ornament and no cause to Poetry: sith there haue beene many most excellent Poets, that neuer versified, and now swarme many versifiers that neede neuer aunswere to the name of Poets. For *Xenophon,* who did imitate so excellently, as to giue vs *effigiem iusti imperii,* the portraiture of a iust Empire vnder the name of *Cyrus,* (as *Cicero* sayeth of him) made therein an absolute heroicall Poem.

So did *Heliodorus* in his sugred inuention of that picture of loue in *Thea-gines* and *Cariclea,* and yet page 28 / both these writ in Prose: which I speak to shew, that it is not riming and versing that maketh a Poet, no more then a long gowne maketh an Aduocate: who though he pleaded in armor should be an Aduocate and no Souldier. But it is that fayning notable images of vertues, vices, or what els, with that delightfull teaching which must be the right describing note to know a Poet by: although indeed the Senate of Poets hath chosen verse as their fittest rayment, meaning, as in matter they passed all in all, so in maner to goe beyond them: not speaking (table talke fashion or like men in a dreame,) words as they chanceably fall from the mouth, but peyzing each sillable of each worde by iust proportion according to the dignitie of the subiect.... page 29 /

The Historian, scarcely giueth leysure to the Moralist, to say so much, but that he loden with old Mouse-eaten records, authorising himselfe (for the most part) vpon other histories, whose greatest authorities, are built vpon the notable foundation of Heare-say, hauing much a-doe to accord differing Writers, and to pick trueth out of partiality, better acquainted with a thou-sande yeeres a goe, then with the present age: and yet better knowing how this world goeth, then how his owne wit runneth: curious for antiquities, and inquisitiue of nouelties, a wonder to young folkes, and a tyrant in table talke, denieth in a great chafe, that any man for teaching of vertue, and ver-tuous actions, is comparable to him....

The Phylosopher (sayth hee) teacheth a disputatiue vertue, but I doe an actiue: his vertue is excellent in the dangerlesse Academie of *Plato,* but mine sheweth foorth her honorable face, in the battailes of *Marathon, Phar-salia, Poitiers,* and *Agincourt.* Hee teacheth vertue by certaine abstract con-siderations, but I onely bid you follow the footing of them that haue gone before you. Olde-aged experience, goeth beyond the fine-witted Phylosopher, but I giue the experience of many ages. Lastly, if he make the Song-booke, I put the learners hande to the Lute: and if hee be the guide, I am the light.

Then woulde hee alledge you innumerable examples, conferring storie by storie, how much the wisest Senatours and Princes, haue beene directed by the credite of history, as *Brutus, Alphonsus* of *Aragon,* and who not, if need

bee? At length, the long lyne **page 31 /** of theyr disputation maketh a
poynt in thys, that the one giueth the precept, and the other the example.

Nowe, whom shall wee finde (sith the question standeth for the highest
forme in the Schoole of learning) to bee Moderator? Trulie, as me seemeth,
the Poet; and if not a Moderator, euen the man that ought to carrie the title
from them both, and much more from all other seruing Sciences. Therefore compare we the Poet with the Historian, and with the Morrall Phylosopher,
and, if hee goe beyond them both, no other humaine skill can match him. For
as for the Diuine, with all reuerence it is euer to be excepted, not only for
hauing his scope as far beyonde any of these, as eternitie exceedeth a moment,
but euen for passing each of these in themselues. . . .

The Philosopher therfore and the Historian, are they which would win
the gole: the one by precept, the other by example. But both not hauing
both, doe both halte. For the Philosopher, setting downe with thorny argument the bare rule, is so hard of vtterance, and so mistie to bee conceiued,
that one that hath no other guide but him, shall wade in him till hee be olde,
before he shall finde sufficient cause to bee honest: for his knowledge standeth so vpon the abstract and generall, that happie is that man who **page 32 /**
may vnderstande him, and more happie, that can applye what hee dooth vnderstand.

On the other side, the Historian wanting the precept, is so tyed, not to what
shoulde bee, but to what is, to the particuler truth of things, . . . that hys
example draweth no necessary consequence, and therefore a lesse fruitfull
doctrine.

Nowe dooth the peerelesse Poet performe both: for whatsoeuer the Philosopher sayth shoulde be doone, hee giueth a perfect picture of it in some
one, by whom hee presupposeth it was done. So as hee coupleth the generall
notion with the particuler example. A perfect picture I say, for hee yeeldeth to the powers of the minde, an image of that whereof the Philosopher be-
stoweth but a woordish description: which dooth neyther strike, pierce,
nor possesse the sight of the soule, so much as that other dooth.

. . . No doubt the Philosopher with his learned definition, bee it of vertue,
vices, matters of publick policie, or priuat gouernment, replenisheth the
memory with many infallible grounds of wisdom: which notwithstanding,
lye darke before the imaginatiue and iudging powre, if they bee not illumi-
nated or figured foorth by the speaking picture of Poesie.

Tullie taketh much paynes and many times not without poeticall helpes,
to make vs knowe the force loue of our Countrey hath in us. Let vs but
heare **page 33 /** old *Anchises* speaking in the middest of *Troyes* flames,
or see *Vlisses* in the fulnes of all *Calipso's* delights, bewayle his absence from
barraine and beggerly *Ithaca.* Anger the *Stoicks* say, was a short maddnes,
let but *Sophocles* bring you *Aiax* on a stage, killing and whipping Sheepe
and Oxen, thinking them the Army of Greeks, with theyr Chiefetaines *Agamemnon* and *Menelaus,* and tell mee if you haue not a more familiar insight
into anger, then finding in the Schoolemen his *Genus* and difference. See
whether wisdome and temperance in *Vlisses* and *Diomedes,* valure in *Achilles,*
friendship in *Nisus,* and *Eurialus,* euen to an ignoraunt man, carry not an apparent shyning: and contrarily, the remorse of conscience in *Oedipus,* the

soone repenting pride of *Agamemnon,* the selfe-deuouring crueltie in his Father *Atreus,* the violence of ambition in the two *Theban* brothers, the sowre-sweetnes of reuenge in *Medaea,* and to fall lower, the *Terentian Gnato,* and our *Chaucers* Pandar, so exprest, that we nowe vse their names to signifie their trades. And finally, all vertues, vices, and passions, so in their own naturall seates layd to the viewe, that wee seeme not to heare of them, but cleerely to see through them. But euen in the most excellent determination of goodnes, what Philosophers counsell can so redily direct a Prince, as the fayned *Cyrus* in *Xenophon?* or a vertuous man in all fortunes, as *Aeneas* in *Virgill?* or a whole Common-wealth, as the way of Sir *Thomas Moores Eutopia?* I say the way, because where Sir *Thomas Moore* erred, it was the fault of the man and not of the Poet, for that way of patterning a Common-wealth was most absolute, though hee perchaunce hath not so absolutely perfourmed it: for the question is, whether the fayned image of Poesie, or the regular instruction of Philosophy, hath the more force in teaching: wherein if the Philosophers haue more rightly shewed themselues Philosophers, then the Poets haue obtained to the high top of their profession. . . .
page 34 /

Certainly, euen our Sauiour Christ could as well haue giuen, the morrall common places of vncharitablenes and humblenes, as the diuine narration of *Diues* and *Lazarus:* or of disobedience and mercy, as that heauenly discourse of the lost Child and the gratious Father; but that hys throughsearching wisdom, knewe the estate of *Diues* burning in hell, and of *Lazarus* being in *Abrahams* bosome, would more constantly (as it were) inhabit both the memory and iudgement. Truly, for my selfe, mee seemes I see before my eyes the lost Childes disdainefull prodigality, turned to enuie a Swines dinner: which by the learned Diuines, are thought not historicall acts, but instructing Parables. For conclusion, I say the Philosopher teacheth, but he teacheth obscurely, so as the learned onely can vnderstande him: that is to say, he teacheth them that are already taught, but the Poet is the foode for the tenderest stomacks, the Poet is indeed the right Popular Philosopher, whereof *Esops* tales giue good proofe: whose pretty Allegories, stealing vnder the formall tales of Beastes, make many, more beastly then Beasts, begin to heare the sound of vertue from these dumbe speakers.

But now may it be alledged, that if this imagining of matters be so fitte for the imagination, then must the Historian needs surpasse, who bringeth you images of true matters, such as indeede were doone, and not such as fantastically or falsely may be suggested to haue been doone. Truely *Aristotle* himselfe in his discourse of Poesie, plainely determineth this question, saying, that Poetry is *Philosophoteron* and *Spoudaioteron,* that is to say, it is more Philosophicall, and more studiously serious, then history. His reason is, because Poesie dealeth with *Katholou,* that is to say, with the vniuersall consideration; and the history with *Kathe-* page 35 / *kaston,* the perticuler; nowe sayth he, the vniuersall wayes what is fit to bee sayd or done, eyther in likelihood or necessity, (which the Poesie considereth in his imposed names,) and the perticuler, onely mark's, whether *Alcibiades* did, or suffered, this or that. Thus farre *Aristotle:* which reason of his, (as all his) is most full of reason. For indeed, if the question were whether it were better to haue a perticular acte truly or falsly set down: there is no doubt which is to be chosen. . . . But if the question be for your owne vse and learning, whether it be better to haue it set downe as it should be, or as it was: then certainely is more doctrinable the fained Cirus of *Xenophon* then the true *Cyrus* in *Iustine:* and the fayned *Aeneas* in *Virgil*, then the right *Aeneas* in *Dares Phrigius*. . . .

If the Poet doe his part a-right, he will shew you in *Tantalus, Atreus*, and such like, nothing that is not to be shunned. In *Cyrus, Aeneas, Vlisses*, each thing to be followed; where the Historian, bound to tell things as things were, cannot be liberall (without hee will be poeticall) of a perfect patterne: but as in *Alexander* or *Scipio* himselfe, shew dooings, some to be liked, some to be misliked. And then how will you discerne what to followe, but by your owne discretion, which you had without reading *Quintus Curtius?* And whereas a man may say, though in vniuersall consideration of doctrine the Poet preuaileth; yet that the historie, in his saying such a thing was doone, doth warrant a man more in that hee shall follow.

The aunswere is manifest, that if hee stande vpon that was; . . . then **page 36 /** indeede it hath some aduantage to a grose conceite: but if he know an example onlie, informes a coniectured likelihood, and so goe by reason, the Poet dooth so farre exceede him, as hee is to frame his example to that which is most reasonable: be it in warlike, politick, or priuate matters; where the Historian in his bare *Was*, hath many times that which wee call fortune, to ouer-rule the best wisedome. Manie times, he must tell euents, whereof he can yeelde no cause: or if hee doe, it must be poeticall; for that a fayned example, hath asmuch force to teach, as a true example: (for as for to mooue, it is cleere, sith the fayned may bee tuned to the highest key of passion). . . .

. . . So then the best of the Historian, is subiect to the Poet; for whatsoeuer action, or faction, whatsoeuer counsell, pollicy, or warre stratagem, the Historian is bound to recite, that may the Poet (if he list) with his imitation make his own; beautifying it both for further teaching, and more delighting, as it pleaseth him: hauing all, from *Dante* his heauen, to hys hell, vnder the authoritie **page 37 /** of his penne. Which if I be asked what Poets haue done so, as I might well name some, yet say I, and say againe, I speak of the Arte, and not of the Artificer.

Nowe, to that which commonly is attributed to the prayse of histories, in respect of the notable learning is gotten by marking the successe, as though therein a man should see vertue exalted, and vice punished. Truely that commendation is peculiar to Poetrie, and farre of from History. For indeede Poetrie euer setteth vertue so out in her best cullours, making Fortune her welwayting hand-mayd, that one must needs be enamored of her. Well may you see *Vlisses* in a storme, and in other hard plights; but they are but exercises of patience and magnanimitie, to make them shine the more in the neerefollowing prosperitie. And of the contrarie part, if euill men come to the stage, they euer goe out (as the Tragedie Writer answered, to one that misliked the shew of such persons) so manacled, as they little animate folkes to followe them. But the Historian, beeing captiued to the trueth of a foolish world, is many times a terror from well dooing, and an incouragement to vnbrideled wickednes.

For, see wee not valiant *Milciades* rot in his fetters? The iust *Phocion*, and the accomplished *Socrates*, put to death like Traytors? The cruell *Seuerus* liue prosperously? The excellent *Seuerus* miserably murthered? *Sylla* and *Marius* dying in theyr beddes? *Pompey* and *Cicero* slaine then, when they would haue thought exile a happinesse?

See wee not vertuous *Cato* driuen to kyll himselfe? and rebell *Caesar* so aduaunced, that his name yet after 1600. yeares, lasteth in the highest honor?.... **page 38** /

For suppose it be granted, (that which I suppose with great reason may be denied,) that the Philosopher in respect of his methodical proceeding, doth teach more perfectly then the Poet: yet do I thinke, that no man is so much *Philophilosophos*, as to compare the Philosopher in moouing, with the Poet.

And that moouing is of a higher degree then teaching, it may by this appeare: that it is wel nigh the cause and the effect of teaching. For who will be taught, if hee bee not mooued with desire to be taught? and what so much good doth that teaching bring forth, (I speak still of morrall doctrine) as that it mooueth one to doe that which it dooth teach? for as *Aristotle* sayth, it is not *Gnosis*, but *Praxis* must be the fruit. And howe *Praxis* cannot be, without being mooued to practise, it is no hard matter to consider. . . . **page 39** /

Nowe therein of all Sciences, (I speak still of humane, and according to the humane conceits) is our Poet the Monarch. For he dooth not only show the way, but giueth so sweete a prospect into the way, as will intice any man to enter into it. . . . He beginneth not with obscure definitions, which must blur the margent with interpretations, and load the memory with doubtfulnesse: but hee commeth to you with words sent in delightfull proportion, either accompanied with, or prepared for the well inchaunting skill of Musicke; and with a tale forsooth he commeth vnto you: with a tale which holdeth children from play, and old men from the chimney corner. And pretending no more, doth intende the winning of the mind from wickednesse to vertue: euen as the childe is often brought to take most wholsom things, by hiding them in such other as haue a pleasant tast: which if one should beginne to tell them, the nature of *Aloes*, or *Rubarb* they shoulde receiue, woulde sooner take their Phisicke at their eares, then at their mouth. So is it in men (most of which are childish in the best things, till they bee cradled in their graues,) glad they will be to heare the tales of *Hercules*, *Achilles*, *Cyrus*, and *Aeneas:* and hearing them, must needs heare the right description of wisdom, valure, and iustice; which, if they had **page 40** / been barely, that is to say, Philosophically set out, they would sweare they bee brought to schoole againe.

That imitation wherof Poetry is, hath the most conueniency to Nature of all other, in somuch, that as *Aristotle* sayth, those things which in themselues are horrible, as cruell battailes, vnnaturall Monsters, are made in poeticall imitation delightfull. Truely I haue knowen men, that euen with reading *Amadis de Gaule*, (which God knoweth wanteth much of a perfect Poesie) haue

found their harts mooued to the exercise of courtesie, liberalitie, and especially courage.

Who readeth *Aeneas* carrying olde *Anchises* on his back, that wisheth not
it were his fortune to perfourme so excellent an acte?. . . Where the Philosophers, as they scorne to delight, so must they bee content little to mooue:
sauing wrangling, whether Vertue bee the chiefe, or the onely good: whether
the contemplatiue, or the actiue life doe excell: which *Plato* and *Boethius*
well knew, and therefore made Mistres Philosophy, very often borrow the
masking rayment of Poesie. . . . **page 41 /**

. . . I think it may be manifest, that the Poet with that same hand of delight,
doth draw the mind more effectually, then any other Arte dooth, and so a
conclusion not vnfitlie ensueth: that as vertue is the most excellent resting
place for all worldlie learning to make his end of: so **page 42 /** Poetrie,
beeing the most familiar to teach it, and most princelie to moue towards it,
in the most excellent work, is the most excellent workman. But I am content,
not onely to decipher him by his workes, (although works in commendation
or disprayse, must euer holde an high authority,) but more narrowly will examine his parts: so that (as in a man) though altogether may carry a presence ful of maiestie and beautie, perchance in some one defectious peece,
we may find a blemish: now in his parts, kindes, or *Species*, (as you list to
terme them) it is to be noted, that some Poesies haue coupled together two
or three kindes, as Tragicall and Comicall, wher-vpon is risen, the Tragi-
comicall. Some in the like manner haue mingled Prose and Verse, as *Sanazzar*
and *Boetius*. Some haue mingled matters Heroicall and Pastorall. But that
commeth all to one in this question, for if seuered they be good, the coniunc-
tion cannot be hurtfull. Therefore perchaunce forgetting some, and leauing
some as needlesse to be remembred, it shall not be amisse in a worde to cite
the speciall kindes, to see what faults may be found in the right vse of them.

Is it then the Pastorall Poem which is misliked? (for perchance, where the
hedge is lowest, they will soonest leape ouer.) Is the poore pype disdained,
which sometime out of *Melibeus* mouth, can shewe the miserie of people,
vnder hard Lords, or rauening Souldiours? And again, by *Titirus*, what bles-
sednes is deriued to them that lye lowest from the goodnesse of them that
sit highest? Sometimes, vnder the prettie tales of Wolues and Sheepe, can
include the whole considerations of wrong dooing and patience. Sometimes
shew, that contention for trifles, can get but a trifling victorie. . . . **page 43 /**

Or is it the lamenting Elegiack, which in a kinde hart would mooue rather
pitty then blame, who bewailes with the great Philosopher *Heraclitus*, the
weakenes of man-kind, and the wretchednes of the world: who surely is to
be praysed, either for compassionate accompanying iust causes of lamenta-
tion, or for rightly paynting out how weake be the passions of wofulnesse.
Is it the bitter, but wholsome Iambick, which rubs the galled minde, in making shame the trumpet of villanie, with bolde and open crying out against
naughtines; Or the Satirick, . . . Who sportingly neuer leaueth, vntil hee make
a man laugh at folly, and at length ashamed, to laugh at himselfe: which he
cannot auoyd, without auoyding the follie. . . . No perchance it is the Comick,
whom naughtie Play-makers and Stage-keepers, haue iustly made odious. To
the argument of abuse, I will answer after. Onely thus much now is to be

said, that the Comedy is an imitation of the common errors of our life, which he representeth, in the most ridiculous and scornefull sort that may be. So as it is impossible, that any beholder can be content to be such a one.

Now, as in Geometry, the oblique must bee knowne as wel as the right: and in Arithmetick, the odde aswell as the euen, so in the actions of our life, who seeth not the filthines of euil, wanteth a great foile to perceiue the beauty of vertue. This doth the Comedy handle so in our priuate and domestical matters, as with hearing it, we get as it were an experience, what is to be looked for of a nigardly *Demea:* of a crafty *Danus:* of a flattering *Gnato:* of a vaine glorious   **page 44** /   *Thraso:* and not onely to know what effects are to be expected, but to know who be such, by the signifying badge giuen them by the Comedian. And little reason hath any man to say, that men learne euill by seeing it so set out. . . . So that the right vse of Comedy will (I thinke) by no body be blamed, and much lesse of the high and excellent Tragedy, that openeth the greatest wounds, and sheweth forth the Vicers, that are couered with Tissue: that maketh Kinges feare to be Tyrants, and Tyrants manifest their tirannicall humors: that with sturring the affects of admiration and commiseration, teacheth, the vncertainety of this world, and vpon how weake foundations guilden roofes are builded. . . . But how much it can mooue, *Plutarch* yeeldeth a notable testimonie, of the abhominable Tyrant, *Alexander Pheraeus;* from whose eyes, a Tragedy wel made, and represented, drew aboundance of teares: who without all pitty, had murthered infinite nombers, and some of his owne blood. So as he, that was not ashamed to make matters for Tragedies, yet coulde not resist the sweet violence of a Tragedie.

And if it wrought no further good in him, it was, that he in despight of himselfe, withdrewe himselfe from harkening to that, which might mollifie his hardened heart. But it is not the Tragedy they doe mislike: For it were too absurd to cast out so excellent a representation of whatsoeuer is most worthy to be learned. Is it the Liricke that most despleaseth,   **page 45** /   who with his tuned Lyre, and wel accorded voyce, giueth praise, the reward of vertue, to vertuous acts? who giues morrall precepts, and naturall Problemes, who sometimes rayseth vp his voice to the height of the heauens, in singing the laudes of the immortall God. Certainly I must confesse my own barbarousnes, I neuer heard the olde song of *Percy* and *Duglas*, that I found not my heart mooued more then with a Trumpet: and yet is it sung but by some blinde Crouder, with no rougher voyce, then rude stile: which being so euill apparrelled in the dust and cobwebbes of that vnciuill age, what would it worke trymmed in the gorgeous eloquence of *Pindar?*. . . .

There rests the Heroicall, whose very name (I thinke) should daunt all back-biters; for by what conceit can a tongue be directed to speake euill of that, which draweth with it, no lesse Champions   **page 46** /   then *Achilles, Cyrus, Aeneas, Turnus, Tideus,* and *Rinaldo?* who doth not only teach and moue to a truth, but teacheth and mooueth to the most high and excellent truth. Who maketh magnanimity and iustice shine, throughout all misty fearefulnes and foggy desires. . . . But if any thing be already sayd in the defence of sweete Poetry, all concurreth to the maintaining the Heroicall, which is not onely a kinde, but the best, and most accomplished kinde of Poetry. For as the image of each action styrreth and instructeth the mind, so the loftie image of such Worthies, most imflameth the mind with desire to be worthy, and informes with counsel how to be worthy. Only let *Aeneas* be worne in the tablet of your memory, how he gouerneth himselfe in the ruine of his Country, in the preseruing his old Father, and carrying away his religious ceremonies: in obeying the Gods commandement to leaue *Dido*, though not onely all passionate kindenes, but euen the humane consideration of vertuous gratefulnes, would haue craued other of him. How in storms, howe in sports, howe in warre, howe in peace, how a fugitiue, how victorious, how besiedged, how besiedging, howe to strangers, howe to allyes, how to enemies, howe to his owne: lastly, how in his inward selfe, and how in his outward gouernment. And I thinke, in a minde not preiudiced with a preiudicating humor, hee will be found in excellencie fruitefull. . . .

But truely I imagine, it falleth out with these Poet-whyppers, as with some good women who often are sicke, but in fayth they cannot tel where. So the name of Poetrie is odious to them, but neither his cause, nor effects, neither the sum that containes him, **page 47 /** nor the particularities descending from him, giue any fast handle to their carping disprayse.

Sith then Poetrie is of all humane learning the most auncient, and of most fatherly antiquitie, as from whence other learnings haue taken theyr beginnings: sith it is so vniuersall, that no learned Nation dooth despise it, nor no barbarous Nation is without it: sith both Roman and Greek gaue diuine names vnto it: the one of prophecying, the other of making. And that indeede, that name of making is fit for him; considering, that where as other Arts retaine themselues within their subiect, and receiue as it were, their beeing from it: the Poet onely, bringeth his owne stuffe, and dooth not learne a conceite out of a matter, but maketh matter for a conceite: Sith neither his description, nor his ende, contayneth any euill, the thing described cannot be euill: Sith his effects be so good as to teach goodnes and to delight the learners: Sith therein (namely in morrall doctrine, the chiefe of all knowledges,) hee dooth not onely farre passe the Historian, but for instructing, is well nigh comparable to the Philosopher: and for mouing, leaves him behind him: Sith the holy scripture (wherein there is no vncleannes) hath whole parts in it poeticall. And that euen our Sauiour Christ, vouchsafed to vse the flowers of it: Sith all his kindes are not onlie in their vnited formes, but in their seuered dissections fully commendable, I think, (and think I thinke rightly) the Lawrell crowne appointed for tryumphing Captaines, doth worthilie (of al other learnings) honor the Poets tryumph. But because wee haue eares aswell as tongues. . . let vs heare, and aswell as wee can ponder, what obiections may bee made against this Arte, which may be worthy, eyther of yeelding, or answering. . . . **page 48 /**

. . . That which gyueth greatest scope to their scorning humors, is ryming and versing. It is already sayde (and as I think, trulie sayde) it is not ryming and versing, that maketh Poesie. One may bee a Poet without versing, and a versifier without Poetry. But yet, presuppose it were inseparable (as indeede it seemeth *Scaliger* iudgeth) truelie it were an inseparable commendation. For if *Oratio*, next to *Ratio*, Speech next to Reason, bee the greatest gyft **page 49 /** bestowed vpon mortalitie: that can not be praiselesse, which dooth most pollish that blessing of speech, which considers each word, not only (as a man may say) by his forcible qualitie, but by his best measured quantitie, carrying euen in themselues, a Harmonie: (without (perchaunce) Number, Measure, Order, Proportion, be in our time growne odious.) But lay a side the iust prayse it hath, by beeing the onely fit speech for Musick, (Musick I say, the most diuine striker of the sences:) thus much is vndoubtedly true, that if reading bee foolish, without remembring, memorie being the onely treasurer of knowled[g]e, those words which are fittest for memory, are likewise most conuenient for knowledge.

Now, that Verse farre exceedeth Prose in the knitting vp of the memory, the reason is manifest. The words, (besides theyr delight which hath a greate affinitie to memory,) beeing so set, as one word cannot be lost, but the whole worke failes: which accuseth it selfe, calleth the remembrance backe to it selfe, and so most strongly confirmeth it; besides, one word so as it were begetting another, as be it in ryme or measured verse, by the former a man shall haue a neere gesse to the follower: lastly, euen they that haue taught the Art of memory, haue shewed nothing so apt for it, as a certaine roome deuided into many places well and throughly knowne. . . . page 50 / Nowe then goe wee to the most important imputations laid to the poore Poets, for ought I can yet learne, they are these, first, that there beeing many other more fruitefull knowledges, a man might better spend his tyme in them, then in this. Secondly, that it is the mother of lyes. Thirdly, that it is the Nurse of abuse, infecting vs with many pestilent desires: with a Syrens sweetnes, drawing the mind to the Serpents tayle of sinfull fancy. And heerein especially, Comedies giue the largest field to erre, as *Chaucer* sayth: howe both in other Nations and in ours, before Poets did soften vs, we were full of courage, giuen to martiall exercises; the pillers of manlyke liberty, and not lulled a sleepe in shady idlenes with Poets pastimes. And lastly, and chiefely, they cry out with an open mouth, as if they out shot *Robin Hood*, that *Plato* banished them out of hys Common-wealth. Truely, this is much, if there be much truth in it. First to the first: that a man might better spend his tyme, is a reason indeede: but it doth (as they say) but *Petere principium:* for if it be as I affirme, that no learning is so good, as that which teacheth and mooueth to vertue; and that none can both teach and moue thereto so much as Poetry: then is the conclusion manifest, that Incke and Paper cannot be to a more profitable purpose employed. . . . To the second therefore, that they should be the principall lyars; I aunswere paradoxically, but truely, I thinke truely; that of all Writers vnder the sunne, the Poet is the least lier: and though he would, as a Poet can scarcely be a lyer. . . . page 51 /

. . . For the Poet, he nothing affirmes, and therefore neuer lyeth. For, as I take it, to lye, is to affirme that to be true which is false. So as the other Artists, and especially the Historian, affirming many things, can in the cloudy knowledge of mankinde, hardly escape from many lyes. But the Poet as I sayd before neuer affirmeth. The Poet neuer maketh any circles about your imagination, to coniure you to beleeue for true what he writes. Hee citeth not authorities of other Histories, but euen for hys entry, calleth the sweete Muses to inspire into him a good inuention: in troth, not labouring to tell you what is, or is not, but what should or should not be: and therefore, though he recount things not true, yet because hee telleth them not for true, he lyeth not.... **page 52** /

Their third is, how much it abuseth mens wit, trayning it to wanton sinfulnes, and lustfull loue: for indeed that is the principall, if not the onely abuse I can heare alledged. They say, the Comedies rather teach, then reprehend, amorous conceits. They say, the Lirick, is larded with passionate Sonnets. The Elegiack, weepes the want of his mistresse. And that euen to the Heroical, *Cupid* hath ambitiously climed.... **page 53** /

For I will not denie, but that mans wit may make Poesie, (which should be *Eikastike*, which some learned haue defined, figuring foorth good things,) to be *Phantastike:* which doth contrariwise, infect the fancie with vnworthy obiects.... But what, shall the abuse of a thing, make the right vse odious? Nay truely, though I yeeld, that Poesie may not onely be abused, but that beeing abused, by the reason of his sweete charming force, it can doe more hurt then any other Armie of words: yet shall it be so far from concluding, that the abuse, should giue reproch to the abused, that contrariwise it is a good reason, that whatsoeuer being abused, dooth most harme, beeing rightly vsed: (and vpon the right vse each thing conceiueth his title) doth most good....

They alledge heere-with, that before Poets beganne to be in price, our Nation, hath set their harts delight vpon action, and not vpon imagination: rather doing　**page 54** /　things worthy to bee written, then writing things fitte to be done. What that before tyme was, I thinke scarcely *Sphinx* can tell: Sith no memory is so auncient, that hath the precedence of Poetrie. And certaine it is, that in our plainest homelines, yet neuer was the *Albion* Nation without Poetrie. Mary, thys argument, though it bee leaueld against Poetrie, yet is it indeed, a chaine-shot against all learning, or bookishnes, as they commonly tearme it.... As for Poetrie it selfe, it is the freest from thys obiection. For Poetrie is the companion of the Campes.

I dare vndertake, *Orlando Furioso*, or honest King *Arthur*, will neuer displease a Souldier.... *Homer* a Greek, florished, before Greece florished. And if to a slight coniecture, a coniecture may be opposed: truly it may seeme, that as by him, their learned men, tooke almost their first light of **page 55** / knowledge, so their actiue men, receiued their first motions of courage. Onlie *Alexanders* example may serue, who by *Plutarch* is accounted of such vertue, that Fortune was not his guide, but his foote-stoole: whose acts speake for him, though *Plutarch* did not: indeede, the Phoenix of warlike Princes. This *Alexander*, left his Schoolemaister, liuing *Aristotle*, behinde him, but tooke dead *Homer* with him: he put the Philosopher *Calisthenes* to death, for his seeming philosophicall, indeed mutinous stubburnnes. But the chiefe thing he euer was heard to wish for, was, that *Homer* had been aliue. He well found, he receiued more brauerie of minde, bye the patterne of *Achilles*, then by hearing the definition of Fortitude.... **page 56** /

But sith I have runne so long a careere in this matter, me thinks, before I giue my penne a fulle stop, it shalbe but a little more lost time, to inquire, why England, (the Mother of excellent mindes,) should bee growne so hard a step-mother to Poets, who certainly in wit ought to passe all other: sith all onely proceedeth from their wit, being indeede makers of themselues, not takers of others. . . . Sweete Poesie, that hath aunciently had Kings, Emperors, Senators, great Captaines, such, as besides a thousand others, *Dauid, Adrian, Sophocles, Germanicus,* not onely to fauour Poets, but to be Poets. And of our neerer times, can present for her Patrons, a *Robert,* king of Sicil, the great king *Francis* of France, King *Iames* of Scotland. Such Cardinals as *Bembus,* and *Bibiena.* Such famous Preachers and Teachers, as *Beza* and *Melancthon.* So learned Philosophers, as *Fracastorius* and *Scaliger.* So great Orators, as *Pontanus* and *Muretus.* So piercing wits, as *George Buchanan.* So graue Counsellors, as besides many, but before all, that *Hospitall* of Fraunce: then whom, (I thinke) that Realme neuer brought forth a more accomplished iudgement: more firmely builded vpon vertue. I say these, with numbers of others, not onely to read others Poesies, but to poetise for others reading, that Poesie thus embraced in all other places, should only finde in our time, a hard welcome in England, I thinke the very earth lamenteth it, and therfore decketh our Soyle with fewer Laurels then it was accustomed. For heertofore, Poets haue in England also florished. . . . **page 60 /**

Chaucer, vndoubtedly did excellently in hys *Troylus* and *Cresseid;* of whom, truly I know not, whether to meruaile more, either that he in that mistie time, could see so clearly, or that wee in this cleare age, walke so stumblingly after him. Yet had he great wants, fitte to be forgiuen, in so reuerent antiquity. I account the *Mirrour of Magistrates,* meetely furnished of beautiful parts; and in the Earle of Surries *Liricks,* many things tasting of a noble birth, and worthy of a noble minde. The *Sheapheards Kalender,* hath much Poetrie in his Eglogues: indeede worthy the reading **page 62 /** if I be not deceiued. That same framing of his stile, to an old rustick language, I dare not alowe, sith neyther *Theocritus* in Greeke, *Virgill* in Latine, nor *Sanazar* in Italian, did affect it. Besides these, doe I not remember to haue seene but fewe, (to speake boldely) printed, that haue poeticall sinnewes in them: for proofe whereof, let but most of the verses bee put in Prose, and then aske the meaning; and it will be found, that one verse did but beget another, without ordering at the first, what should be at the last: which becomes a confused masse of words, with a tingling sound of ryme, barely accompanied with reason.

Our Tragedies, and Comedies, (not without cause cried out against,) obseruing rules, neyther of honest ciuilitie, nor of skilfull Poetrie, excepting *Gorboduck,* (againe, I say, of those that I haue seene,) which notwithstanding, as it is full of stately speeches, and well sounding Phrases, clyming to the height of *Seneca* his stile, and as full of notable moralitie, which it doth most delightfully teach; and so obtayne the very end of Poesie: yet in troth it is very defectious in the circumstaunces; which greeueth mee, because it might not remaine as an exact model of all Tragedies. For it is faulty both in place, and time, the two necessary companions of all corporall actions. For where the stage should alwaies represent but one place, and the vttermost time presupposed in it, should be, both by *Aristotles* precept, and common reason, but one day: there is both many dayes, and many places, inartificially imagined. But if it be so in *Gorboduck,* how much more in al the rest? where you shal haue *Asia* of the one side, and

Affrick of the other, and so many other vnder-kingdoms, that the Player, when he commeth in, must euer begin with telling where he is: or els, the tale wil not be conceiued. Now ye shal haue three Ladies, walke to gather flowers, and then we must beleeue the stage to be a Garden. By and by, we heare newes of shipwracke in the same place, and then wee are to blame, if we accept it not for a Rock.   **page 63** /

Vpon the backe of that, comes out a hidious Monster, with fire and smoke, and then the miserable beholders, are bounde to take it for a Caue. While in the mean-time, two Armies flye in, represented with foure swords and bucklers, and then what harde heart will not receiue it for a pitched fielde? Now, of time they are much more liberall, for ordinary it is that two young Princes fall in loue. After many trauerces, she is got with childe, deliuered of a faire boy, he is lost, groweth a man, falls in loue, and is ready to get another child, and all this in two hours space: which how absurd it is in sence, euen sence may imagine, and Arte hath taught, and all auncient examples iustified: and at this day, the ordinary Players in Italie, wil not erre in. . . . But they wil say, how then shal we set forth a story, which containeth both many places, and many times? And doe they not knowe, that a Tragedie is tied to the lawes of Poesie, and not of Historie? not bound to follow the storie, but hauing liberty, either to faine a quite newe matter, or to frame the history, to the most tragicall conueniencie. Againe, many things may be told, which cannot be shewed, if they knowe the difference betwixt reporting and representing. . . . So was the manner the Auncients tooke, by some *Nuncius*, to recount thinges done in former time, or other place. Lastly, if they wil represent an history, they must not (as *Horace* saith) beginne *Ab ouo:* but they must come to the principall poynt of that one action, which they wil represent. . . .   **page 64** /   But besides these grosse absurdities, how all theyr Playes be neither right Tragedies, nor right Comedies: mingling Kings and Clownes, not because the matter so carrieth it: but thrust in Clownes by head and shoulders, to play a part in maiesticall matters, with neither decencie, nor discretion. So as neither the admiration and commiseration, nor the right sportfulnes, is by their mungrell Tragy-comedie obtained. I know *Apuleius* did some-what so, but that is a thing recounted with space of time, not represented in one mo-ment: and I knowe, the Auncients haue one or two examples of Tragy-comedies, as *Plautus* hath *Amphitrio:* But if we marke them well, we shall find, that they neuer, or very daintily, match Horn-pypes and Funeralls. So falleth it out, that hauing indeed no right Comedy, in that comicall part of our Tragedy, we haue nothing but scurrility, vnwoorthy of any chast eares: or some extreame shew of doltishnes, indeed fit to lift vp a loude laughter, and nothing els: where the whole tract of a Comedy, shoulde be full of delight, as the Tragedy shoulde be still maintained, in a well raised admiration. But our Comedians, thinke there is no delight without laughter, which is very wrong, for   **page 65** /   though laughter may come with de-light, yet commeth it not of delight: as though delight should be the cause of laughter. . . .   **page 66** /

. . . I haue lauished out too many wordes of this play matter. I doe it be-cause as they are excelling parts of Poesie, so is there none so much vsed in England, and none can be more pittifully abused. . . . Other sorts of Poetry almost haue we none, but that Lyricall kind of Songs and Sonnets: which, Lord, if he gaue vs so good mindes, how well it might be imployed, and with howe heauenly fruite, both priuate and publique, in singing the prayses of the immortall beauty: the immortall goodnes of that God, who gyueth vs hands to write, and wits to conceiue, of which we might well want words, but neuer matter, of which, we could turne our eies to nothing, but we should euer haue new budding occasions. But truely many of such writings, as come vnder the banner of vnresistable loue, if I were a Mistres, would neuer perswade mee they were in loue: so coldely they apply fiery speeches, as men that had rather red Louers writings; and so caught vp certaine swell-ing phrases, which hang together, like a man which once tolde mee, the winde was at North, West, and by South, because he would be sure to name windes enowe: then that in truth they feele those passions, which easily (as I think) may be bewrayed, by that same forcibleness, or *Energia*, (as the Greekes cal it) of the   page 67 /   writer. But let this bee a sufficient, though short note, that wee misse the right vse of the materiall point of Poesie.

Now, for the out-side of it, which is words, or (as I may tearme it) *Diction*, it is euen well worse. So is that honny-flowing Matron Eloquence, apparelled, or rather disguised, in a Curtizan-like painted affectation: one time with so farre fette words, they may seeme Monsters: but must seeme straungers to any poore English man. Another tyme, with coursing of a Letter, as if they were bound to followe the method of a Dictionary: an other tyme, with figures and flowers, extreamelie winter-starued. But I would this fault were only peculier to Versifiers, and had not as large possession among Prose-printers; and, (which is to be meruailed) among many Schollers; and, (which is to be pittied) among some Preachers. . . .

. . . Now for similitudes, in certaine printed discourses, I thinke all Herbarists, all stories of Beasts, Foules, and Fishes, are rifled vp, that they come in page 68 /   multitudes, to waite vpon any of our conceits; which certainly is as absurd a surfet to the eares, as is possible: for the force of a similitude, not being to prooue anything to a contrary Disputer, but onely to explane to a willing hearer, when that is done, the rest is a most tedious pratling: rather ouer-swaying the memory from the purpose whereto they were ap-plyed, then any whit informing the iudgement, already eyther satisfied, or by similitudes not to be satisfied. . . .   page 69 /

Now, of versifying there are two sorts, the one Auncient, the other Moderne: the Auncient marked the quantitie of each silable, and according to that, framed his verse: the Moderne, obseruing onely number, (with some regarde of the accent,) the chiefe life of it, standeth in that lyke sounding of the words, which wee call Ryme. Whether of these be the most excellent, would beare many speeches. The Auncient, (no doubt) more fit for Musick, both words and tune, obseruing quantity, and more fit liuely to expresse diuers passions, by the low and lofty sounde of the well-weyed silable. The latter likewise, with hys Ryme, striketh a certaine musick to the eare: and in fine, sith it dooth delight, though by another way, it obtaines the same purpose: for beeing in eyther sweetnes, and wanting in neither maiestie.

Truely the English, before any other vulgar language I know, is fit for both sorts: for, for the Ancient, the Italian is so full of Vowels, that it must euer be cumbred with *Elisions*. The Dutch, so of the other side with Consonants, that they cannot yeeld the sweet slyding, fit for **page 70 /** a Verse. The French, in his whole language, hath not one word, that hath his accent in the last silable, sauing two, called *Antepenultima*, and little more hath the Spanish: and therefore, very gracelesly may they vse *Dactiles*. The English is subiect to none of these defects.

Nowe, for the ryme, though wee do not obserue quantity, yet wee ob-serue the accent very precisely: which other languages eyther cannot doe, or will not doe so absolutely. That *Caesura*, or breathing place in the mid-dest of the verse, neither Italian nor Spanish haue, the French, and we, neuer almost fayle of. Lastly, euen the very ryme it selfe, the Italian cannot put in the last silable, by the French named the Masculine ryme, but still in the next to the last, which the French call the Female; or the next before that, which the Italians terme *Sdrucciola*. The example of the former, is *Buono, Suono*, of the *Sdrucciola, Femina, Semina*. The French, of the other side, hath both the Male, as *Bon, Son*, and the Female, as *Plaise, Taise*. But the *Sdrucciola*, hee hath not: where the English hath all three, as *Due, True, Father, Rather, Motion, Potion;* with much more which might be sayd, but that I finde already, the triflingnes of this discourse, is much too much enlarged. So that sith the euer-praise-worthy Poesie, is full of vertue-breeding delightfulnes, and voyde of no gyfte, that ought to be in the noble name of learning: sith the blames laid against it, are either false, or feeble: sith the cause why it is not esteemed in Englande, is the fault of Poet-apes, not Poets: sith lastly, our tongue is most fit to honor Poesie, and to bee honored by Poesie, I coniure you all . . . no more to scorne the sacred misteries of Poesie: no more to laugh at the name of Poets, as though they were next inheritours to Fooles: no more to iest at the reuerent title of a Rymer: but to beleeue with *Aristotle*, that they were the auncient Treasurers, of the Graecians Diuinity. To beleeue with *Bembus*, that they were first bringers **page 71 /**   in of all ciuilitie. To beleeue with *Scaliger*, that no Philosophers precepts can sooner make you an honest man, then the reading of *Virgill*. To beleeue with *Clauserus*, the Translator of *Cornutus*, that it pleased the heauenly Deitie, by *Hesiod* and *Homer*, vnder the vayle of fables, to giue vs all knowledge, Logick, Rethorick, Philosophy, naturall, and morall. . . . To beleeue with me, that there are many misteries contained in Poetrie, which of purpose were written darkely, least by prophane wits, it should bee abused. To beleeue with *Landin*, that they are so beloued of the Gods, that whatsoeuer they write, proceeds of a diuine fury. Lastly, to beleeue themselues, when they tell you they will make you immortall, by their verses.

Thus doing, your name shal florish in the Printers shoppes; thus doing, you shall bee of kinne to many a poeticall Preface; thus doing, you shall be most fayre, most ritch, most wise, most all, you shall dwell vpon Super-latiues. . . . Thus doing, your soule shal be placed with *Dantes Beatrix*, or *Virgils Anchises*. But if, (fie of such a but) you be borne so neere the dull making *Cataphract* of *Nilus*, that you cannot heare the Plannet-like Musick of Poetrie, if you haue so earth-creeping a mind, that it cannot lift itselfe vp, to looke to the sky of Poetry: or rather, by a certaine rusticall disdaine, will become such a Mome, as to be a *Momus* of Poetry: then, though I will not wish vnto you, the Asses eares of *Midas*, nor to bee driuen by a Poets verses, (as *Bubonax* was) to hang himselfe, nor to be rimed to death, as is sayd to be doone in Ireland: yet thus much curse I must send you, in the behalfe of all Poets, that while you liue, you liue in loue, and neuer get fauour, for lacking skill of a *Sonnet:* and when you die, your memory die from the earth, for want of an *Epitaph.*   **page 72 /**

Edmund Spenser (1552–1599), one of the most learned of the English poets, was also among those most generally admired. While at Pembroke Hall, Cambridge, he formed an intimate friendship with Gabriel Harvey and Edward Kirke, who first recognized and encouraged his poetic genius. He lived for a time at Leicester House and formed a close association with Sir Philip Sidney. He was a member of the Areopagus, which apparently met at Leicester House in 1578–1579, where he, Sidney, Dyer, Drant, and others debated and experimented with the application of classical rules of quantity to English meter. Letters exchanged between Spenser and Harvey in 1579–1580 make reference to this interest. The correspondence was published in 1580 by Henry Bynneman in two volumes: "Three proper and wittie familiar Letters: lately passed betwene two Universitie men: touching the Earthquake in Aprill last, and our English refourmed Versifying. — With the Preface of a wellwiller to them both" and "Two other very commendable Letters, of the same mens writing: both touching the foresaid Artificiall Versifying, and certain other Particulars. — More lately delivered unto the Printer." The letters dealt principally with the questions of versification and Spenser's literary projects, the latter subject especially intriguing; for example, the Nine Comedies, the Dreames, and the Dying Pellicane cannot now be identified. Other references suggest works which seem to have been incorporated into later poems.

The Shepherd's Calendar, a series of twelve eclogues in the pastoral tradition of Theocritus, Bion, Marot, and Mantuan, dedicated to Sidney, brought general literary acclaim to Spenser. An interesting feature of the work is the "Epistle," notes, and glossary appended by E. K. (generally identified as Edward Kirke), who analyzes Spenser's relationship to the pastoral tradition, the language and intent of the eclogues, and the poet's particular contribution.

The "Letter to Sir Walter Raleigh" might well be supplemented by the October eclogue of the Shepherd's Calendar in order to gain a fuller view of Spenser's critical position. As the letter suggests, Spenser requires his poem to serve a didactic purpose — the Faerie Queene is in design a moral treatise, "the general end ... is to fashion a gentleman or noble person in virtuous and gentle discipline."

Spenser's contribution to the language is immeasurable. His contemporaries regarded him as Chaucer's successor, and his continuing influence upon succeeding poets has proved the appropriateness of the judgment.

Edmund Spenser. *The Shepheardes Calendar* (1579) in *The Complete Works of Edmund Spenser*. Edited by R. Morris, London, 1869.

"The Epistle"

To the Most Excellent and Learned, Both Orator and Poete, Mayster Gabriell Harvey, His Verie Special and Singular Good Frend E. K. Commendeth the Good Lyking of This His Labour, and the Patronage of the New Poete.

Uncouthe, unkiste, sayde the old famous Poete Chaucer: whom for his excellencie and wonderfull skil in making, his scholler Lidgate, a worthy scholler of so excellent a maister, calleth the Loadestarre of our Language: and whom our Colin Clout in his Aeglogue calleth Tityrus the God of shepheards, comparing hym to the worthines of the Roman Tityrus, Virgile. Which proverbe, myne owne good friend Ma. Harvey, as in that good old Poete it served well Pandares purpose for the bolstering of his baudy brocage, so very well taketh place in this our new Poete, who for that he is uncouthe (as said Chaucer) is unkist, and unknown to most men, is regarded but of few. But I dout not, so soone as his name shall come into the knowledge of men, and his worthines be sounded in the tromp of fame, but that he shall be not onely kiste, but also beloved of all, embraced of the most, and wondred at of the best. No lesse, I thinke, deserveth his wittinesse in devising, his pithinesse in uttering, his complaints of love so lovely, his discourses of pleasure so pleasantly, his pastoral rudenesse, his morall wisenesse, his dewe observing of Decorum everye where, in personages, in seasons, in matter, in speach; and generally, in al seemely simplycitie of handeling his matter, and framing his words: the which of many thinges which in him be straunge, I know will seeme the straungest, the words them selves being so auncient, the knitting of them so short and intricate, and the whole Periode and compasse of speache so delightsome for the roundnesse, and so grave for the straungenesse. And firste of the wordes to speake, I graunt they be something hard, and of most men unused, yet both English, and also used of most excellent Authors, and most famous Poetes. In whom, whenas this our Poet hath bene much traveiled and throughly redd, how could it be, (as that worthy Oratour sayde) but that walking in the sonne, although for other cause he walked, yet needes he mought be sunburnt; and, having the sound of those auncient Poetes still ringing in his eares, he mought needes, in singing, hit out some of theyr tunes. But whether he useth them by such casualtye and custome, or of set purpose and choyse, as thinking them fittest for such rusticall rudenesse of shepheards, eyther for that theyr rough sounde would make his rymes more ragged and rustical, or els because such olde and obsolete wordes are most used of country folke, sure I think, and think I think not amisse, that they bring great grace, and, as one would say, auctoritie to the verse. For albe, amongst many other faultes, it specially be objected of Valla against Livie, and of other against Saluste, that with over much studie they affect antiquitie, as coveting thereby credence and honor of elder yeeres, yet I am of opinion, and eke the best learned are of the lyke, that those auncient solemne wordes are a great ornament, both in the one, and in the other;

the one labouring to set forth in hys worke an eternall image of antiquitie, and the other carefully discoursing matters of gravitie and importaunce. For, if my memory faile not, Tullie, in that booke wherein he endevoureth to set forth the paterne of a perfect Oratour, sayth that ofttimes an auncient worde maketh the style seeme grave, and as it were page 441 / reverend, no otherwise then we honour and reverence gray heares, for a certein religious regard, which we have of old age. Yet nether every where must old words be stuffed in, nor the common Dialecte and maner of speaking so corrupted therby, that, as in old buildings, it seme disorderly and ruinous. But all as in most exquisite pictures they use to blaze and portraict not only the daintie lineaments of beautye, but also rounde about it to shadowe the rude thickets and craggy clifts, that, by the basenesse of such parts, more excellency may accrew to the principall; for oftimes we fynde our selves, I know not how, singularly delighted with the shewe of such naturall rudenesse, and take great pleasure in that disorderly order. Even so doe those rough and harsh termes enlumine, and make more clearly to appeare, the brightnesse of brave and glorious words. So oftentimes a dischorde in Musick maketh a comely concordaunce: so great delight tooke the worthy Poete Alceus to behold a blemish in the joynt of a wel shaped body. But, if any will rashly blame such his purpose in choyse of old and unwonted words, him may I more justly blame and condemne, or of witlesse headinesse in judging, or of heedelesse hardinesse in condemning; for, not marking the compasse of hys bent, he wil judge of the length of his cast: for in my opinion it is one special prayse of many, whych are dew to this Poete, that he hath laboured to restore, as to theyr rightfull heritage, such good and naturall English words, as have ben long time out of use, and almost cleane disherited. Which is the onely cause, that our Mother tonge, which truely of it self is both ful enough for prose, and stately enough for verse, hath long time ben counted most bare and barrein of both. Which default whenas some endevoured to salve and recure, they patched up the holes with peces and rags of other languages, borrowing here of the French, there of the Italian, every where of the Latine; not weighing how il those tongues accorde with themselves, but much worse with ours: So now they have made our English tongue a gallimaufray, or hodgepodge of al other speches. Other some, not so wel seene in the English tonge as perhaps in other languages, if they happen to here an olde word, albeit very naturall and significant, crye out streightway, that we speak no English, but gibbrish, or rather such as in old time Evanders mother spake: whose first shame is, that they are not ashamed, in their own mother tonge, to be counted straungers and alienes. The second shame no lesse then the first, that what so they understand not, they streight way deeme to be senselesse, and not at al to be understode. . . . The last, more shameful then both, that of their owne country and natural speach, which together with their Nources milk they sucked, they have so base regard and bastard judgement, that they will not onely themselves not labor to garnish and beautifie it, but also repine, that of other it shold be embellished. . . .

Now, for the knitting of sentences, whych they call the joynts and members therof, and for al the compasse of the speach, it is round without roughnesse, and learned without hardnes, such indeede as may be perceived of the leaste, understoode of the moste, but judged onely of the learned. For what in most English wryters used to be loose, and as it were ungyrt, in this Authour is well grounded, finely framed, and strongly trussed up together. In regard wherof, I scorne and spue out the rakehellye route of our ragged rymers (for so themselves use to hunt the letter) which without learning boste, without judgement jangle, without reason rage and fome, as if some instinct of Poeticall spirite had newly ravished them above the meanenesse of common capacitie. And being, in the middest of all theyr bravery, sodenly, eyther for want of matter, or of ryme, or having forgotten theyr former conceipt, they seeme to be so pained and traveiled in theyr remembrance, as it were a woman in childebirth. . . .

Nethelesse, let them a Gods name feede on theyr owne folly, so they seeke not to darken the beames of others glory. As for Colin, under whose person the Authour selfe is shadowed, how furre he is from such vaunted titles and glorious showes, both him selfe sheweth, where he sayth,

'Of Muses Hobbin, I conne no skill.

And

'Enough is me to paint out my unrest, &c.'

And also appeareth by the basenesse of the name, wherein it semeth he chose rather to unfold great matter of argument covertly then,   **page 442 /** professing it, not suffice thereto accordingly. Which moved him rather in Aeglogues then other wise to write, doubting perhaps his habilitie, which he little needed, or mynding to furnish our tongue with this kinde, wherein it faulteth; or following the example of the best and most auncient Poetes, which devised this kind of wryting, being both so base for the matter, and homely for the manner, at the first to trye theyr habilities; and as young birdes, that be newly crept out of the nest, by little first to prove theyr tender wyngs, before they make a greater flyght. So flew Theocritus, as you may perceive he was all ready full fledged. So flew Virgile, as not yet well feeling his winges. So flew Mantuane, as not being full somd. So Petrarque. So Boccace. So Marot, Sanazarus, and also divers other excellent both Italian and French Poetes, whose foting this Author every where followeth; yet so as few, but they be wel sented, can trace him out. So finally flyeth this our new Poete as a birde whose principals be scarce growen out, but yet as one that in time shall be hable to keepe wing with the best.

 . . . And thus recommending the Author unto you, as unto his most special good frend, and my selfe unto you both, as one making singuler account of two so very good and so choise frends, I bid you both most hartely farwel, and commit you and your commendable studies to the tuicion of the Greatest.

Your owne assuredly to be commaunded,

E. K.   **page 443 /**

"Letters From Spenser (Immerito) to Gabriel Harvey." Reprinted in *The Complete Works of Edmund Spenser*. Edited by R. Morris, London, 1869.

To the Worshipfull His Very Singular Good Friend, Maister G. H.
Fellow of Trinitie Hall in Cambridge.

Good Master G. I perceive by your most curteous and frendly Letters your good will to be no lesse in deed than I alwayes esteemed. In recompence wherof, think I beseech you, that I wil spare neither speech nor wryting, nor aught else, whensoever, and wheresoever occasion shal be offred me: yea, I will not stay, till it be offred, but will seeke it in al that possibly I may. And that you may perceive how much your Counsel in al things prevaileth with me, and how altogither I am ruled and over-ruled thereby: I am now determined to alter mine owne former purpose, and to subscribe to your advizement: being notwithstanding resolved stil, to abide your farther resolution. My principal doubts are these. First, I was minded for a while to have intermitted the uttering of my writings: leaste by over-much cloying their noble eares, I should gather a contempt of myself, or else seeme rather for gaine and commoditie to doe it, for some sweetnesse that I have already tasted. Then also, meseemeth, the work too base for his excellent Lordship, being made in honour of a private Personage unknowne, which of some yl-willers might be upbraided not to be so worthie, as you knowe she is: or the matter not so weightie, that it should be offred to so weightie a Personage: or the like. The selfe former Title still liketh me well ynough, and your fine Addition no lesse. If these, and the like doubtes, maye be of importaunce in your seeming, to frustrate any parte of your advice, I beseeche you without the least selfe love of your own purpose, councell me for the beste: and the rather doe it faithfullye and carefully, for that, in all things I attribute so muche to your judgement, that I am evermore content to annihilate mine owne determinations, in respecte thereof. And indeede for your selfe to, it sitteth with you now, to call your wits and senses togither (which are alwaies at call) when occasion is so fairely offered of Estimation and Preferment. For whiles the iron is hote, it is good striking, and minds of Nobles varie as their Estates....

I pray you bethinke you well hereof, good Maister G. and forthwith write me those two or three special points and caveats for the nonce.... Your desire to heare of my late being with hir Majestie muste dye in it selfe. As for the twoo worthy Gentlemen, Master *Sidney* and Master *Dyer*, they have me, I thanke them, in some use of familiarity: of whom and to whome, what speache passeth for youre credite and estimation, I leave to your selfe to conceive, having alwayes so well conceived of my unfained affection and zeale towardes you. And nowe they have proclaimed...a generall surceasing and silence of balde Rymers, and also of the verie beste to: in steade wherof they haue, by authoritie of their whole Senate, prescribed certaine Lawes and rules of Quantities of Englishe sillables for English Verse: having had thereof already great practise, and drawen mee to their faction. Newe Bookes I heare of none, but only of one, that writing a certaine Booke, called *The Schoole of Abuse,* and dedicating it to Maister

Sidney, was for his labor scorned: if at leaste it be in the goodnesse of that nature to scorne. Suche follie is it, not to regarde aforehande the inclination and qualitie of him to whome wee dedicate oure Bookes. Suche mighte I happily incurre entituling *My Slomber* and the other Pamphlets unto his honor. I meant them rather to Maister *Dyer.* But I am of late more in love wyth my Englishe Versifying than with Ryming: whyche I should haue done long since, if I would then haue followed your councell. . . .
page 706 /

·   ·   ·   ·   ·   ·   ·   ·   ·   ·   ·   ·   ·

Leycester House, this 5 [?16] of October, 1579.

> *Per mare, per terras,*
> *Vivus, mortuusque*
> *Tuus Immerito.*

To My Long Approoved and Singular Good Frende, Master G. H.

Good Master H. I doubt not but you have some great important matter in hande, which al this while restraineth your Penne, and wonted readinesse in provoking me unto that, wherein your selfe nowe faulte. If there bee any such thing in hatching, I pray you hartily, lette us knowe, before al the worlde see it. But if happly you dwell altogither in Justinians Courte, and give your selfe to be devoured of secreate Studies, as of all likelyhood you doe: yet at least imparte some your olde, or newe Latine or Englishe, Eloquent and Gallant Poesies to us, from whose eyes, you saye, you keepe in a manner nothing hidden. Little newes is here stirred: but that olde great matter still depending. His Honoure never better. I thinke the *Earthquake* was also there wyth you (which I would gladly learne) as it was here with us: overthrowing divers old buildings and peeces of Churches. Sure verye   page 708 /   straunge to be hearde of in these Countries, and yet I heare some saye (I knowe not howe truely) that they have knowne the like before in their dayes. . . . I like your late Englishe Hexameters so exceedingly well, that I also enure my Penne sometime in that kinde: whyche I fynd indeede, as I have heard you often defende in worde, neither so harde, nor so harshe, that it will easily and fairely yeelde it selfe to our Moother tongue. For the onely, or chiefest hardnesse, whych seemeth, is in the Accente: whyche sometime gapeth, and, as it were, yawneth ilfavouredly, comming shorte of that it should, and sometime exceeding the measure of the Number, as in *Carpenter,* the middle sillable being used shorte in speache, when it shall be read long in Verse, seemeth like a lame *Gosling that draweth one legge after hir:* and *Heaven* being used shorte as one sillable, when it is in verse stretched out with a Diastole, is like a *lame dogge that holdes up one legge.* But it is to be wonne with Custome, and rough words must be subdued with Use. For, why a Gods name, may not we, as else the Greekes, have the kingdome of oure owne Language, and measure our Accentes by the sounde, reserving the Quantitie to the Verse? Loe, here I let you see my olde use of toying in Rymes

turned into your artificial straightnesse of Verse by this *Tetrasticon*. I beseech you tell me your fansie without parcialitie.

> See yee the blindfoulded pretie God, that feathered Archer,
> Of Lovers Miseries which maketh his bloodie game?
> Wote ye why, his Moother with a Veale hath coovered his Face?
> Trust me, least he my Loove happely chaunce to beholde.

Seeme they comparable to those two, which I translated you *ex tempore*
in bed, the last time we lay togither in Westminster?

> That which I eate did I joy, and that which I greedily gorged,
> As for those many goodly matters leaft I for others.

I would hartily wish, you would either send me the Rules and Precepts
of Arte, which you observe in Quantities, or else follow mine, that M.
Philip Sidney gave me, being the very same which M. Drant devised, but
enlarged with M. Sidneys own judgement, and augmented with my Observations, that we might both accorde and agree in one: leaste we over-
throwe one an other, and be overthrown of the rest. Trust me, you will
hardly beleeve what greate good liking and estimation Maister *Dyer* had of
your *Satyricall Verses*, and I, since the viewe thereof, having before of my
selfe had speciall liking of *Englishe Versifying*, am even nowe aboute to
give you some token, what, and howe well therein I am able to doe: for,
to tell you trueth, I minde shortely at convenient leysure, to sette forth a
Booke in this kinde, whiche I entitle *Epithalamion Thamesis;* whyche Booke,
I dare undertake wil be very profitable for the knowledge, and rare for
the Invention and manner of handling. For in setting forth the marriage of
the Thames: I shewe his first beginning, and offspring, and all the Countrey, that he passeth thorough, and also describe all the Rivers throughout
Englande, whyche came to this Wedding, and their righte names, and right
passage, &c. A worke, beleeve me, of much labour, wherein notwithstanding Master *Holinshed* hath muche furthered and advantaged me, who therein
hath bestowed singular paines, in searching oute their firste heades and
sources: and also in tracing and dogging oute all their Course, til they fall
into the Sea. . . . Nowe, my *Dreames* and *Dying Pellicane*, being fully finished (as I partelye signified in my laste Letters) and presentlye to bee
imprinted, I wil in hande forthwith with my *Faery Queene*, whyche I
praye you hartily send me with al expedition: and your frendly Letters, and
long expected Judgement wythal, whyche let not be shorte, but in all pointes
suche, as you ordinarilye use, and I extraordinarily desire. *Multum vale.*
Westminster. Quarto Nonas Aprilis 1580. . . .

Yours alwayes to commaunde,

Immerito.

Postscripte.

I take best my *Dreames* shoulde come forth alone, being growen by
meanes of the Glosse (running continually in maner of a Paraphrase) full as

great as my *Calendar*. Therin be some things excellently, and many things wittily discoursed of E.K. and the pictures so singularly set forth and purtrayed, as if Michael Angelo were there, he could (I think) nor amende the beste, nor reprehende the worst. I know you woulde lyke them passing wel. Of my *Stemmata Dudleiana*, and especially of the sundry Apostrophes therein, addressed you knowe to whome, must more advisement be had, than so lightly to sende them abroade: howbeit, trust me (though I doe never very well) yet, in my owne fancie, I never dyd better. . . .

EXTRACT FROM HARVEY'S REPLY.

But Master *Collin Cloute* is not every body, and albeit his olde Companions, *Master Cuddy* and *Master Hobbinoll* be as little beholding to their *Mistresse Poetrie*, as ever you writ: yet he peradventure by the meanes of hir special favour, and some personall priviledge, may happely live by *Dying Pellicanes*, and purchase great landes, and lordshippes, with the money, which his *Calendar* and *Dreames* have, and will affourde him. *Extra jocum*, I like your *Dreames* passingly well: and the rather, bicause they savour of that singular extraordinarie veine and invention, which I ever fancied moste, and in a maner admired onelye in *Lucian, Petrarche, Aretine, Pasquill*, and all the most deli-   page 709 /   cate, and fine conceited Grecians and Italians: (for the Romanes to speake of, are but verye ciphars in this kinde:) whose chiefest endevour, and drifte was, to have nothing vulgare, but in some respecte or other, and especially in *lively hyperbolicall amplifications*, rare, queint, and odde in every pointe, and as a man would saye, a degree or two at the leaste, above the reache, and compasse of a common schollers capacitie. In whiche respecte notwithstanding, as well for the singularitie of the manner, as the Divinitie of the matter, I hearde once a Divine, preferre *Saint Johns Revelation* before al the veriest *Metaphysicall Visions*, and jollyest conceited *Dreames* or *Extasies*, that ever were devised by one or other, howe admirable, or super excellent soever they seemed otherwise to the worlde. And truely I am so confirmed in this opinion, that when I bethinke me of the verie notablest, and moste wonderful Propheticall, or Poeticall Vision, that ever I read, or hearde, me seemeth the proportion is so unequall, that there hardly appeareth anye semblaunce of Comparison: no more in a maner (especially for Poets) then doth betweene the incomprehensible Wisdome of God, and the sensible Wit of man.

But what needeth this digression between you and me? I dare saye you wyll holde yourselfe reasonably wel satisfied, if youre *Dreames* be but as well esteemed of in Englande, as *Petrarches Visions* be in Italy: which I assure you, is the very worst I wish you. But, see, how I have the Arte *Memorative* at commaundement. In good faith I had once againe nigh forgotten your *Faerie Queene:* howbeit by good chaunce, I have nowe sent hir home at the laste, neither in better nor worse case, then I founde hir. And must you of necessitie have my judgement of hir indeede? To be plaine, I am voyde of al judgement, if your *Nine Comedies*, whereunto in imitation of *Herodotus*, you give the names of the *Nine Muses* (and in one mans fansie not unworthily) come not neerer *Ariostoes Comoedies*, eyther for the finenesse of plausible Elocution, or the rarenesse of Poetical Invention, then that *Elvish Queene* doth to his *Orlando Furioso,* which notwithstanding, you wil needes seeme to emulate, and hope to overgo, as you flatly professed yourself in one of your last Letters.

Besides that you know, it hath bene the usual practise of the most exquisite and odde wittes in all nations, and specially in *Italie,* rather to shewe, and advaunce themselves that way, then any other: as namely, those three notorious dyscoursing heads, *Bibiena, Machiavel,* and *Aretine* did, (to let *Bembo* and *Ariosto* passe) with the great admiration, and wonderment of the whole country: being in deede reputed matchable in all points, both for conceyt of Witte and eloquent decyphering of matters, either with *Aristophanes* and *Menander* in Greek, or with *Plautus* and *Terence* in Latin, or with any other, in any other tong. But I wil not stand greatly with you in your owne matters. If so be the *Faerye Queene* be fairer in your eie than the *Nine Muses,* and *Hobgoblin* runne away with the Garland from *Apollo:* Marke what I saye, and yet I will not say that I thought, but there an End for this once, and fare you well, till God or some good Aungell putte you in a better minde.   **page 710 /**

Edmund Spenser. "A Letter of the Authors, ... to the Right Noble and
     Valorous Sir Walter Raleigh. . . ." in *The Complete Works of Edmund
     Spenser.* Edited by R. Morris, London, 1869.

Sir, knowing how doubtfully all Allegories may be construed, and this booke of mine, which I have entituled the Faery Queene, being a continued Allegory, or darke conceit, I haue thought good, as well for avoyding of gealous opinions and misconstructions, as also for your better light in reading thereof, (being so by you commanded,) to discover unto you the general intention and meaning, which in the whole course thereof I have fashioned, without expressing of any particular purposes, or by accidents, therein occasioned. The generall end therefore of all the booke is to fashion a gentleman or noble person in vertuous and gentle discipline: Which for that I conceived shoulde be most plausible and pleasing, being coloured with an historicall fiction, the which the most part of men delight to read, rather for variety of matter then for profite of the ensample, I chose the historye of King Arthure, as most fitte for the excellency of his person, being made famous by many mens former workes, and also furthest from the daunger of envy, and suspition of present time. In which I have followed all the antique Poets historicall; first Homere, who in the Persons of Agamemnon and Ulysses hath ensampled a good governour and a vertuous man, the one in his Ilias, the other in his Odysseis: then Virgil, whose like intention was to doe in the person of Aeneas: after him Ariosto comprised them both in his Orlando, and lately Tasso dissevered them againe, and formed both parts in two persons, namely that part which they in Philosophy call Ethice, or vertues of a private man, coloured in his Rinaldo; the other named Politice in his Godfredo. By ensample of which excellente Poets, I labour to pourtraict in Arthure, before he was king, the image of a brave knight, perfected in the twelve private morall vertues, as Aristotle hath devised; the which is the purpose of these first twelve bookes: which if I finde to be well accepted, I may be perhaps encoraged to frame the other part of polliticke vertues in his person, after that hee came to be king.

To some, I know, this Methode well seeme displeasaunt, which had rather have good discipline delivered plainly in way of precepts, or sermoned at large, as they use, then thus clowdily enwrapped in Allegoricall devises. But such, me seeme, should be satisfide with the use of these dayes, seeing all things accounted by their showes, and nothing esteemed of, that is not delightfull and pleasing to commune sence. For this cause is Xenophon preferred before Plato, for that the one, in the exquisite depth of his judgement, formed a Commune welth, such as it should be; but the other in the person of Cyrus, and the Persians, fashioned a government, such as might best be: So much more profitable and gratious is doctrine by ensample, then by rule. So haue I laboured to doe in the person of Arthure: whome I conceive, after his long education by Timon, to whom he was by Merlin delivered to be brought up, so soone as he was borne of the Lady Igrayne, to have seene in a dream or vision the Faery Queen, with whose excellent beauty ravished, he awaking resolved to seeke her out; and so being by Merlin armed, and by Timon throughly instructed, he went to seeke her forth in Faerye land. In that Faery Queene I mean glory in my generall intention, but in my particular I conceive the most excellent and glorious person of our soveraine the Queene, and her kingdome in Faery land. And yet, in some places els, I doe otherwise shadow her. For considering she beareth two persons, the one of a most royall Queene or Empresse, the other of a most vertuous and beautifull Lady, this latter page 3 / part in some places I doe expresse in Belphoebe, fashioning her name according to your owne excellent conceipt of Cynthia, (Phoebe and Cynthia being both names of Diana.) So in the person of Prince Arthure I sette forth magnificence in particular; which vertue, for that (according to Aristotle and the rest) it is the perfection of all the rest, and conteineth in it them all, therefore in the whole course I mention the deedes of Arthure applyable to that vertue, which I write of in that booke. But of the xii. other vertues, I make xii. other knights the patrones, for the more variety of the history: Of which these three bookes contayn three.

The first of the knight of the Redcrosse, in whome I express Holynes: The seconde of Sir Guyon, in whome I sette forth Temperaunce: The third of Britomartis, a Lady Knight, in whome I picture Chastity. But, because the beginning of the whole worke seemeth abrupte, and as depending upon other antecedents, it needs that ye know the occasion of these three knights seuerall adventures. For the Methode of a Poet historical is not such, as of an Historiographer. For an Historiographer discourseth of affayres orderly as they were donne, accounting as well the times as the actions; but a Poet thrusteth into the middest, even where it most concerneth him, and there recoursing to the thinges forepaste, and divining of things to come, maketh a pleasing Analysis of all. . . .

Thus much, Sir, I have briefly overronne to direct your understanding to the wel-head of the History; that from thence gathering the whole intention of the conceit, ye may as in a handfull gripe al the discourse.... So, humbly craving the continuance of your honorable favour towards me, and th' eternall establishment of your happines, I humbly take leave.

23. Ianuary 1589,

Yours most humbly affectionate,

Ed. Spenser. page 4 /

John Stow (1525?–1605), chronicler and antiquarian, began in 1560 to collect printed books, legal and literary documents, charters, and transcriptions of ancient MSS and inscriptions. In 1565 he published A Summary of English Chronicles; *later he contributed to the enlarged second edition of Holinshed's* Chronicle (1587). *One of his major works was* The Chronicles of England from Brute unto this present year... 1580, *revised and brought up to date under the new title* The Annals of England (1592), *and continued after Stow's death by Edmund Howe, beginning in 1615. The* Svrvay of London (1598), *perhaps his greatest work, is invaluable for detailed information about the city and English customs during Elizabeth's reign.*

John Stow. *A Svrvay of London, Contayning the Originall, Antiquity, Increase, Moderne Estate, and Description of that Citie,* Written in the Year 1598. Edited by Henry Morley, London, 1893.

Sports and Pastimes of old Time used in this City.

...Of late time...hath been used comedies, tragedies, interludes, and histories, both true and feigned; for the acting whereof certain public places, as the Theatre, the Curtain, &c., have been erected. Also cocks of the game are yet cherished by divers men for their pleasures, much money being laid on their heads, when they fight in pits, whereof some be costly made for that purpose. The ball is used by noblemen and gentlemen in tennis courts, and by people of meaner sort in the open fields and streets.

The marching forth of citizens' sons, and other young men on horseback, with disarmed lances and shields, there to practise feats of war, man against man, hath long since been left off, but in their stead they have used on horseback to run at a dead mark, called a quintain. . . . **page 119 /** This exercise of running at the quintain was practised by the youthful citizens as well in summer as in winter, namely, in the feast of Christmas, I have seen a quintain set upon Cornhill, by the Leadenhall, where the attendants on the lords of merry disports have run, and made great pastime; for he that hit not the broad end of the quintain was of all men laughed to scorn, and he that hit it full, if he rid not the faster, had a sound blow in his neck with a bag full of sand hung on the other end. I have also in the summer season seen some upon the river of Thames rowed in wherries, with staves in their hands, flat at the fore end, running one against another, and for the most part, one or both overthrown, and well ducked.

On the holy days in summer the youths of this city have in the field exercised themselves in leaping, dancing, shooting, wrestling, casting of the stone or ball, &c. **page 120 /**

. . . .

Farringdon Ward.

... Then is the north churchyard of Paul's, in the which standeth the cathedral church, first founded by Ethelbert, king of Kent, about the year of Christ 610. ...   **page 307 /**

[The] steeple was repaired in the year 1462, and the weathercocks again erected. ... Since the which time, needing reparation, it was both taken down and set up in the year 1553. At which time it was found to be of copper, gilt over; and the length from the bill to the tail being four feet, and the breadth over the wings three feet and a half, it weighed forty pounds; the cross from the bowl to the eagle, or cock, was fifteen feet and six inches of assize; the length thereof overthuart was five feet and ten inches, and the compass of the bowl was nine feet and one inch.

The inner body of this cross was oak, the next cover was lead, and the uttermost was of copper, red varnished. The bowl and the eagle, or cock, were of copper, and gilt also.

The height of the steeple was five hundred and twenty feet, whereof the stone work is two hundred and sixty feet, and the spire was likewise two hundred and sixty feet. The length of the whole church is two hundred and forty tailors' yards, which make seven hundred and twenty feet; the breadth thereof is one hundred and thirty feet; and the height of the body of that church is one hundred and fifty feet. The church hath a bishop, a dean, a precentor, chancellor, treasurer, and five archdeacons; to wit, of London, Middlesex, Essex, Colchester, and St. Albans. It hath prebendaries thirty, canons twelve, vicars choral six, &c. ...

There was also one great cloister, on the north side of this church, environing a plot of ground, of old time called Pardon Churchyard, whereof Thomas More, Dean of Paul's, was either the first builder, or a most especial benefactor, and was buried there. About this cloister was artificially and richly painted the Dance of   **page 309 /**   Machabray, or Dance of Death, commonly called the Dance of Paul's, like whereof was painted about St. Innocent's cloister at Paris, in France. The metres, or poesy of this dance, were translated out of the French into English by John Lidgate, monk of Bury, and with the picture of death leading all estates, painted about the cloister, at the special request and at the dispence of Jenkin Carpenter, in the reign of Henry VI. In this cloister were buried many persons, some of worship, and others of honour, the monuments of whom, in number and curious workmanship, passed all other that were in that church.

Over the east quadrant of this cloister was a fair library . . . , which hath been well furnished with fair written books in vellum, but few of them now do remain there. ...   **page 310 /**

At the west end of this Jesus' Chapel, under the choir of Paul's, also was a parish church of St. Faith, commonly called St. Faith under Paul's, which served for the stationers and others dwelling in Paul's Churchyard, Paternoster Row, and the places near adjoining. ...

Then was there on the north side of this churchyard a large charnel house for the bones of the dead, and over it a chapel, . . . all of which were pulled down in the year 1549. The bones of the dead couched up in a charnel under the chapel, were conveyed from thence to Finsbury field, by report of him who paid for the carriage, amounting to more than one thousand cart-loads, and there laid on a moorish ground, in short space after **page 311 /** raised, by soilage of the city upon them, to bear three windmills. The chapel and charnel were converted into dwelling-houses, ware-houses, and sheds before them, for stationers, in place of the tombs.

In the east part of this churchyard standeth Paul's School, lately new built, and endowed in the year 1512 by John Colet, Doctor of Divinity and Dean of Paul's, for one hundred and fifty-three poor men's children, to be taught free in the same school, for which he appointed a master, a sur-master, or usher, and a chaplain, with large stipends for ever, committing the oversight thereof to the masters, wardens, and assistants of the mercers in London, because he was son to Henry Colet, mercer, sometime mayor. He left to these mercers lands to the yearly value of one hundred and twenty pounds, or better. **page 312 /**

Philip Stubbes (fl. 1581–93), Puritan pamphleteer, is noted primarily for his Anatomy of Abuses *(1583), in which he denounced what he felt to be the evil customs of the times. In the preface to the first edition, Stubbes announced that his purpose was not to secure the abolition of all amusements, but only the abuses of them. For example, he admitted that some plays were useful, that dancing in private was permissible, that gaming was wrong only when inflamed with covetousness. Written as a dialogue in which Philoponus, who spent seven years in Ailgna (Anglia), describes to Spudeus the general evil conditions he observed, the work is now valuable as one of the principal sources of information about the manners, fashions, social and economic conditions of England in the late sixteenth century.*

Inasmuch as the dialogue as such is unimportant, only the words of Philoponus are herein reproduced.

Philip Stubbes. *The Anatomie of Abuses.* Reprinted from the third edition of MDLXXXV, under the Superintendence of William B.D.D. Turnbull, Esq., W. Pickering, London: and W. & D. Lang, Edinburgh, MDCCCXXXVI.

Consideryng the innumerable meryades of sondrie fashions daiely inuented. . . . Wherefore, to begin firste with their hattes.

Sometymes they vse them sharpe on the croune, pearking vp like the spere, or shaft of a steeple, standying a quarter of a yarde aboue the crowne of their heades, some more, some lesse, as please the phantasies of their inconstant mindes. Othersome be flat and broad on the crowne, like the battlemētes of a house. An other sorte haue rounde crownes, sometymes with one kinde of band, sometymes with an other, now blacke, now white, nowe russed, now redde, now grene, nowe yellowe, now this, now that, neuer content with one colour or fashion two daies to an ende. . . . And as the fashions bee rare and straunge, so is the stuffe whereof their hattes be made diuers also; for some are of silke, some of ueluet, some of taffatie, some of sarcenet, some of wooll, and, which is more cu- **page 38 /** rious, some of a certaine kinde of fine haire; these they call beuer hattes, of xx. xxx. or xl. shillinges price, fetched from beyonde the seas, from whence a greate sorte of other vanities doe come besides. And so common a thing it is, that euery seruyng man, countrieman, and other, euen all indefferently, dooe weare of these hattes. For he is of no account or estimation amongst men if he haue not a ueluet or taffatie hat, and that must be pincked, and cunnyngly carued of the beste fashion. And good profitable hattes be these, for the longer

The diuersie of hattes in Ailgna.

The sundrie things whereof hattes be made.

you weare thē the fewer holes they haue. Besides this, of late there is a
new fashion of wearyng their hattes sprong vp amongst them, which they
father vpon the Frenchmen, namely, to weare them without bandes, but
how vnsemely (I will not saie how assie) a fashion that is, let the wise
iudge; notwithstanding, howeuer it be, if it please them, it shall not displease
me. And an other sort (as phantasticall as the rest) are content with no
kinde of hat without a greate bunche of feathers of diuers and sondrie
colours, peakyng on top of their heades, not vnlike (I dare not saie) cockes-
combes, but as sternes of pride, and ensignes of vanity. And yet, notwithstanding these flutteryng sailes, and feathered flagges of defiaunce to vertue
(for so they be) are so aduanced in Ailgna, that euery child hath them in
his hat or cap: many get good liuing by dying and selling of them, and not
a few proue thēselues more than fooles in wearyng of them.   page 39 /

Wearyng of hattes without bandes.

Wearyng of feathers in hattes.

[Ruffes:]

They haue great and monsterous ruffes, made either of cambrike, holland, lawne, or els of sōe other the finest cloth that can be got for money,
whereof some be a quarter of a yarde deepe, yea, some more, very fewe
lesse, so that they stande a full quarter of a yearde (and more) from their
necks, hanging ouer their shoulder points in steade of a vaile. But if Æolus
with his blasts, or Neptune with his stormes, chaunce to hit vpon the crasie
barke of their brused ruffes, then they goe flip flap in the winde like ragges
that flew abroade lying vpon their shoulders like the dishcloute of a slut.
But wot you what? the deuill, as he, in the fulnesse of his malice, first inuented these great ruffes, so hath he now found out also two great pillers
to beare vp and maintaine this his kingdome of pride withal (for the deuill
is kyng and prince ouer al the children of pride). The one arch or piller,
whereby his kyngdome of great ruffes is vnderpropped, is a certaine kind
of liquid matter, whiche they call starch, wherein the deuill hath willed
them to washe and diue their ruffes well, whiche, beeyng drie, will then
stande stiffe and inflexible about their neckes. The other piller is a certaine
deuice made of wiers crested for the purpose, whipped ouer either with
gold, thred, siluer, or silke, and this he calleth a supportasse or vnder-
propper; this is to bee applied round about their neckes vnder the ruffe,
vpon the out side   page 40 /   of the bande, to beare vp the whole frame
and bodie of the ruffe, from fallyng and hangyng doune.

Great ruffes deformed and ill fauoured.

Two arches or pillers to vnder- proppe the kingdome of great ruffes with- all vide- licet, supportasses and starche.

So fewe haue of them as almost none is without them, for euery one, how
meane or simple soeuer they bee otherwise, will haue of them three or
fowre a peece for failyng.

Euery pesant hath his stately bandes and monstrous ruffes, how costly soeuer they bee.

Their shirtes, whiche all in a maner doe weare (for if the nobilitie or
gentrie onely did weare them, it were some deale more tollerable), are either
page 41 /   of camericke, hollād, lawne, or els of the finest cloth that maie
be got. And of these kindes of shirtes euery one now doethe weare alike;
so, as it maie be thought, our forefathers haue made their bands and ruffes

The shirtes vsed in Ailgna.

(if they had any at all) of grosser clothe, and baser stuffe, then the worst of our shirtes are now made of nowe a daies. And these shirtes (sometymes it happeneth) are wrought throughout with needle worke of silke, and such like, and curiously stitched with open seame, and many other knackes besides, more than I can describe; in so much, as I haue heard of shirtes that haue cost some ten shillynges, some twenty, some forty, some fiue pound, some twenty nobles, and (which is horrible to heare) some ten pounde a pece — yea, the meanest shirt that commonly is worne of any doth cost a crowne or a noble at the least; and yet this is scarsly thought fine enough for the simplest person that is. **page 42 /**

[Doublets.]

Their dublets are no lesse monstrous thē the rest; for now the fashion is to haue them hang downe to the middle of their theighes, or at least to their priuie members, being so hard quilted, stuffed, bombasted, and sewed, as they can neither worke, nor yet well playe in them, through the excessiue heate thereof; and therefore are forced to weare thē lose about them for the most part, otherwise they could very hardly eyther stoupe or decline to the grounde, so stiffe and sturdy they stand about them. **page 44 /** *The monsterous dublets in Ailgna.*

... I say nothing of what their dubletes be made, some of saten, taffatie, silke, grograine, chamlet, gold, siluer, and what not! slashed, iagged, cut, carued, pincked, and laced with all kinde of costly lace of diuers and sondry colours. ... *Dublets of diuers fashions.*

[Hose.]

Then haue they hosen, whiche, as they be of diuers fashions, so are they of sundry names. Some be called Frenche hose, some Gallie, and some Venetians. The Frenche hose are of two diuers makinges, for the common Frenche hose (as they list to call them) containeth length, breadth, and sidenesse sufficient, and is made very rounde. The other contayneth neyther length, breadth, nor sidenesse (being not past a quarter of a yarde side), whereof some be paned, cut, and drawen out with costly ornamentes, with canions annexed, reaching downe beneath their knees. The Gally hosen are made very large and wide, reaching downe to their knees onely, with three or foure gardes a peece laid downe along either hose. And the Venetian ho- **page 45 /** sen they reach beneath the knee, to the gartering place of the legge, where they are tyed finely with silke poyntes, or some such like, and layde on also with rewes of lace or gardes, as the other before. And yet, notwithstanding, all this is not sufficient, except they be made of silke, ueluet, saten, damaske, and other like precious thinges beside; yea, euery one, seruing man, and other inferiour to them in euery condition, will not sticke to flaunt it out in these kinde of hosen, with all other their apparell sutable thereunto. In tymes past, kynges (as olde historiographers in theyr bookes, yet extant, doe recorde) woulde not disdayne to weare a payre of hosen of a noble, ten shillinges, or a marke price, with all the rest of their apparell after the same rate; but now it is a small matter to bestowe twenty nobles, tenne pounde, twenty pounde, forty pounde, yea a hundred pounde, *Hosen of diuers and sondry fashions.* *French hosen of two sortes.* *Gally hosen.* *The great excesse vsed in hosen.*

of one payre of breeches (God be mercifull vnto us!) and yet is this thought no abuse neither.

. . . .

The diuersity of nether-stocks worne in Ailgna.

Then haue they nether-stocks to these gaie hosen, not of cloth (though neuer so fine), for that is thought too base, but of jarnsey, worsted, cre-well, silke, thred, and such like, or els at the least of the finest yearne that can be got, and so curiously knitte with open seame downe the legge, with quirks and clocks about the anckles, and sometime (haply) **page 46 /** interlaced with golde or siluer threds, as is wonderfull to behold . . .

. . . .

Corked shoes, pantoffles, and pinsnets.

To these their nether-stockes they haue corked shoes, pinsnets, and fine pantoffles, whiche beare them vppe a finger or two from the ground, whereof some be of white leather, some of blacke, and some of red; some of black veluet, some of white, some **page 47 /** of red, some of greene, razed, carued, cut, and stitched all ouer with silke, and layd on with golde, siluer, and such like. . . . **page 48 /**

. . . .

[Coats.]

The varietie of coates and ierkins.

Their coates and ierkīs, as they be diuers in colours, so be they diuers in fashions; for some be made with collors, some without, some close to the body, some loose, which they cal mandilians, couering the whole body down to the thigh, like bags or sacks, that were drawne ouer them, hiding the dimensions and lineaments of the body; some are buttoned down the brest, some vnder the arme, and some downe the backe, some with flaps ouer the brest, some without; some with great sleeues, some with small, and some with none at all; some pleated and crested behinde, and curiously gathered, some not. . . . **page 49 /**

. . . .

The sundry fashions of clokes.

They haue clokes there also in nothing discrepant from the rest, of diuers and sundrye colours, white, red, tawnie, blacke, greene, yellow, rus-set, purple, violet, and infinite other colours; — some of clothe, silke, veluet, taffetie, and such like, whereof some be of the Spanishe, French, and Dutch fashions — some shorte, scarsly reaching to the girdlestead or waste, some to the knee, and othersome trailing vppon the grounde (almost), liker gownes then clokes: then are they garded with veluette gardes, or els laced with costly lace, either of golde, siluer, or at the least of silke, three or foure fingers broade, downe the balke, about the skirts, and euery where els. And nowe of late they vse to garde their clokes rounde about the skirtes with

Bugled clokes.

(bables), **page 51 /** I should saie bugles, and other kinde of glasse, and all to shine to the eye. Besides al this, they are so faced, and withall so lined, as the inner side standeth almost in as muche as the outside; some haue sleeues, other some haue none; some haue hoodes to pull ouer the head, some haue none; some are hāged with poyntes and tassells of golde, siluer, or silke, some without all this. But how euer it be, the day hath bene, when one might haue bought him two clokes for lesse then nowe he can haue one of these

clokes made for, they haue suche store of workmanship bestowed vpon
them.

. . . .

They haue also bootehoose, whiche are to be wondred at, for they be of
the finest clothe that may be got, yea, fine enough to make any band,
ruffe, or shirte, needefull to be worne; yet this is bad enough to weare
next their greasie bootes. And would to God this were all; but (oh phy
for shame!) they must be wrought all ouer, from the gartering place vp-
warde, with needle woorke, clogged with silke of all colours, with byrdes,
foules, beastes, and antiques purtraied all ouer in sumptuous sorte. So that I
haue knowne the very needle worke of some one payre of these bootehoose to stand, some in foure **page 52 /** pounde, six pounde, and some
in ten pound a peece. Besides this, they are made so wide to draw ouer all,
and so long, to reach vp to the waste, that as little or lesse clothe would
make one a reasonable large shirte.

. . . .

To these haue they their rapiers, swordes, and daggers, gilt twise or thrise *Swordes and*
ouer the hiltes with good angell golde, or els argented ouer with siluer *dagger gilt*
and damasked.
both within and without; and if it be true, as I heare say it is, there be some
hiltes made all of pure siluer it selfe, and couered with golde. Othersome at the least are damasked, vernished, and ingrauen meruilous goodly;
and least any thing shoulde be wanting to set forth their pride, their scab-
erdes and sheathes are of veluet, or the like; for leather, thoughe it be more
profitable and as seemely, yet wil it not carie suche a porte or countenaunce
as the other. And will not these golden swords and daggers almost appale
a man, think you (though otherwise neuer so stout a martialist), to haue
any dealyng with them? for either to that ende they be worne, or els other *Why gilt*
page 53 / swordes, daggers, and rapers of bare iron and steel were as hand- *swordes and*
daggers be
some as they, and much more conducible to that ende whereto swordes *worne.*
and rapiers should serue, namely, for a man's lawfull and godly defence
against hys aduersarie, in time of necessitie. But wherefore they be so
clogged with golde and siluer I know not, nor yet whereto this excesse
serueth I see not. . . . **page 54 /**

The women . . . (many of them) vse to colour their faces with certaine *Colouring of*
faces with
oyles, liquors, *vnguentes*, and waters made to that end, whereby they thinke *oyntmentes*
their beautie is greatly decored . . . . **page 55 /** *and waters.*

. . . .

Then followeth the trimming and tricking of their heades, in laying out *Trimming of*
their heades.
their haire to the shewe, whiche of force must be curled, fristed, and crisped,
laid out (a world to see) on wreathes and borders, from one eare to an other. *Laying oute of*
And least it should fall down, it is vnder propped with forks, wiers, and I *their haire.*
cannot tell what . . . . Then, on the edges of their boulstered hair (for it standeth crested rounde about their frontiers, and hanging ouer their faces like *Golde*
wreathes en-
pendices or uailes, with glasse windowes on euery side) there is laied great *cumbering the*
temples of
wreathes of golde and siluer, curiously wrought, and cunningly applied to the *their heads.*
temples of their heades. And for feare of lacking any thinge to set forthe
their pride withall, at their haire, thus wreathed and creasted, are hanged

Gewgawes ranged about their frontiers.

bugles (I dare not say bables), ouches, rynges, gold, siluer, glasses, and suche other childishe gewgawes, and foolish trinkets besides . . . .   **page 60 /**

Curling, displaying, and laying out of haire.

If curling and laying out their owne naturall haire were all (which is impious, and at no hande lawfull, being, as it is, an ensigne of pride, and the sterne of wantonnesse to all that behold it), it were the lesse matter; but thei are not simplie content with their owne haire, but buye other haire, either of horses, mares, or any other straunge beastes, dying it of what colour they list themselues. And if there be any poore woman (as now and then, we see, God doth bless them with beautie as well as the riche) that hath faire haire, these nice dames will not rest till they haue bought it. Or if any children haue faire haire, they will entice them into a secret place, and for a penie or two they will cut of their haire . . . .   **page 61 /**

Bought haire and coloured, intended to be worne.

Capitall ornamentes for the head.

Then on toppes of these stately turrets (I meane their goodly heades, wherein is more vanitie than true philosophie, nowe and then) stand their other capitall ornaments, as Frēch-hood, hatte, cappe, kercher, and such like, whereof some be of veluet, some of taffatie, some (but few) of wooll, some of this fashion, some of that, and some of this colour, some of that, accordyng to the variable phantasies of their serpentine mindes. And to suche excesse it is growne, as euery artificer's wife (almost) will not sticke to goe in her hat of veluet euery day, euery merchant's wife, and meane gentlewomen, in her French-hoode, and euery poore cottager's daughter in her taffatie hat, or els of wooll at least, well lined with silke, veluet, or taffatie . . . .

Hattes of veluet, taffatie, worne in common.

They haue also other ornamentes besides these to   **page 62 /**   furnishe forthe their ingenious heades, whiche they call (as I remember) cawles, made netwise, to the ende, as I thinke, that the clothe of golde, clothe of siluer, or els tinsell (for that is the worst wherewith their heads are couered and attired withall vnderneath their caules), may the better appeare, and shew it selfe in the brauest maner; so that a man that seeth them (their heades glister and shine in such sorte) would thinke them to haue golden heades. And some weare lattice cappes with three hornes, three corners I should say, like the forked cappes of popishe priestes with their perriwinckles, chitterlinges, and the like apishe toyes of infinite varietie.

Cawles made netwise.

Golden heads fraught with leaden wit.

. . . .

Making of holes in their ears, to hang rings and jewelles by.

An other sort of dissolute minions, and wanton sempronians (for I can terme them no better), are so farre bewitched as they are not ashamed to make holes in their eares, whereat they hang ringes and other jewels of gold and precious stones. . . .   **page 63 /**

Great ruffes, neckerchers, and partlets, vsed of women.

The women . . . vse great ruffes and neckerchers of holland, laune, camericke, and such clothe, as the greatest threed shall not be so big as the least haire that is; and lest they should fall downe, they are smeared and starched in the deuil's liquor, I meane starche — after that dried with great diligence, streaked, patted, and rubbed very nicely, and so applied to their goodly necks, and, withal, vnderpropped, with supportasses (as I told you before), the stately arches of pride; beyond all this, they haue a further fetche, nothyng inferiour to the rest, as,   **page 64 /**   namely, three or foure degrees of minor ruffes, placed *gradatim*, one beneath an other, and al vnder the mayster deuilruffe; the skirtes then of these great ruffes are long and side euery way pleated, and crested full curiously, God wot. Then, last of all, they are

Starche, the deuil's liquor.

Supportasses the pillers of pride.

Minor ruffes.

either clogged with gold, siluer, or silke lace of stately price, wrought all ouer with needle worke, speckeled and sparkeled here and there with the sunne, the mone, the starres, and many other antiques strange to beholde. Some are wrought with open worke downe to the midst of the ruffe and further; some with close woorke, some wyth purled lace so cloied, and other gewgawes so pestered, as the ruffe is the least parte of it selfe. Sometimes they are pinned vpp to their eares, sometimes they are suffered to hãge ouer theyr shoulders, like windemill sails fluttering in the winde . . . . **page 65 /**

The great curiositie in ruffes and neckerchers.

. . . .

Their gownes be no lesse famous then the rest, for some are of silke, some of veluet, some of grograine, some of taffatie, some of scarlet, and some of fine clothe, of x. xx. or xl. shillinges a yarde. But if the whole gowne be not silke or veluet, then the same shall be layd with lace, two or three fingers broade, all ouer the gowne, or els the moste parte; or if not so (as lace is not fine enough sometimes), then it must bee garded with great gardes of veluet, euery gard fower or sixe fingers broad at the least, and edged with costly lace; and as these gownes be of diuers and sondry colours, so are they of diuers fashions, chaunging with the moone — for some be of the new fashion, some of the olde, some of thys fashion, and some of that, some with sleeues hanging downe to their skirtes, trailing on the ground, and cast ouer their shoulders like cowe tailes. Some haue sleeues muche shorter, cut vp the arme, and poincted with silke ribbons very gallantly, tied with true loues knottes (for so they call them). Some haue capes reachyng downe to the middest of their backes, faced with veluet, or els with some fine wrought silke taffatie, at the least, and fringed about very brauely: and (to shut vp all in a worde) some are pleated, and rinsled downe the backe wonder- **page 69 /** fully, with more knackes then I can declare. Then haue they petticoates of the beste clothe that can be bought, and of the fay-rest dye that can be made. And sometimes they are not of clothe neither, for that is thought to base, but of scarlet, grograine, taffatie, silke, and such like, fringed about the skirtes with silke fringe, of chaungeable colour. But whiche is more vayne, of whatsoeuer their petticoates be, yet must they haue kirtles (for so they call them) either of silke, veluett, grograine, taffatie, satten, or scarlet, bordered with gardes, lace, fringe, and I cannot tell what besides . . . . So farre hath this canker of pride eaten into the body of the common wealth, that euery poore yeoman his daughter, and euery husband-man his daughter, and euery cottager his daughter, will not stick to flaunt it out in such gownes, petticoates, and kirtles, as these. **page 70 /**

The diuersity of gownes.

Costly gownes.

Diuerse fashions of gownes.

Petticoates.

Kirtles.

Poor men's daughters excesse.

. . . .

Their netherstockes, in like maner, are either of silke, iearnsey, worsted, crewell, or, at least, of as fine yearne, thread, or cloth, as is possible to be hadde; yea, they are not ashamed to weare hoase of all kinde of chaungeable colours, as green, red, white, russet, tawny, and els what. . . . Then these delicate hosē must bee cunningly knit, and curiously indented in euery point with quirkes, clockes, open seame, and euery thing els accordingly — wherto they haue corked shoes, pinsnets, pantoffles, and slippers; some of blacke veluet, some of white, some of greene, and some of yellowe — some of Spanishe leather, and some of Englishe, stitched with silke, and imbrodered

Netherstocks of iearnsey or silke.

Corked shoes, pinsnettes, pantoffles, and such like for women.

with golde and siluer all ouer the foot, with other gewgaws innumerable . . . .
page 72 /

The vayne gestures and coynes of women in the midst of their pecocke feathers.

. . . After all this, when they haue attired themselues thus, in the middest of their pride, it is a world to consider their **page 74 /** coienesse in gestures, their mincednesse in words and speaches, their gingernesse in tripping on toes like young goates, their demure nicitie and babishnesse, and withall their hautie stomackes, and more then cyclopical countenaunces; their fingers must

Fingers clogged with ringes.

be decked with golde, siluer, and precious stones, their wreastes with brace-lettes, and armelettes of golde, and other costly jewelles, their hādes couered with their sweet washed gloues imbrodered with golde, siluer, and what not;

Women's trinkets.

and to suche abhomination it is growen, as they must haue their looking-glasses caried with them wheresoeuer they goe; and good reason, for els how could they see the deuil in them? For, no doubt, they are the deuilles spec-

Sweeted gloues.

tacles, to allure vs to pride, and consequently to destruction for euer.

Looking-glasses the devill's spectacles.

.   .   .   .

Then must they haue their silke scarffes cast about their faces, and fluttering in the wind **page 75 /** with great tassels at euery ende, eyther of gold,

Silke scarffes.

siluer, or silke. But I know wherefore they will say they weare these scarffes, namely, to keep them from sunne burning. But I would aske these niselinges one question, wherein if they can resolue me, then I will say, as they say, that scarffes are necessarie, and not flagges of pride. Can that thing which is most glorious and fayre of itselfe make any thing foule or ill fauoured? The sunne is a most glorious and fayre creature, and therefore cannot make them fouler then they are of their owne nature . . . .

.   .   .   .

Visours, or inuisories of veluet to ride abroad in.

When they vse to ride abroad, they haue visors made of veluet (or in my iudgement they may rather be called inuisories) wherewith they couer all their faces, hauing holes made in them agaynst their eies, whereout they looke . . . . **page 76 /**

Stage Plaies and Enterludes, with Their Wickednesse.

All stage playes, enterludes, and commedies, are eyther of diuine or pro-phane matter: If they bee of diuine matter, then are they most intollerable, or rather sacrilegious, for that the blessed word of God is to be handled reuerently, grauely, and sagely, with veneration to the glorious maiestie of God, whiche shineth therein, and not scoffingly, floutingly, and iybingly, as it is vppon stages in playes and enterludes, without any reuerence, wor-shippe, or veneration at all done to the same: For it is most certaine the worde of oure saluation, the price of Christ his bloude, and the merites of his passion, were not geuen to bee derided and iested, or to bee mixt and interlaced with

The deriding of the word of God in stage plaies.

bawdrie, wanton shewes, and vncomely gestures, as is vsed (euery man know-eth) in these playes and enterludes, vppon stages and scaffoldes made for that purpose. . . . **page 160 /**

A warning to players

. . . Beware, therefore, you masking plaiers, you painted sepulchres, you double dealyng ambodexters, be warned betimes, and like good computists, cast your accompts before what will bee the reward thereof in the ende, least God destroye you in his wrathe: abuse God no more, corrupt his people no

longer with your dregges, and intermingle not his blessed worde with such *Not lawful to intermixt diuinitie with scurrilitie.*
prophane vanities. For, at no hande, it is not lawfull to mixt scurrilitie with
diuinitie, nor diuinitie with scurrilitie. . . . **page 161 /**

. . . .

. . . It is more then manifest that they are noe fit exercises for Christian men
to followe. But if there were no euill in them **page 163 /** saue this, namely,
that the arguments of tragedies, anger, wrathe, immunitie, crueltie, iniurie, *The arguments of tragedies.*
incest, murther, and suche like; the persons or actors are gods, goddesses, furies,
findes, hagges, kynges, queenes, or potentates. Of commedies, the matter
and ground is loue, bawdrie, cosenage, flatterie, whordome, adulterie; the
persons or agentes, whores, queanes, bawdes, scullions, knaues, curtizans, *The ground of comedies.*
lecherous olde men, amorous yong men, with suche like of infinite varietie.
If, I saie, there were nothing els but this, it were sufficient to with draw a good
Christian from the vsyng of them. For, so often as they goe to those houses
where plaiers frequent, they goe to Venus' pallace and Sathan's sinagogue,
to worship deuilles and betraie Christ Jesus. . . . **page 164 /**

. . . There is no mischiefe which these playes maintaine not. For, doe they
not nourishe idlenesse? . . . Doe they not drawe the people from hearyng the
word of God, from godly lectures and sermons? For you shall haue them
flocke thether thicke and threefolde, when the churche of God shall be bare *The fruites of theaters and playes.*
and emptie; and those that will neuer come at sermons will flow thether
apace. . . . Doe they not maintaine bawdrie, insinuat foolerie, and renue the re-
membraunce of heathen idolatrie? Doe they not induce whoredome and
vncleannesse? Nay, are they not rather plaine deuourers of maidenly vir-
ginitie and chastitie? For proofe whereof, but marke the flockyng and *The goodly demeanoures vsed at plaies and enter-ludes.*
runnyng to theaters and curtens, daylie and hourelie, night and daie, tyme
and tide, to see plaies and enterludes, where suche wanton gestures, suche
bawdie speeches, suche laughyng and flearyng, **page 165 /** suche kissyng
and bussyng, suche clippyng and culling, such wincking and glauncing of
wanton eyes, and the like, is vsed, as is wonderfull to beholde. Then these *The goodly examples of plaies and enterludes.*
goodly pageantes beeyng ended, euery mate sortes to his mate, euery one
bringes an other homewarde of their waie very freendly, and in their secrete
conclaues (couertly) they plaie the Sodomits, or worse. And these be the
fruites of plaies and enterludes, for the most parte. And whereas you saie
there are good examples to be learned in them, truely so there are: if you
will learne falshood; if you will learne cosenage; if you will learne to de- *What thinges are to be learned at plaies.*
ceiue; if you will learn to plaie the hipocrite, to cogge, to lye and falsifie; if
you will learne to iest, laugh, and fleere, to grinne, to nodd, and mowe; if you
will learne to plaie the vice, to sweare, teare, and blaspheme both heauen
and earth; if you will learne to become a bawde, vncleane, and to diuerginate
maides, to deflowre honest wiues; if you will learne to murther, slaie, kill,
picke, steale, robbe, and roue; if you will learne to rebell against princes, to
commit treason, to consume treasures, to practise idlenesse, to sing and talke
of bawdie loue and venerie; if you will learne to deride, scoffe, mocke, and
floute, to flatter and smooth; if you will learne to plaie the whoremaister,
the glutton, drunkard, or incestuous person; if you will learne to become
proude, hautie, and arrogant; and, finally, if you will learne to contemne God

and all his lawes, to care neither for heauen nor hell, and to commit all kind of sinne and mischeefe, you neede to goe to no other page 166 / schoole, for all these good examples maie you see painted before your eyes in enterludes and plaies. . . .

Therefore, I beseeche all plaiers, founders, and maintainers of plaies and enterludes, in the bowelles of Iesus Christ, as they tender the saluation of their soules, and others, to leaue of that cursed kinde of life, and giue themselues to suche honest exercises, and godly misteries, as God hath commaunded them in his worde to get their liuynges withall. For who will call him a wise man that plaieth the parte of a foole and a vice? Who can call hym a Christian who plaieth the parte of a deuill, the sworne enemie of Christ? Who can call hym a iust man that plaieth the parte of a dissemblyng hipocrite? And to bee breefe, who can call him a straight dealyng man who plaieth a cosener's tricke? And so of all the rest. Awaie, therefore, with this so infamous an art! for goe they neuer so braue, yet are they counted and taken but for beggars. And is it not true? page 167 / Liue they not vppon begging of euery one that comes? Are they not taken by the lawes of the realme for roagues and vacabounds? (I speake of suche as trauailethe countreis with plaies and enterludes, making an occupation of it), and ought so to bee punished, if they had their deserts. But hopyng that they will be warned now at the last, I will say no more of them, beseeching them to consider what a fearfull thing it is to fall into the handes of God, and to prouoke his wrath and heauie displeasure against them selues and others. Which the Lorde of his mercie tourne from vs! page 168 /

page 166 /
page 167 /
page 168 /

Marginal notes:
An exhortation to players.
The ignominy due to players.
Players liue vpon begging.
Players counted rogues by the lawes of the realm.

Cardes, Dice, Tables, Tennisse, Boules, And Other Exercises, Vsed Vnlawfully in Ailgna.

To plaie at tables, cardes, dice, bowles, or the like (though a good Christian man will not so idly and vainely spende his golden daies), one Christian with an other, for their priuate recreations, after some oppression of studie, to driue awaie fantasies and suche like, I doubt not but they maie, vsing it moderatly, with intermission and in the feare of God. But to plaie for lucre of gaine, and for desire onely page 206 / of his brother's substance (rather then for any other cause), it is at no hande lawfull, or to be suffered.

For as it is not lawfull to robbe, steale, and purloine by deceite or slaight, so is it not lawfull to get thy brother's goodes from hym by cardyng, dicyng, tablyng, bowlyng, or any other kind of theft; for these games are no better, nay, worser then open theft, for open theft euery man can beware of, but this beyng a craftie politicke theft, and commonly doen vnder pretence of freendship, fewe or none at all can beware of it. The commaundement saieth, Thou shalt not couet, nor desire any thyng that belongeth to thy neighbour. Now, it is manifest that those that plaie for money not onely couet their brother's money, but also vse craft, falshoode, and deceite, to winne the same. page 207 /

page 206 /
page 207 /

Marginal notes:
Vnlawful for one Christian to plaie with an other to winne his money.
Gamyng worse then open theft.

. . . For, as concernyng footeball playing, I protest vnto you, it maie rather bee called a freendly kynde of fight then a plaie or recreation, a bloudie and murtheryng practise, then a fellowlie sporte or pastyme. For, dooeth not *Football a freendly kind of fight.* euery one lye in waite for his aduersarie, seekyng to ouerthrowe hym, and to picke hym on his nose, though it bee vpon harde stones, in ditche or dale, in valley or hill, or what place so euer it be, he careth not, so he maie haue him downe? And he that can serue the moste of this fashion, he is counted the onely fellowe, and who but he? So that by this meanes, sometymes their neckes are broken, sometymes their backes, sometymes their legges, some- *Hurt by football playing.* time their armes, sometyme one part thrust out of ioynte, sometyme an other, sometyme their noses gush out with bloud, sometyme their eyes starte out; and sometymes hurt in one place, sometymes in an other. But who so euer scapeth awaie the best, goeth not scotfree, but is either sore wounded and bruzed, so as he dieth of it, or els scapeth very hardlie: And no meruaile, for they haue sleightes to meete one betwixte twoo, to dashe hym against the *Foote ball playing a murtheryng plaie.* harte with their elbowes, to hitte hym vnder the shorte ribbes with their griped fistes, and with their knees, to catche him vpon the hip, and to picke him on his necke; with an hundred suche murderyng deuises: And hereof groweth enuie, malice, rancour, cholour, hatred, displeasure, enmitie, and what not els? And sometymes fightyng, **page 220 /** braulyng, contention, quarrell pickyng, murther, homicide, and great effusion of bloud, as experience daiely teacheth. **page 221 /**

Petruccio Ubaldino was an Italian scholar and an illuminator to Edward VI. A native of Florence, he resided in England from 1545. His description of the battle between the English and the Spanish fleets seems to have been borrowed in part from Camden's account. The work was originally printed with illustrations showing the positions of the fleets in the various actions.

Petruccio Ubaldino. *A Discourse, concerning the* Spanish *Fleet invading* England, *in the year 1588, and overthrown by her Majesty's Navy, under the Conduct of the Right Honourable the Lord* Charles Howard, *High-Admiral of* England; *written in* Italian, *by* Petruccio Ubaldino, *Citizen of* Florence, *and translated for* A. Ryther. . . . *MDXC. Reprinted in The Harleian Miscellany.* Vol. I, pp. 115–128. London, 1745.

. . . The Spanish Fleet being manifestly discovered about a Hundred and forty Miles from *Edestone,*   page 119 /   and clearly seen of every one, towards the West, and so far off from *Foy,* as the *English* Fleet was, that is twenty-five ordinary *English* Miles: The next Morning, being the twenty-first of *June,* all the Ships, which were now come out of the Haven, had gotten the Wind of the *Spaniards,* and, approaching somewhat nearer, found, that their Fleet was placed in Battle Aray after the Manner of a Moon crescent, being ready with her Horns, and her inward Circumference, to receive either all, or so many of the *English* Navy, as should give her Assault, her Horns being extended in Wideness about the Distance of eight Miles, if the Information given have not deceived my Pen. The Reason of their arranging, in this Order, arose upon the Foresight of the Duke of *Medina Sidonia* General of the *Spanish* Fleet, who, approaching the Coast, sent out a small Ship, to espy somewhat concerning the *English* Fleet, and hearing by certain Fishermen taken Prisoners, that our Fleet was in *Plymouth,* he prepared himself as aforesaid, for the Avoiding of all such Chances as might after befal. Whereupon, about Nine of the Clock, before Noon, the Lord Admiral commanded his Pinnace, called the *Disdain,* to give the Defiance unto the Duke of *Medina:* After which, he himself, in the Queen's ship called the *Ark,* went foremost, as was convenient, and began hotly to fight with a great Ship, which was Admiral of the *Spanish* Fleet, in which Ship, he thought, by Reason of certain likely Conjectures, the Duke of *Medina* to be, considering also the said Ship was so well accompanied by others. The Fight with her continued so long, and so hot, that divers other Ships, yea, the most Part of the *Spanish* Fleet, came to her Succour.

In the mean Season, the Vice-Admiral Sir *Francis Drake,* with Master *John Hawkins* and Master *Martin Frobisher,* fought with a Galleon of *Portugal,* wherein they thought *Don Martin de Ricaldes* the Vice-Admiral to be.

This Fight was so well maintained for the Time it continued, that the Enemy was inforced to leave his Place, and to give Way, gathering towards the East. In the which Point of Removing, a great Galleon, wherein *Don Pedro de Valdes* went as Captain, falling foul with another Ship of their Fleet, was deprived of her Foremast, so that she could not follow the Body of the Fleet that forsook her, to the great Marvel of the *Englishmen* themselves, whereby *Don Pedro* became Prisoner. . . .

Furthermore also, there was, at this Time, a great Ship of *Biscay*, about eight hundred Ton in Burthen, that was spoiled by Fire upon this Occasion: The Captain of the Soldiers that went in her . . . did insolently beat a certain *Flemish* Gunner. . . . Whereupon, the perplexed Man . . . set himself on Fire, in a Barrel of Gunpowder, procuring thereby, through the Loss of his own Life, and the extreme Hazard of those that belonged unto him, and the Loss of many Men's Lives besides, a cruel Revenge of his Injuries received by one only Man. . . . This first Skirmish continued not above two Hours, because the Lord Admiral, considering, that he wanted as yet forty Ships, which could not so readily come forth of the Haven, thought he should do better Service, if he stayed their Coming, before he proceeded any further, beating behind upon the Enemy, lest he should bring the rest too much in Hazard, and, therefore, he thought it not profitable, too much, to embolden and prick those forward that he had with him. . . . **page 120 /**

The next Day, the Vice-Admiral, Sir *Francis Drake*, being in the Queen's Ship, called the *Revenge*, having also the *Roebuck* and a Pinnace or two in his Company, took Don *Pedro de Valdes*, who . . . had lost the Foremast of his Ship. . . .

The same Day, being the Twenty-second of the Month, a little before the Vice-Admiral, Sir *Francis Drake*, was returned unto the Fleet, the *Spaniards* forsook the Ship, which the Day before was spoiled by Fire. To the which Ship, the Lord Admiral sent the Lord *Thomas Howard*, and with him, Mr. *John Hawkins*, who, being in the Cockboat of the *Victory*, went a-board her, and there found a lamentable Sight. For, all the uppermost Decks of her being torn and spoiled by the Fire, there were in her fifty Men miserably burnt with the Powder. The Stink in her was so great, and the Ship itself so filthy, that the Lord *Howard* departed presently from her: And returning, with Mr. *John Hawkins*, to the Lord Admiral, they informed him of that they found and saw there. For which Cause, there was presently Commandment given, that the little Pinnace of Captain *Fleming* should conduct her into some Port of *England*. . . . **page 121 /**

The Morning following being *Tuesday*, the twenty-third of the Month, the Wind was at North-East, whereupon the *Spaniards* came back upon the *Englishmen*, with the Advantage of the Wind, directing their Course toward the Land; the which Course was not profitable for the *Englishmen*. Therefore, to take the Advantage of the Enemy, they cast about toward the West, with a reasonable Compass, their Ships being very good both of Sail and Stirrage, that they might bring about their Purpose. Now the *Spaniards*, to hinder their Intent, after they perceived it, offered to come near a-board to fight with them, trusting in the huge Greatness and Height of their Ships. The which Offer of theirs the *Englishmen* refused not, but began presently to bring themselves into Battle Aray, which the enemy perceiving he also did the like.

In this Case the *Ark*, the *Lion*, the *Bear*, the *Elizabeth Jonas*, the *Victory*, and certain other Ships were content to follow the Ship, called the *Non Pariglia.*

In the mean Season the *Triumph*, with other five Ships of *London*, namely the Merchant *Royal*, the *Centurion*, the *Margery Joan*, the *Mary Rose*, and the *Golden Lion*, were so far to the Rereward, and so far severed from the rest of the Fleet, that the Galliasses undertook to give them an hard Assault. But they were well entertained by the Ships, for the Space of an Hour and an Half, until at the Length, some of the Queen's Ships, coming to succour the *Triumph* and the *Londoners*, dealt so well in the Matter, that the Galliasses were driven to retire. The Wind came about at this Present, to the South-east, and afterwards, to the South-west and by South, at which Time a certain Number, or Squadron of the Queen's, together with other Merchants Ships, gave Assault unto the *Spanish* Fleet, and that, so furiously to the Westward of them, that the *Spaniards* were all inforced to give them Way: For which Cause, the Lord Admiral considering both the Discommodity and Danger, whereinto the *Triumph*, and the other five Ships were come, he called other of the Queen's Ships that were not far off, and gave them straight Commandment to follow him, and to charge the Enemies which were to the Westward with all their Force; giving further Order to them all, not to discharge any one Piece of Ordnance, before they should come within a Musket-shot of the Enemy, inasmuch, as that was the only Way to succour the Ships of their Friends with the greater Damage of the Enemy. This was well performed by the *Ark*, the *Elizabeth Jonas*, the Galleon *Leicester*, the *Golden Lion*, the *Victory*, the *Mary Rose*, the *Dread-nought*, and the *Swallow*. Which Thing the Duke of *Medina* perceiving, he also came forth with sixteen of his best Galleons, to hinder and impeach the *Englishmen* in the Defence of the *Triumph*, seeming in this Case to pretend, that the Reason of the Fight did so require. . . . Howbeit that fell out in the end . . . that the Success of the Conflict falling out on his Side, as hardly, as in such a Case might be, the *Spaniards*, in the End, were inforced to give Place, and to retire unto their Aray of Battle. . . .

Toward the Evening, four or five *Spanish* Ships came out from the rest of the Fleet, from the South-eastward, against whom, certain of the *English* Ships came, and namely, the *Mayflower*, of *London*, which discharged certain Pieces upon the Enemy, with a very honourable Declaration of the Marine Discipline; and being accompanied by other Ships, that were there found, they all behaved themselves no less   page 122 /   diligently . . . . The Conflict continued from the Morning unto the Evening. . . . It might well be said, that, for the Time, it was not possible to see, before this Battle, in this Sea so hard a Conflict, nor so terrible a Spoil of Ships, by Reason of the *Pellets* * that flew so thick every Way: To conclude, there was never seen so vehement a Fight, either Side endeavouring through an headstrong and deadly Hatred the other's Spoil and Destruction. For, albeit the Musquettiers and Harquebusiers were in either Fleet many in Number, yet could they not be discerned or heard, by Reason of the more violent and roaring Shot of the

* *i.e.* Bullets. [*Footnotes are from the source.* — Ed.]

greater Ordnance, that followed so thick one upon another, and played so well that Day, on either Side, that they were thought to be equal in Number, to common Harquebusiers in an hot Skirmish. The Battle was not only long, but also near at Hand, within half a Musket-shot, and that to the great Advantage of the *Englishmen,* who with their Ships, being . . . excellent of Sail and Stirrage, yet less a great Deal, than the *Spanish* Ships, and therefore, more light and nimble, sought not at all, according to their Manner otherwise, to board them, but keeping themselves aloof at a reasonable Distance, continually beat upon the Hull and Tacklings of their Enemies Ships, which being a great Deal higher, could not so conveniently beat the *English* Ships, with their Ordnance. This long Conflict being finished . . . the next Day following (which was *Wednesday,* the twenty-fourth of the Month) was passed without any Thing done . . . . **page 123** /

. . . The Lord Admiral, having, by certain Notice, understood, that the Duke of *Parma* had prepared a great Number of Tuns of Water, and ten Thousand chosen Footmen, to be embarked for the Joining with the Fleet . . . , knowing also the evident Peril, that was to be feared, if the *Spanish* Fleet should be suffered to refresh itself, and to be furnished with so many Soldiers, he applied his Wits so, in the Deliberation of these Matters of Weight and Importance, having the Consent of others more practised, that no Time might be lost, for the Furtherance of this Service; and, for so much as the Forces of the Enemy were not yet united and joined together, therefore the twenty-eighth of this Month, at Midnight, he provided eight small Ships, dressed with artificial Fire,* to the Intent to drive the same upon the *Spanish* Fleet. This Thing was diligently and effectually brought to pass, under the Charge of Captain *Young* and Captain *Prewse,* two valiant and courageous Men. By Reason hereof, the Enemy was not only inforced to break his Sleep, but, the Fire coming so suddenly upon him, . . . to cut his Cables, to let slip his Anchors, and to hoist up Sails, as the only Way to save his Fleet from so imminent and unexpected a Mischief. Furthermore, by means of this Tumult and Confusion . . . the chief Galliass fell foul with another Ship, upon the Cable of whose Anchor, her Stern was set so fast, that they could not loose her all the Night long, so that the next Day following she was inforced with her Oars to make toward the Land . . . , but, not knowing that Water . . . , she fell upon a Shelf. This Thing being, in good Time, espied by the Lord Admiral, he sent thither his greatest Boat . . . who fought with her, but unequally, for that the Ship, being gravelled, could . . . prevail but little. . . . The *Englishmen* being more secure, took her, and sacked her to their great Commodity. . . .
page 125 /

During the Time of surprising of which Galliass, Sir *Francis Drake,* Vice-Admiral, being in the Ship called *The Revenge,* accompanied with *Tho. Fenner,* Captain of the *Non Pariglia,* with the rest of that Squadron, set upon the *Spanish* Fleet, giving them a hot Charge. Within a While after, Sir *John Hawkins,* in the *Victory,* accompanied with *Edward Fenton,* Captain of the *Mary Rose,* with *George Beeston,* Captain in the *Dreadnought,* and *Richard Hawkins,* in the *Swallow,* with the rest of the Squadron, put themselves for-

* This is the first Occasion on which we read that Fire-ships were used in a Sea-Fight.

ward, and broke thro' the Midst of the *Spanish* Fleet; where there began a vehement Conflict continuing all the Morning, wherein every Captain did very honourable Service. . . .

It seemeth hereby that we may with Reason gather, that in these Conflicts many of the *Spanish* Ships perished, albeit that most Men think, that few of them miscarried. After this Battle, which was made the Twenty-ninth of the Month, the Lord Admiral the thirtieth Day ordained, that the Lord *Seymer* and Sir *William Winter* should return with their Fleet unto their appointed Office in the Channel, which was to keep the Coast from the Danger that the Duke of *Parma* seemed to threaten. The which Duke had already lost the Opportunity of being able to do any Thing for the Accomplishing of the common Intention of the *Spaniards* . . . because the sudden and unlooked for Departure of the Duke of *Medina* with the whole Fleet, from the Coast of Calais. . . . **page 126 /**

The Lord Admiral, therefore, determined to follow the *Spanish* Fleet only so long until they might be shut up to the Northward, whither the *Spanish* Fleet directed her Course. . . . The *Spaniards* kept their Course about the Islands of *Orkney*, declaring thereby, that they minded to return that Way into *Spain*, along by the North-coast of *Scotland*. . . .

The *Spanish* Fleet, passing, as aforesaid, into those Seas, which, for the most Part, are quiet and calm enough, whether it were driven to and fro in them with contrary Winds, or by some other fatal Accident that fell out, it continued therein tossed up and down until the End of *September*, with fearful Success and deadly Shipwrack along the whole Coast of *Ireland*, so that the Duke of *Medina Sidonia* was inforced to leave there behind him about the Number of seventeen good Ships, besides those fifteen that were thought to be lost in the Months of *July* and *August*, and so to return into *Spain*.

The Persons, lost in *Ireland*, were esteemed to be about 5500. So that, all being accounted together, it is certainly avouched, that all the Ships that were lost amount unto the Number of thirty-two, and the Men accounted, one with another, arise to the Number of 13500 or more. The Prisoners also of all Sorts, in *England*, *Ireland*, and the *Low Countries*, arise to the Number of 2000 and more. . . . **page 127 /**

Certain Advertisements out of Ireland, *concerning the Losses and Distresses happened to the* Spanish *Navy, upon the West Coasts of* Ireland, *in their Voyage intended from the Northern Isles beyond* Scotland, *toward* Spain. Imprinted at London, by *J. Vautrollier, for Richard Field.* 1588. Reprinted in *The Harleian Miscellany,* Vol. I, pp. 128–137.

Ships and Men sunk, drowned, killed, and taken upon the Coast of Ireland, *in the Month of* September, 1588.

In *Tyrconnel*	In *Loughfoyle*	1 Ship	1100	Men, of that Ship and others that escaped.
	In *Sligo* Haven	3 great Ships	1500	
	In *Tirawley*	1 Ship	400	
	In *Clare* Island	1 Ship	300	
In *Connaught*	In *Finglas*	1 Ship	400	
	In *Oflarty*	1 Ship	200	
	In *Irrise*	2 Ships		The Men fled into other Vessels
	In *Galway* Bay	1 Ship	70	

page 136 /

	In the *Shannon*	2 Ships	600	
	In *Traylie*	1 Ship	24	
In *Munster*	In *Dingle*	1 Ship	500	
	In *Desmond*	1 Ship	300	
	In the *Shannon*	1 Ship burnt		The Men embarked in another Ship

Total 17 Ships   5,394 Men

Before the Loss of the aforesaid seventeen Ships in Ireland, *there perished, in* July *and* August, *fifteen other great Ships in the Fight betwixt the* English *and* Spanish *Navies in the narrow Seas of* England.

First Gallies		4 Ships	1622 Men
Near *Ediston*, by *Plymouth*, at the first Conflict		1	0000

The same Time was distressed and taken Don *Pedro de Valde's* Ship }	1	422 } These two
At the same Time by Fire a great *Biscay* Ship	1	289 } remain in *England*
Before *Calais*, spoiled the principal Galliass of *Naples* }	1	686
In the Conflict was sunk a great *Biscayan*	1	000
The Galleon St. *Philip*	1	532 } These two forced into
St. *Matthew*	1	397 } *Flushing* being fore beaten by the *English* great Shot.
A *Biscayan* wrecked before *Ostend*	1	000
The Day after the Fight there sunk two *Venetians*	2	843
A great *Biscayan* forced by two of the Queen's Ships to perish at *Newhaven* }	1	000

Total	15 Ships	4791	Men
The above Loss	17	5394	

Total of both these Losses Besides many Ships not yet heard of, thought to be lost.

32 Ships 10185 Men, whereof there are Prisoners in *England* and *Zeland* at least 1000, besides a great Multitude of Men not here accounted, that were slain in the Fight, and that have died of Famine . . . . page 137 /

Shakespeare's Will in *The Works of Shakespeare*, Vol. I. Edited by Lewis
   Theobald, London, 1773.*

In the name of God, *Amen*. I *William Shakspeare* of *Stratford upon Avon*
in the county of *Warwick*, Gent. in perfect health and memory, God be
praised, do make and ordain this my last Will and Testament in manner and
form following; that is to say:

First, I commend my Soul into the hands of God my Creator, hoping and
assuredly believing, through the only merits of Jesus Christ my Saviour, to
be made partaker of life everlasting; and my body to the earth whereof that
is made.

Item, I give and bequeath unto my daughter *Judith* one hundred and fifty
pounds of lawful *English* money, to be paid unto her in manner and form
following;/ that is to say, one hundred Pounds in discharge of her marriage portion within one year after my decease, with considerations after the
rate of two shillings in the pound for so long time as the same shall be unpaid
unto her after my decease; and the fifty pounds residue thereof upon her
surrendring of or giving of such sufficient security as the overseers of this
my Will shall like of, to surrender or grant all her estate and right that shall de-
scend or come unto her after my decease, or that she now hath of, in, or
to one copyhold tenement, with the appurtenances lying and being in
Stratford upon Avon aforesaid, in the said county of *Warwick*, being parcell
or holden of the Manor of *Rowington*, unto my daughter *Susannah Hall*,
and her heirs for ever.

Item, I give and bequeath unto my said daughter *Judith*, one hundred and
fifty pounds more, if she, or any issue of her body, be living at the end of
three years next ensuing the day of the date of this my Will, during which
time my executors to pay her consideration from my decease according to
the rate aforesaid: And if she die within the said term without issue of her
body, then my Will is, and I do give/ and bequeath one hundred pounds
thereof to my niece *Elizabeth Hall*, and the fifty pounds to be set forth by
my executors during the life of my sister *Joan Harte*, and the use and profit
thereof coming, shall be paid to my said sister *Joan*, and after her decease the
fifty pounds shall remain amongst the children of my said sister, equally to
be divided amongst them; but if my said daughter *Judith* be living at the
end of the said three years, or any issue of her body, then my Will is, and so I
devise and bequeath the said hundred and fifty Pounds to be set out by my
executors and overseers for the best benefit of her and her issue, and the
stock not to be paid unto her so long as she shall be married and covert
baron; but my Will is that she shall have the consideration yearly paid
unto her during her life, and after her decease the said stock and consideration

---

* The prefatory section in Theobald's edition is not numbered. The end of a page will
be indicated in this present draft by a (/).

to be paid to her children, if she have any, and if not, to her executors and assigns, she living the said term after my decease; provided that if such husband as she shall at the end of the said three years be married unto, or at and after, do sufficiently assure unto her and the issue of her body, land answerable/ to the portion by this my Will given unto her, and to be adjudged so by my executors and overseers, then my Will is, that the said hundred and fifty pounds shall be paid to such husband as shall make such assurance, to his own use.

Item, I give and bequeath unto my said sister *Joan* twenty pounds, and all my wearing apparel, to be paid and delivered within one year after my decease; and I do will and devise unto her the house with the appurtenances in *Stratford*, wherein she dwelleth, for her natural life, under the yearly rent of twelve pence.

Item, I give and bequeath unto her three sons, *William Hart*, —— *Hart*, and *Michael Hart*, five pounds apiece, to be paid within one year after my decease.

Item, I give and bequeath unto the said *Elizabeth Hall* all my plate that I now have, except my broad silver and gilt boxes, at the date of this my Will.

Item, I give and bequeath unto the poor of *Stratford* aforesaid ten pounds, to Mr. *Thomas Combe* my sword, to *Thomas Russel*, Esq; five pounds, and to *Francis Collins* of the borough of *Warwick*, in the county of *Warwick*, Gent. thirteen pounds six/shillings and eight pence, to be paid within one year after my decease.

Item, I give and bequeath to *Hamlett Sadler* twenty-six shillings, eight pence, to buy him a ring; to *William Reynolds*, Gent. twenty six shillings, eight pence, to buy him a ring; to my godson *William Walker* twenty shillings in gold; to *Anthony Nash*, Gent. twenty-six shillings, eight pence; and to Mr. *John Nash* twenty-six shillings, eight pence; and to my fellows *John Hemynge*, *Richard Burbage*, and *Henry Cundell*, twenty-six shillings, eight pence apiece to buy them rings.

Item, I give, will, bequeath, and devise, unto my daughter *Susannah Hall*, for the better enabling of her to perform this my Will, and towards the performance thereof, all that capital messuage or tenement, with the appurtenances in *Stratford* aforesaid, called the *New Place*, wherein I now dwell, and two messuages or tenements, with the appurtenances, situate, lying, and being in *Henley Street*, within the borough of *Stratford* aforesaid; and all my barns, stables, orchards, gardens, lands, tenements, and hereditaments whatsoever, situate, lying, and being, or to be had, reserved, preserved/or taken within the towns, hamlets, villages, fields, and grounds of *Stratford upon Avon*, *Old Stratford*, *Bushaxton*, and *Welcombe*, or in any of them, in the said county of *Warwick*; and also all that messuage or tenement, with the appurtenances, wherein one *John Robinson* dwelleth, situate, lying and being in the *Black Friers* in *London* near the *Wardrobe*; and all other my lands, tenements, and hereditaments whatsoever; to have and to hold all and singular the said premises, with their appurtenances, unto the said *Susannah Hall*, for and during the term of her natural life; and after her decease to the first son of her body lawfully issuing, and to the heirs males of the body of the said first son lawfully issuing; and for default of such issue, to the second son of her body lawfully issuing, and to the heirs males of the body of the said second son lawfully issuing; and for default of such heirs to the third son of the body of the said *Susannah* lawfully issuing; and of the heirs males of the body of the said third son lawfully issuing; and for default of such issue, the same to be and remain to the fourth, fifth, sixth, and seventh sons of her body, lawfully issuing one after another,/and to the heirs males of the bodies of the said fourth, fifth, sixth, and seventh sons lawfully issuing, in such manner as it is before limited to be and remain to the first, second, and third sons of her body, and to their heirs males; and for default of such issue, the said premises to be and remain to my said Niece *Hall*, and the heirs males of her body lawfully issuing; and for default of such issue, to my daughter *Judith*, and the heirs males of her body lawfully issuing; and for default of such issue, to the right heirs of me the said *William Shakspeare* for ever.

Item, I give unto my wife my brown best bed with the furniture.

Item, I give and bequeath to my said daughter *Judith* my broad silver gilt bole. All the rest of my goods, chattels, leases, plate, jewels, and household-stuff whatsoever, after my debts and legacies paid, and my funeral expences discharged, I give, devise, and bequeath to my son-in law *John Hall*, Gent. and my daughter *Susannah* his wife, who I ordain and make executors of this my last Will and Testament. And I do intreat and appoint the said *Thomas Russel*, Esq; and *Francis Collins*,/Gent. to be overseers hereof. And do revoke all former Wills, and publish this to be my last Will and Testament. In witness whereof I have hereunto put my hand, the day and year first abovewritten, by me

William Shakspeare.

Witness to the publishing hereof,
Fra. Collins,
Julius Shaw,
John Robinson
Hamlett Sadler,
Robert Whattcott.

Probatum coram Magistro William Byrde Legum Doctore Commissario &c. vicesimo secundo die Mensis Junii Anno Domini 1616. Juramento Johannis Hall unius ex. et cui &c. de bene et Jurat Reservata potestate et Susannae Hall alt ex. &c. cu. vendit &c. petitur. |

SUGGESTED TOPICS FOR PAPERS

LIST ONE: LIMITED TOPICS

Topics in this list may be used (1) for short papers stressing particular aspects of research technique using only materials in this collection, or (2) for longer papers requiring additional reading in literary or historical sources.

English Inns
Sports and Games
Affectation of Foreign Dress and Manners
English Dress
The Italianate Englishman
A Characterization of Elizabeth
The Death of Elizabeth
The Battle Against the Armada
Middle-Class Standards of Living
Food and Drink
Crime and Punishment
A Comparison of Modern and Sixteenth Century Forms of Punishment
Sixteenth Century Education
Entertainments: Public and Private
Definition and Function of a Poet

Interest in and Evidences of Wealth and Love of Display
Sixteenth Century Attitudes Toward Chaucer and Other Ancient Poets
The Sixteenth Century as a Period of Literary Experiment
The Sixteenth Century Contribution to the Development of Modern English
Foreign and Native Influence on Sixteenth Century Language Habits
The Contemporary Comparison of English and Foreign Languages
Sir Philip Sidney As the Exemplar of the Age
Debate Over the Usefulness of Literature
The Purpose of Literature
Criticism of Literary Affectations

LIST TWO: GENERAL TOPICS

Topics in this list may be used for longer papers (1) limited to materials in this collection or (2) supplementing these materials with further reading in literary or historical sources.

Elizabethan Theaters
The Theater Audience
Puritan Antagonism to Theaters
Travel in England
Eagerness of Englishmen for Foreign Travel

Antagonism to Foreign Travel
England Through Foreign Eyes
The Queen's Court
The Elizabethan Courtier
English Humanism in the Sixteenth Century

Growth of English Nationalism in the Sixteenth Century

Education: Schools, Theories, Practices, Studies, Scholars

Living Standards: Middle Class and Nobility

Trade and Tradesmen

The Character of a Nobleman and Magistrate

Middle-Class Prosperity

Middle-Class Economy

Native and Imported Products

Foreign Influences on English Literature in the Sixteenth Century

Introduction of an Experimentation with Foreign Literary Forms (e.g., the sonnet and the heroic poem)

Spenser's Contribution to English Letters

Spenser and the Pastoral Tradition

Literature as a Profession

Shakespeare as Actor, Entrepreneur, Playwright

Critical Theories Concerning the Function and Position of the Poet

CDEFGHIJ-B-743210/698765